When you were a child, I crept into your dreams. Dazzlingly attractive, glamorous, and mysterious, I promised to make you happy forever after.

When you grew up, I kept beckoning. I would sweep you off your feet, make your pulse race and your spirits soar. I thrilled you with excitement, romance, and passion. I vowed the spell would never fade — and then I broke your heart.

I AM FALSE LOVE.

FALSE LOVE

AND OTHER ROMANTIC ILLUSIONS

WHY LOVE GOES WRONG
AND HOW TO MAKE IT RIGHT

DR. STAN J. KATZ AND AIMEE E. LIU

TICKNOR & FIELDS
NEW YORK · 1988

For
Jennifer, Jamie, and Jordan
and
Graham and Daniel

May your lives be filled with
joy, happiness, and love.

Library of Congress Cataloging-in-Publication Data

Katz, Stan J.
  False love and other romantic illusions : why love goes
wrong, and how to make it right / Stan J. Katz and
Aimee E. Liu.
    p.   cm.
  ISBN 0-89919-538-5
    1. Love.   2. Interpersonal relations.   I. Liu,
Aimee E.   II. Title.
HQ801.K36 1988
306.7 — dc19   88-9407
                                      CIP

Printed in the United States of America

Q 10 9 8 7 6 5 4 3 2 1

CONTENTS

ACKNOWLEDGMENTS

We owe a debt of gratitude to all the people who lent us their support during the months of planning, writing, and editing required to produce this book. In particular, we'd like to thank Richard Pine for the introduction that brought us together and the encouragement that kept us moving forward; Katrina Kenison for her unflagging enthusiasm, commitment, and editorial comments; the patients whose lives provided the cases for this book; and Deborah and Martin, who are our own true loves.

FALSE
LOVE
AND OTHER
ROMANTIC
ILLUSIONS

INTRODUCTION

What comes to mind when you hear the words *true love*? Ingrid Bergman and Humphrey Bogart? White knights and maidens in distress? Candlelit dinners? Electric passion? Obsessive desire? These are all part of the picture we're taught to call true love. Unfortunately, this image is as misleading as the myths and fairy tales on which it is based. It is a composite of illusions that guide us not toward the truly loving, committed relationships we want but to their opposite — false love.

False love is the affair that dries up inexplicably three weeks after you decide it's the greatest romance of the century. It's the marriage that cruises effortlessly for ten years until you discover that your husband has a lover half your age. For him, of course, false love is also the relationship for which he leaves you. False love may be your first, your latest, or every romance you've ever known. Often exciting, sometimes glamorous, it is always seductive, because it's based on some of your favorite illusions. Unfortunately, it's so seductive that it can become addictive, sabotaging your opportunities for true love.

Unlike false love, the real thing involves mature choice as well as emotion. It recognizes that feelings as well as people develop and change over time, and it accommodates changes by preserving an intimacy that runs deeper than lust. True love is mutual, honest, and highly complex. It may have all the bells and whistles of a storybook courtship, but it may also appear rather mundane. People truly in love have enough faith in each other that they need neither elaborate gifts nor public swooning. It doesn't matter what others think of their relationship.

What does matter is trust, respect, sharing, and commitment. True love is a union of two individuals, not a show. It is a choice, not a feeling or a magical state of existence. It makes life more satisfying and richer for both lovers, but it is not a panacea for all their problems. Unfortunately, true love does *not* conquer all.

Some say the problem with romantic relationships is that dessert comes first and makes the rest of the meal unappetizing by comparison. No one can keep the honeymoon going forever. In fact, the key difference between true love and false is that false love often *ends* with the honeymoon. If the relationship lingers longer, it's usually because the lovers are trying vainly to recapture their initial passion. True love, on the other hand, presses forward without mourning the past. The spark of excitement comes and goes, the trust deepens, and the stakes get higher. Living happily ever after requires a lot more hard work than magic.

It's small wonder, then, that false love is so distracting. It glitters with romantic trappings. It makes delicious promises that true love never does. It feels good and impresses the people around you. Perhaps most compelling of all, it reinforces the fractured images of love you've been fed from childhood. Beginning with myths of sleeping princesses and visions of starry-eyed TV newlyweds, you absorbed one set of ideals for romance. Later, secret peeks at porno magazines, adult movies, and "dirty" books may have paved the way for quite a separate notion of sex. Meanwhile, your parents and other real-life couples presented altogether different and more bewildering images of marital love — images that usually are completely unacceptable to a young person transfixed by the lure of a "perfect" love. If you're like most people, you've spent a good share of your life trying to weave these contradictory impressions into something that looks and feels good, something you think might actually be true love. Sometimes your feelings of love might be based on good sex, sometimes on the infatuation that comes with "falling in love," and sometimes on beauty, power, wealth, social status, or security. Many of these romantic illusions are reflections of the love lies you were taught as a child.

What do *you* look for in love? Would you agree that true love means:

- Finding the one person who is right for you
- Being intensely attracted to your partner
- Feeling excited whenever you're with your partner
- Rarely fighting
- Rarely wanting to be apart from your partner
- Having great sex
- Never being sexually attracted to anyone else
- Enjoying constant romance
- Never needing anyone but your partner in your life
- Complete fulfillment

If this describes the relationship you've been seeking, you may be caught in the false love syndrome, for these criteria describe not lasting love, but illusion — illusion so powerful that it becomes difficult even to imagine any more realistic kind of love. In your quest for this impossible devotion, you probably have created a trail of unsatisfactory affairs, each of which superficially meets your expectations for a while and then crumbles, leaving you mystified as to what went awry and why you keep choosing partners who turn out to be "wrong" for you. If you are in a promising relationship right now but are afraid it will end as the others did, the unhappy truth is that your fears probably will be borne out unless you adjust your expectations and begin moving toward a more realistic and enduring love.

As unromantic as it may seem, true love revolves around shared goals and commitment more than around passion. This is not to say that passion is absent in genuine love, but it inevitably fades in and out. When it wanes, lovers make the active choice to continue giving each other affection, encouragement, support, and attention. In genuine love there's a balance between mutual supportiveness and independence. Change and personal growth challenge the relationship instead of threatening it. Lack of change is viewed as a warning sign that the relationship is too tight. Because both partners are committed to loving each other *and understand that this balance is an important part of true love*, they can accept the challenges that arise. False love's greatest downfall is that it retreats from problems instead of confronting and resolving them.

Analyze your own behavior in relationships past and present. Forget about the feelings. Focus instead on your actions toward your lovers and their responses to you. What do you look for in a lover that's different from what you seek in a friend? What level of commitment are you really looking for, and what are you willing to do to get it? How well do you know your lovers before you start talking about "love"? Are your demonstrations of love all kisses and flowers, or do you both actively support each other as separate individuals beyond your relationship?

If you keep asking and answering these questions honestly, you'll eventually start to see a pattern in your behavior that may help explain why true love keeps slipping through your fingers. Perhaps you are attracted to people who avoid commitment because you're afraid of the honesty that true love requires. Maybe you keep choosing lovers who make you look good to your friends but don't truly interest you. Or are you just so afraid of being alone that you grab the first attractive offer that comes along — and then feel trapped by both your lover and your fear? If you don't have a balanced give-and-take of understanding, trust, intimacy, and enjoyment with your partner, you don't have love. If you don't *demand* that balance when you begin a serious relationship, you're perpetuating the false love syndrome.

Once you've identified the illusions that have governed your love life in the past, it's not so hard to figure out if your current love is true or false. What's different this time around? If it's the intensity of the feelings, the quality of the sex, or the fabulous time you have when you're on vacation together, take a closer look. Accepting each other as individuals is as important as adoring each other as lovers. Listening to each other and responding openly is more important than exciting each other. And selflessness and commitment to a future together is critical for both of you if you're to call this true love.

If you are not in a relationship right now or if you already know that your current partner is not right for you, then you must find someone who *is* appropriate before you can start to build true love. This person could be anywhere — cruising the neighborhood singles bars, joking around the office water cooler, shopping in your corner deli, or even appearing in the local video dating service. No one can tell you where or when you'll meet your beloved, but you can reshape your expectations so that you recognize a compatible partner when one appears.

Remember that you cannot find love. What you're searching for is a person with whom you can establish a lasting and loving relationship. So stop thinking in terms of superficial attractions, and consider first whether you yourself are prepared to invest the time, energy, and dedication that love requires. Only when you accept this responsibility can you reasonably expect to find someone to reciprocate your love.

Before you open your arms to anyone, ask questions and demand answers. Assess each new person using a list of realistic and honest priorities, not appearances. Your list naturally will reflect your personal values, beliefs, and goals for your own life as well as the requirements of true love, but remember that the more exacting you are, the more difficult it will be for you to find appropriate partners. Everyone — including you — has imperfections. While it is not wise to enter into love with someone who lacks the characteristics you consider critical, neither is it sensible to create a fixed image of your "ideal beloved." Being willing to accept some blemishes and accommodate them through concession and compromise is a prerequisite for loving.

This book will help you break the false love syndrome and acquire the tools you need to develop a truly loving relationship the next time around. The conclusions are based on years of clinical experience. The cases you'll read here are based on those of my patients (names and identifying details have been changed), but it is almost impossible to write about love without being influenced by one's own experience. My co-author, Aimee Liu, and I both fell for many of the illusions that perpetuate the false love syndrome, and we both eventually broke through the syndrome by reluctantly giving up these illusions in favor of a more realistic and rewarding model of true love. How well have we succeeded? Let our stories speak for themselves.

Dr. Stan Katz

A brilliant blue sky studded with cloud puffs and radiant with warm Mediterranean sunshine. Gently rolling hills thick with olive trees. Here and there the proud remnants of an ancient city whispering suggestions of romance for all time. It was an enchanted setting, the only truly appropriate setting for lovers truly in love.

Or so I thought at age thirteen watching *Roman Holiday* for the first time. As Gregory Peck and Audrey Hepburn headed off on their scooter and faded into the sunset, I knew I had witnessed true love in the making. Who could question the intensity and desire with which they gazed into each other's eyes? Or the romantic phrases that passed between them? It was clear that they were made for each other. It was also clear to me that I'd instantly find my own true love if I just moved to Rome, dressed like Gregory Peck, and started riding a Vespa scooter.

By age seventeen I'd figured out that true love might not be restricted to Italy, but I reached this conclusion only because *The Graduate* had persuaded me that California breeds lovers as well. There was Dustin Hoffman relentlessly pursuing the irresistible Katharine Ross all the way to the altar, where he stole her away from her obviously inappropriate fiancé and captured her heart forever. This, I was sure, was true love in its purest form. Watching Hoffman and Ross bumping along in the back of a bus after their escape from Mr. Wrong, how could anyone question that they'd live happily ever after?

These cinematic images still haunt me. Their indelibility serves as a constant reminder of my naiveté and ignorance about love and of the failure of society, parents, and adults in general to teach me what true love is and how to find and maintain it. My own parents did have an extremely loving and sincere relationship, but there was no passion between them that I could see. I wanted the passion, lust, and infatuation all within a framework of total acceptance and undying supportiveness. Without any more persuasive models to set me on a realistic course toward love, I willingly let the movies convince me that true love would deliver all my requirements with the sudden force of a lightning bolt.

This fantasy shadowed me all through high school. The girls I dated were pleasant company, but they were not romantic leading ladies. Despite the fact that I was an unassuming, average-looking kid with occasional acne, it seemed perfectly reasonable that my true love should be a cross between Julie Christie and Sophia Loren, who on our first meeting would instantly feel as attracted and as passionately committed to me as I would to her.

By the time I got to college it was beginning to dawn on me that I could have intense sexual attractions without true love. Though on one level I was still holding out for my "perfect love," on another I was running wild. Bent on sexual excitement, I dated voraciously and frequently, falling "in lust" hundreds of times without ever seeing the fireworks I knew would signal the arrival of my one and only. My growing list of "conquests" did wonders for my ego but threatened my grand illusions of love. No matter what wonderful traits a woman possessed, she inevitably was missing some key element that, to me, was a requirement. I continued to insist that my ideal partner have an IQ in the stratosphere, the face, figure, and fashion sense of a model, and the social consciousness to singlehandedly eliminate world hunger, poverty, and the nuclear threat.

True to my fond memories of Hepburn and Peck, I spent my junior year in Italy and shrugged off the deepening suspicion that my notion of true love was an impossible dream. While in Italy, I fell prey to many new illusions, including the one that the right lover would elevate my social and economic status. After a whirlwind relationship with a young woman whose father was an official in the Johnson administration, I finally realized that I was much more impressed with the father than with the daughter. Fortunately, I was not foolish enough to let my lust for prestige override my lack of feeling for the relationship.

Then in Florence, at the American Express office, I honestly thought I'd found love at first sight. I discarded my travel plans, followed her to Switzerland, and spent one glorious week with her before realizing that my enthusiasm was driven primarily by the idea of being in love with a future social worker. A sucker for the rhetoric of the late sixties, I fantasized that we'd heal the world together. When I tried to fantasize our *living* together, I hit a wall.

By the time I turned twenty-three, many of my illusions about love were starting to dim. I suspected I might have to tone down a few of my standards and accept the possibility that love might not make the earth move after all. I even entertained the notion that *I* might have to change to accommodate true love. I was not prepared, however, to find my personal leading lady in a bar. The evening I met my future wife, finding a permanent mate was far removed from my nocturnal ambitions. My primary feeling for her was a physical attraction — strong enough that I asked her out the next night, but certainly not enough to set me dreaming about a shared future. I was a cocky graduate student who had lived abroad, and I was not about to settle down with a twenty-one-year-old college student I'd met at a bar, no matter how pretty she was. Had anyone ventured a wager, I would have bet my prized possession, a rusty orange Porsche, against this absurd notion.

But cocky as I was, I was also getting sick of chasing illusions. This quest for perfection in others and in myself was both exhausting and fruitless. Even if I wasn't ready to stop deluding myself entirely, I was ready to start letting my defenses down. My future wife was the first woman I ever dated for more than a few months. The longer I stayed with her, the more I realized that the time had come to get past the myths of love and start working on a truly loving relationship. I needed that emotional connection with another person.

The woman I had chosen possessed many of the qualities I desired, but also a few that irritated me. Accepting these "imperfections" in her, as well as the flaws she pinpointed in me, was a continual struggle for me during our courtship. I also had trouble figuring out what to say and how to behave in order to develop a mature relationship with her. We had fun together, enjoyed a lot of the same activities, and had a wonderful physical relationship, but we stayed away from the hard issues about the future. What kind of lifestyle we wanted, how we'd raise our kids, and, most important of all, what we expected of each other all remained large question marks for some time. We both entered the relationship still clinging to our idealized visions of the perfect mate. If we didn't come that way, then we'd change each other to fit the molds.

Now, changing someone is no small task. It demands that you know precisely what needs to be changed and how it should be "fixed." It also demands that the other person be perfectly compliant. Fortunately, I never had to test my wife's compliance because I never really figured out what I wanted her to be. There were times when I toyed with the notion of a wife who would devote her entire life to me, but this prospect always made me uneasy because I was so attracted to independence in women. Sometimes I wanted a wife who was glamorous, but when I was around women who were truly glamorous I always felt slightly uncomfortable. Girl-next-door types put me at ease, but they didn't excite me. Flipping back and forth between these sorts of fantasies, I gradually realized that even if I found the ideal woman, I'd consider her ideal only for that moment. I also realized that this quest for perfection was my way of avoiding the real demands of love. If I wanted a truly successful relationship, I was going to have to accept my future wife as she came, prepare to make some sacrifices myself, and get down to the hard work of building love.

We'd been dating for over a year when she first told me she loved me. Still unable to say the "L" word myself, I was touched but somewhat unsettled by this pronouncement. From the start, she had been as cautious and uncertain as I, but now she had made the choice to love me. I wanted to reciprocate but honestly didn't know how. Fortunately, she was able to guide me toward mutual love. By being honest, committed, and willing to compromise, she showed me how to let my defenses down in return. By being patient and respecting my reluctance, she gave me the breathing room I needed to make my own choice to love her.

By the time we married, three years after first meeting, we were both equally committed to building a strong relationship that would endure over time. This commitment proved far more powerful than the petty grievances and self-serving illusions that clouded our early years. We still had our share of problems. Accepting each other remained difficult at times, and there were still those fleeting doubts that tempted us to run from the marriage, but we now knew enough to expect and accept these lapses without capitulating to them.

For my part, seeing couples in marital and relationship therapy actually enhanced my commitment to my own wife. Treating couples in trouble gave me a front row seat on the mistakes that so often ruin marriages. I saw how many people resist commitment and sharing even after years together. I realized how dangerous romantic illusions can be and how few people have any idea what true love is all about. And the more couples I saw who lacked commitment in love, the more confident I became that my wife and I could succeed in our own relationship if only we both believed in our choice and were willing to invest the faith and devotion that would keep renewing our love.

Now after twelve years of marriage and three children, I've finally learned that there are no perfect lovers, husbands, or wives. There are no perfect, unchanging couples. We all have flaws, we all change, and our relationships must adjust with us in order to survive. It may not be very romantic, but it's true. Love requires more than a European scooter and a brilliant sunset. It requires mutual dedication and trust.

Aimee Liu

The way my husband and I tell it, our early courtship sounds like a fairy tale. We first met on the Great Wall of China in 1979. He was scouting locations for a movie he was producing. I was there with my parents to tour the country and search for the home in Shanghai where my father grew up (we found it). My future husband spotted me from a distance. I didn't actually notice him but flirted with some of the other men in his group. It was one of a hundred encounters on such a trip. Statistically, our groups should never have met again. After that day, his group proceeded down the Yangtze River and mine flew several thousand miles to the interior of China.

Two weeks later in Shanghai, I saw them again, having lunch at my hotel. This time, I noticed him. When his group invited me to a banquet across town, I accepted without hesitation.

Like most of the hotels for foreigners in Shanghai, the guesthouse where the banquet was held had been built by Europeans decades before the Chinese Revolution, and its architecture was lavish. A porte-cochère protected the entrance, and just inside the door a majestic flight of carpeted stairs led up to the reception hall. I stepped out of my cab just as my future husband started down the stairs to greet me. There, in that setting reminiscent of a thirties Bogart-Bacall movie, we both felt lightning strike.

We shared a total of three evenings in Shanghai, touring the city by foot (including the black-as-pitch "lover's lane" where Chinese lovers secretly make out away from the watchful and disapproving gazes of parents and Communist party cadres) and exchanging the fundamental details of our respective pasts and plans for the future. He'd married first at age twenty-one and had divorced fifteen years later to enter another inappropriate relationship, which had recently ended. I was a veteran of countless misguided short-term relationships and was looking for something more stable. It was by no means a perfect match. Had we been on home ground, we might have pursued it just to see what would happen. As it was, our travel schedules prevailed and I headed for New York, he to Los Angeles. It was obvious to me that we'd never see each other again.

He had other plans. A postcard arrived from Hong Kong shortly after I arrived home. A phone call came several days later. The phone calls proliferated, and in about a month he arrived on my doorstep for a week in New York. As romantic as that first week together was, it was also an opportunity for reality-testing. I discovered that he had a two-year-old son. He learned that I was virtually penniless after working for a year on a novel that never sold. I faced the fact that he was fourteen years older. And then there was the conflict over location. Born in New York, he had left the city many years before and was now committed to the urban-suburban Los Angeles lifestyle. I, having grown up in suburban Connecticut, was reveling in my new identity as a young Manhattanite. While it was delightful to be with him, I realized the deck was stacked against us in many ways. If we were to survive, it would be a constant negotiation.

What I didn't realize at the time is that true love is always based largely on negotiation. Compromise and mutual adjustment are intrinsic to any successful relationship, *especially* a love relationship. But then I was still buying into all the myths and illusions with which I'd grown up.

I believed the lyrics of every love song I'd ever heard, as well as the plots of every romantic movie I'd ever seen. (I drew the line at romance novels, but that's not saying much.) In keeping with most of my generation, at age twenty-two I considered myself "sexually liberated," but when my liaisons broke up, as they inevitably did, I rarely was as philosophical or cavalier as the men. They seemed to treat their relationships as a game, a temporary pastime until they were ready for a more substantial commitment. Early in my twenties, I was no more prepared for a permanent commitment than they, but the notion of true love still seemed damnably attractive. So attractive, in fact, that it destroyed some perfectly acceptable relationships that might have become permanent friendships if I hadn't tried to turn them into passionate love affairs.

The fact is, I had not been all that discerning about the men I considered "prospects." My desire for love was so strong that it obscured my judgment and cost me a great deal of time, unhappiness, and humiliation. By the time I reached the Great Wall at age twenty-five, I'd chalked up a list of ex-lovers full of classic mistakes:

- The bright young doctor, a future plastic surgeon, who pointed to a model in a magazine ad and announced, "With a few tucks, you could look like that."
- The Harvard M.B.A. who culminated a three-month relationship by vanishing one day without a word of warning or explanation. He remained invisible until I bumped into him at a party three years later. "That was one of my disappearing acts," he explained, shrugging and smiling.
- The talented painter who lived in a loft in downtown Manhattan and had a longstanding relationship with a woman in

Philadelphia who viewed him as the father and brother she'd never had. He warned me from the start that those ties were much too strong to break, but I continued to hope he'd leave her. Finally, the split schedule of weekends with her and weekdays with me became too much for him. Weekends won out.

- The successful restaurateur almost twice my age who escorted me to some of the most exclusive clubs and restaurants in the city but could never look me in the eye. When his eighteen-year-old girlfriend came back from modeling in Europe, I was history. (Dumped at age twenty-two for a younger woman!)
- The male model who dealt and used cocaine. Why I don't know, but I took him home to Connecticut to meet my parents. Afterward, my mother said through her tears, "You can't stay with him. He's such a *type!*" Although I refused to admit it at the time, she was absolutely right. I've since met numerous young men who could be his clones.

In each case, there was that very specific initial jolt of attraction, that moment of "love at first sight." With my husband, that moment of electricity was canonized by the fact that our relationship survived and grew into true love, but it was never a guarantee of true love and, in fact, it probably was no more "magic" than any of my first encounters with other lovers. The difference lay in the peculiar way our personal objectives meshed and in our mutual desire to make this relationship work. While we recognized and enjoyed the chemistry, we soon realized that our feelings alone would never conquer all the obstacles in our path. We each would have to make some very big concessions, and we'd have to keep making them as long as we were together.

After just two week-long visits from him in New York, I began packing to move to Los Angeles. It was impetuous. My parents, having met him only once, were distraught by the age difference and what they viewed as the irresponsible haste with which I was going to live with him. To mollify them and give myself a fallback, I did keep my apartment for another six months, but long before my lease was up I knew I'd be staying in California for good.

By then I'd met his little boy, his ex-wives, his dying mother, and his aged father. This was a man with a lot of personal baggage, which overwhelmed me because I had relatively little, and what I had I'd left three thousand miles away. At the same time, the complications made him more interesting and allowed me to understand him much better than if he'd had a perfectly clean slate. Besides, knowing what had gone wrong in his past gave me an inkling of what he was looking for in his next relationship — stability, maturity, companionship, mutual supportiveness, caring, and respect. That matched my own goals almost perfectly. The one problem was that I still cared a little too much about romance.

Over the next few years, my romantic memories of our fairy-tale meeting occasionally threatened the relationship. I was particularly guilty of comparing the present with the past. If the beginning was so wonderfully easy, why was our later relationship so often difficult and annoying? This desire for the illusion nearly cost us our marriage at one point. Fortunately, after the strained period was over and we'd renewed our commitment, it made us both appreciate each other even more.

The adjustments have continued in intervening years. We both have made numerous career shifts, which in turn have slightly altered our images of each other and subtly affected the balance between us. We had to compromise socially by establishing friendships both separately and as a couple. The negotiations over marriage lasted more than four years before we finally agreed to tie the knot. But by far the most sensitive issue was whether or not to have children. I was determinedly childless for our first few years together, so much so that I had trouble making room emotionally for my stepson when he came to visit. We each struggled to accommodate everyone's needs, and eventually the presence of the child and my husband's visible

love for him rubbed off on me. Then I began hungering for a
child of my own — after he'd decided he was out of the baby
business. We had to start negotiating all over again. It took us
another two years to reach agreement, but the result was another son and an even further strengthening of our love.

Is this a true love that will last "as long as we both shall
live"? We didn't have the courage to make that promise in our
wedding vows, and I can't make it now. Not even true love is
guaranteed to last forever. It often does, but not always. At any
rate, that's not the most important issue. Far more important
is the fact that we are building both a relationship and a family
on a base of true love. If we are successful in sustaining our
love and teaching our children the right way to build love, we
will have finally conquered the illusions, myths, and desires
that dogged us in our early years and threatened to cost us true
love. In many ways, our children will be the ultimate measure
of how well we succeed.

True love can be the most exciting and rewarding element in
life. It can involve great passion and adventure and on the surface resemble the greatest love stories ever told. The secret of
true love is not that it must be *all* hard work, struggle, and sacrifice, but that it cannot consist *solely* of illusion. The initial
superficial attraction between two people may be the spark,
but only the spark, for an enduring relationship. What then
turns that relationship into true love is the shared process of
loving.

Those who are caught in the false love syndrome often claim
that they "love too much" or that they simply cannot find partners who love "enough" in return. In fact, most of these people
don't understand how to love at all. And many actively seek
out partners whose sense of loving is as misguided as their
own. Breaking the false love syndrome means not only over-
coming the myths that contribute to false love but also learning
how to demonstrate, demand, and live true love. This is the ultimate message of this book.

PART I
THE SEARCH

LOOKING FOR LOVE

THEY FIRST SAW EACH OTHER at a party. She was smiling and talking to the host. He caught her gaze and held it. Her smile broadened, and he headed across the crowded room to meet her.

They struck up a conversation about movies, TV shows, women's rights, and dogs. John was a golden retriever fanatic and Kate preferred poodles. She was a devoted Steven Spielberg fan; he saw only foreign films. He thought the whole idea of the ERA was foolish; she was deeply committed to the fight for its passage. They agreed on nothing.

Nevertheless, as rapidly as their discussion shifted to argument, their attraction to each other ignited. She was drawn to his cool blue eyes and the way he threw back his head when he laughed. His husky voice mesmerized her even when his words contradicted her heartfelt beliefs. As they talked, he found himself admiring the graceful curve of her cheekbones and the long creamy sweep of her neck. His gaze trained downward, lingering on her abundant curves. She had an earthiness and strength that made her very different from the other women in his life — different and, at the moment, dazzlingly attractive. Perhaps, he told himself, he'd finally found the woman he could marry.

Their conversation pitched and turned as they discovered more and more things about which they disagreed. Kate was fiery and filled with conviction about almost everything, but John refused to be baited. His mouth constantly twitched in merriment as if teasing her to erupt. As opposites, they were well matched. Long before the party was over, they knew they would leave together.

They would not sleep together, though, Kate reminded herself. She who had once jumped into bed routinely on the first date now had a firm policy of caution. Herpes, AIDS, and VD had her spooked. She would rather wait until she knew her partners, preferably until they'd taken a blood test. She voiced her concerns as they walked out into the summer evening. He didn't object, though he did mention that he carried condoms with him. Then he asked if it would be all right to kiss her. Kate was so relieved at his understanding attitude and yet so full of pent-up desire that she responded by throwing her arms around him.

The kiss cast a spell on them both. Cars were honking and people were shouting across the street, but the noise vanished as their bodies met. For a moment, they were conscious only of each other's smell and touch and the pounding of their hearts. Then they pulled apart, joined hands, and walked silently toward Kate's apartment. Despite her good intentions, the condoms worked that night.

The next morning Kate floated into work. "What's with you?" her assistant asked. "Love?"

"Afraid so," sighed Kate. "I feel like I'm falling down a rabbit's hole."

She couldn't stop thinking about him all day. She was barely able to concentrate on her paperwork and had to pinch herself to pay attention during the afternoon's business meetings. At five o'clock, she bolted home to shower, change, and make herself into the most ravishing woman in John's life. She labored over her makeup and scoured her wardrobe for just the right combination. The final effect was sensuous and, she hoped, provocative. This was the relationship she'd been waiting for, and she wasn't going to let it get away from her.

He arrived bearing a dozen white roses and looking like Don Johnson. They had dinner reservations at one of the city's trendiest new restaurants. He wanted to show off his new girl.

Kate was more than willing to appear on his arm and meet his friends. He had money and was willing to spend it on her. She liked that. It also set him apart from the men she usually dated. She had known from that first glance that John was different, and it was good to have her expectations confirmed.

Over a dinner which Kate was too nervous to eat, they told each other about their families and work, passions and dreams. He said he was a disenchanted VP with one of Madison Avenue's top ad agencies. She told him she was a frustrated artist passing time as a copy editor for one of the lesser known teenage fashion magazines. He held her hand and she stroked his leg under the table.

Intermittently, John's well-heeled friends stopped by the table to say hello. They shot her a glance, chatted with him, then sauntered back to their own tables. He was obviously a regular here, and Kate was impressed — but she was also annoyed at the offhand way his friends seemed to be sizing her up.

As soon as they were back in her apartment, her annoyance melted into passion. They were more relaxed and familiar with each other now. They took their time and played more. If every man made love like this, thought Kate, she'd have been married years ago.

John left around one o'clock. An early business meeting tomorrow, he explained. There wouldn't be time for him to go home and change in the morning. But he kissed her and told her she was sensational. He said he'd call her at work to arrange for tomorrow night.

When Kate arrived in the office a message was waiting. "Can't make it tonight. Call you later. John." By the end of the day, there was still no call. By midnight, when she finally forced herself to fall asleep, she'd heard nothing. She waited another day and then called his office. His secretary told her he was on the road. That made her feel somewhat better, though she still was miffed that he hadn't at least said goodbye.

John meanwhile was fielding calls from everyone who had seen them together. Most of his friends clearly thought he was making a mistake. One said bluntly, "Nice jugs, but a little below your class, old buddy." Unfortunately, he agreed with them. Not that he doubted that initial rush of excitement he'd felt when he first laid eyes on her. He had pushed to get her into the sack and hoped it would lead to love. After all, years of TV movies had trained him that opposites attract. And the first night was good — special, really. The idea of going out with someone as raw and forceful as Kate appealed to him.

The trouble was, she never let up, and she was too eager. Much as he enjoyed enthusiasm in bed, he hated having women grope him in public, and in a restaurant where he knew everyone in sight it was especially irritating. At the same time she was pawing him, she never stopped sparring, goading him into arguments about trivial points. The first night, that banter was fun. It made her seem more challenging. But two days later, enough was enough.

He went to bed with her the second night because that's what she wanted and she was, after all, a good lay. But he couldn't stomach waking up with her in the morning, so he made up an excuse to leave early and for the next couple of days arranged to visit clients out of town.

He'd pulled these disappearing acts before and in the long run, he felt, they made things easier on both sides. At least there were none of those drawn-out dissections of the affair, and he didn't have to face the word *love*. Admittedly, he'd entertained that this *might* be love, so strong was their initial attraction. But he'd been mistaken. It was just a physical thrill. When he fell in love for real, he told himself, he'd know it. In the meantime, he refused to let a woman like Kate force him to analyze "where our love went wrong." "Our love," he thought, had never existed.

When a week later she still hadn't heard from John, Kate

started to worry. What if he's been killed? What if he's on a trip around the world? What if . . . ? She screwed up her courage and called his office again. This time he was in a meeting. How long had he been back? Four days. The secretary took her message.

Kate debated whether to shoot him or herself first. Grudgingly, she decided bloodshed wasn't necessary. She would give him one last chance to answer her. The hurt and hope were both subsiding, but she'd need a damn good explanation to quell her anger.

Neither the call nor the explanation came. He had simply cut her off.

In the following weeks, Kate struggled through as many possible explanations as she could imagine. Maybe she wasn't good enough in bed. Or not up to his high-class standards. Maybe she came on too strong. For a long while she blamed herself and tried to figure out what she'd done wrong. Then she exonerated herself and turned the full blame on him. He was the one who had conned her into falling in love, she reassured herself. He was the one who had the problem. But, she vowed, this was the last time she'd be the sucker. Next time she was struck by love at first sight, she'd ignore it . . . well, at least be more cautious.

Once her bruised ego had begun to heal, Kate was able to take a clearer look at what had happened, and she started to see that she and John both were responsible. What had really brought them together, however briefly, was their mutual illusion that love could be found — fully formed — on a warm summer night across a crowded room. They had been so eager to believe in the magic that they'd refused to see how little they had in common simply as *people*. There was hardly any basis for friendly conversation, much less a life together. In style and income, they were worlds apart. He was a cavalier playboy, she an earnest activist. Yet that fleeting spark of attraction had jolted them so that they became blind to their differences and threw themselves eagerly into a situation that was destined to cause disappointment and hurt. John certainly could have been more courteous, but the fact that he realized the truth first did not make him responsible for Kate's illusions, or for her heartbreak.

For Kate and John to move beyond this kind of doomed liaison, they would have to relinquish their faith in instantaneous love and accept that a lasting relationship is based on much more than an exchange of glances. Unfortunately, the myth of love at first sight was so deeply ingrained in both of them that it continued to drive their relationships for several years afterward. They each would keep chasing this illusion partly because the chase itself was so exciting, partly because this was what they'd been taught to believe, but mostly because they *wanted* love to be mystical, immediate — and effortless.

As often as you may be "burned" in love, it can be difficult — and painful — to learn from your mistakes. If you're like Kate and John and many others, you repeatedly venture forth "looking for" love as if it were a commodity you could purchase with the right kind of look, conversation, or sexual performance. Instead of searching for a person with whom you can build an honest, lasting relationship, you "shop" for a ready-made attraction that matches your illusion of love. Whenever you cross paths with someone who returns your interest, you may hopefully call it love at first sight or, if you're more restrained, say that you're falling in love. Here at last is that special person — The One. Days, weeks, months, or even years later, when the relationship breaks up, you realize that your interest was superficial all along, and you start searching all over again. This false love syndrome feeds on the romantic myths we all learned as children, myths that are as enticing as they are dangerous. To break the cycle, you first need to recognize and then move beyond these myths.

The Myth of Love at First Sight

"Love at first sight" is a delicious sensation. Your heart does a flutter kick. Your skin tingles. Your body aches with desire. It's like being simultaneously lifted off your feet and clobbered with a baseball bat. Few experiences in life are as thrilling, overwhelming, or deceptive.

What we routinely call love at first sight is not love at all. Usually, as with Kate and John, it's little more than a powerful attraction. Sometimes the draw is wealth, power, mystique, or some idea the other person represents to you. Ironically, many of the reasons you're initially attracted to a person are likely to be red flags. These warning signals include most of the romantic formulas that work so beautifully in the movies. Verbal fencing between two lovers produces great film dialogue, but in real life it becomes very tedious very quickly. When a wealthy boy meets a struggling girl on screen, the plot gets interesting, but off screen the two generally have so little in common that the plot disintegrates. In the movies, lovers expect each other to look glamorous all the time because the makeup artist and costumer are on standby, but in true love, anyone who expects a lover to look as good in the morning as the night before should not expect the relationship to last long. Realistically, it makes more sense to take several steps backward than to plunge headlong into a love affair based on instantaneous attraction.

There is no great mystery or magic to love at first sight. You probably have had this pleasure many times and perhaps will have it many times more. The requirements are minimal: a little time, attention, and sexual desire. Combine a certain level of lust with an attractive appearance, and you could generate this brand of false love several times a day.

Truly loving someone is an altogether different story. Despite all the romantic mythology, it does not happen in an instant. While you may meet a potential partner anywhere, no one finds *love* while walking on the beach, entering a party, or surveying the crowd at a singles bar. True love is not a feeling that seizes you magically when one particular person walks into your life. Certainly, you can have loving feelings toward people whom you admire or lust after, but the real bond of true love must be secured and developed over time by two committed and trusting partners.

True love may or may not start with "love at first sight." It usually does involve an initial period of infatuation when you tell yourself you're falling in love, but this is not a prerequisite. Some people quietly love each other for many years without ever feeling the earth move. Loving friendships can easily blossom into true love. In other cultures, true love often develops in arranged marriages, even when the bride and groom meet for the first time on their wedding day. If both partners understand what's involved in love and sincerely want to build a life together, the fanfare or lack of it in the beginning is irrelevant.

The Myth of the One True Love

The myth of love at first sight goes hand in hand with the myth that each person has one true love. According to this theory, if you just find the right partner, everything else will take care of itself. The search, in other words, is the key to love.

When she was a child, Nancy lay in bed at night dreaming of the man she would marry. He would be dark, handsome, wealthy, loving, and absolutely devoted to her. Somewhere out there, he too was growing up, and one day their paths would cross.

If there was just one perfect mate for her, she reasoned, he was probably many thousands of miles away. She might have to circle the globe to find him. This notion made him seem all the more glamorous and exciting. It also made her leery of the boys in her hometown. In high school she knew young men who were gorgeous to look at, athletic, and popular, and she was tempted. But the laws of probability were against them and, besides, none of them fit her ideal perfectly. When I meet my one true love, she told herself, there will be no doubt in my mind or his. In the meantime, she held herself aloof.

The waiting game continued through college, where she acquired a reputation for being frigid because she refused to sleep with any of the men she dated. It wasn't so much that she was saving herself; she just didn't feel like exposing so much of herself to men she knew were transient in her life. Sex, to her, would be a union of spirits, something very ethereal, and not at all like the "scoring" these guys were after.

After college, Nancy took a job in Chicago as secretary for one of the handsomest and wealthiest men in the city. In these respects, he fit her image of perfection. But he was also much older, very domineering — and married. Nevertheless, while one part of her resented and resisted him, she was attracted physically as she never had been to any other man. When he made a play for her, she consented and was quickly hooked. He was an experienced, confident lover. When he realized how inexperienced she was, he became gentle and generous in bed. She had never imagined that sex could be this physically exciting. Maybe she had been too rigid in her search for perfection. Maybe *this* was her sign.

Their affair intensified while remaining absolutely secret. They spent three evenings a week together yet never touched in public. For a while, Nancy relished the masquerade. In a strange way the notion that she had stolen into his life and swept him off his feet suited her fantasy. As soon as he could get out of his marriage, she convinced herself, they would become the perfect couple. And yet for a long while she didn't dare ask about the rest of his personal life. Deep down, she knew that his answers would violate her dream.

The affair lasted three months. Toward the end, Nancy began declaring her undying love, and he told her she was the most special woman in his life. She asked him about his wife. He explained that their marriage was troubled, but the kids kept them together. She asked for more time together. He promised to bring her along on his next business trip. She asked when he would be ready to divorce his wife. He patiently reminded her that he was a Catholic and was under intense pressure from both family and business associates to maintain a "dignified" image. She pressed the issue. He informed her that he had never had any intention of getting a divorce.

Nancy retreated with her pride smashed and her self-esteem torn to shreds, but the illusion of her one true love persisted. She had had no business taking a lover who wasn't perfect, she told herself. She should have left it in the hands of destiny. Never again would she compromise her faith in love.

Five years later, Nancy entered therapy in an attempt to understand why her faith in true love had failed her. Now a moderately successful insurance executive with a passion for gardening and cooking and a small group of close women friends, she had had no more than a handful of intimate relationships with men, all of which she'd chosen to end because the men weren't "special" enough. Even though she badly wanted to experience love, she still was terrified of settling for a partner who was not "meant for her."

Nancy clung to her imaginary true love largely because she subconsciously believed that the man who was destined to become her husband would automatically forgive her flaws and consider her as perfect as she fancied him. Whenever she was with a man whom she considered less than ideal, she was painfully aware of her own inadequacies. Her illusion of love contained no such awkwardness; she and her beloved would bathe each other in unconditional acceptance and affection because, in each other's eyes, they would have no faults. The resulting relationship would be free of stress or conflict and would be a permanent source of emotional validation.

As unrealistic as this concept of love might be, it protected Nancy from the kind of rejection she had experienced in her first affair. Before having her heart broken, her mythical image of love had been little more than a child's fancy which she accepted because she'd never experienced anything compelling enough to persuade her otherwise. Afterward, however, it became her retreat. Now she was convinced that there was something deeply wrong with her — something that only her one true love could undo. It was as if she'd cast herself in the role of Frog Princess awaiting her Prince to transform her into his beloved. Unwittingly, she'd chosen to hide behind this myth so that she wouldn't have to confront what really was wrong with her: lack of self-confidence.

Once Nancy recognized the falseness of her illusion, she could no longer hide behind it, nor could she continue to ignore the insecurity that had bound her to it for so long. She was not yet ready to accept the responsibility of true love, and she would not be ready until she developed the inner strength to accept some level of emotional risk. But she had taken an important first step toward moving beyond false love.

People respond to the myth of the one true love in different ways. Some people search the world and test hundreds of partners to find the one that "feels right." When Cupid's arrow hits its mark, they tell themselves, it will create such a surge of delight that they'll know the search is over. Others, like Nancy, create a superficial image of The One and then either search for the person who most closely matches it or assign the whole matter to fate. But even when the myth betrays them and the ideal lover fails to materialize, most of these true believers still cling to the fantasy. They would rather chase magic and repeatedly fail than face the test of true love.

In fact, there is very little magic to choosing an appropriate partner. The world is full of acceptable candidates. Theoretically, you could create true love with any number of people over the course of a lifetime. The catch is that true love is exclusive. Because of the commitment, respect, and sheer energy required, no one can be truly in love with more than one person simultaneously. True love is also something that evolves over time, not overnight. It builds gradually in strength and intensity so that there is less and less temptation to start fresh with another partner.

When true love is ended prematurely, by death or forced separation, for example, even the most devoted lover can find a new partner and start over again. The new partner needn't be a duplicate of the first, and the new relationship inevitably will be different from the first, but it can still be true love. It's the *process* of loving that creates true love, not merely the selection of the loved one.

The Illusion of Falling in Love

Even more misleading than the myths of love at first sight and the one true love is the illusion that you "fall in love." The phrase conjures up images of Disneyesque couples with animated hearts pounding and bluebirds whirling about. The idea is that love is like a state of grace. It's something that happens *to* you instead of something you *make* happen.

The appeal of this illusion is that it leaves you free of responsibility. All you have to do is relax and enjoy the rather dizzying sensation of what, in fact, is infatuation. For a while the excitement and elation can eclipse almost everything else — including problems, career concerns, family, and friends. The sensation of infatuation is so consuming that you may not believe you'll ever be unhappy again. Unfortunately, this freefall never lasts forever, and when you come back to earth, you're forced to choose between the illusion and the relationship.

George and Nora were friends for years before they became lovers. George and his young family lived on Nora's block. Nora saw them at the grocery store. She babysat for the kids. It was a neighborly relationship until Nora moved away and they lost touch with each other.

She was out of work, contemplating a career change, and facing a wide open future when she returned to her old neighborhood at Christmastime eight years later. George heard she was back and invited her to a New Year's Eve party.

Nora barely recognized his children, now in their teens, but she was even more surprised by George. He'd lost a great deal of weight, and his sandy hair had turned a distinguished white. He'd shaved his beard and was wearing tweed and corduroy instead of polyester.

"Where have you been all my life?" she joked.

"Married," he replied with a wink, "but I'm not anymore. Want to dance?"

They danced, joked, drank champagne, and brought each other up to date. While she'd been keeping company with an assortment of men and establishing herself as a television publicist, he had become an extremely successful building contractor and had watched his wife slip irretrievably into the clutches of a religious cult. When his wife moved to an ashram, George was left to raise the children alone. They were good kids, but they had their share of trouble. His son at fifteen was talking about dropping out of school. His twelve-year-old daughter was asking about birth control. George really wasn't sure how to handle these issues.

Listening, Nora was struck by an openness and vulnerability she'd never sensed before. He was genuinely worried about his children and his role as a father. He now was wealthy and had even picked up a sense of style along the way, yet he seemed more gentle and sensitive than she remembered him.

They talked and continued to dance, moving closer and closer as the night progressed. George had forgotten how feminine Nora was on the outside — and how strong inside. She felt soft in his arms, but her conversation was tough and self-confident. He found himself laughing as he hadn't for months, perhaps years. She made him feel secure and comfortable.

Still together for the midnight toast, they were about to kiss when George's daughter cut in.

"I haven't seen you all night, Daddy!" she cried. "Happy New Year!" And she jumped into his arms, pushing Nora out of the way.

Over the next two months, George and Nora saw each other several times a week. At first they went out to restaurants. Then she started coming over for dinner. For the youngsters, it was almost like old times. Nora was familiar, friendly, and supportive. She knew where to tickle them and what jokes they liked. She helped George's daughter learn to use makeup and worked with his son on model airplanes. They thought she was terrific until she started sleeping with their father.

Both Nora and George were oblivious to any dissent in the ranks. George felt that Nora had turned his life into a dream. Just seeing her made his pulse race with desire. They made love morning and night and occasionally slipped away when the kids were watching TV or doing their homework. His excitement and eagerness made Nora feel deliciously out of control. She had chased other men and had been chased herself many times before, but no one had ever worked so hard to please her or welcomed her into his life as lovingly as George.

By the time she moved in, they were talking seriously about marriage, and Nora had visions of becoming a housewife. She had no urgent desire to go back to work, and they didn't need the money. She wasn't going to have any children of her own, and George's kids needed a second parent. She wasn't about to mother them, but she could offer guidance and friendship. They were part of George's life, and she would make them part of hers, too. In the haze of love, it all sounded ideal.

The children, unfortunately, refused to be persuaded. Instead of warming up to Nora over time, they became increasingly resentful, and their resentment began to show in their behavior. They skipped school and stayed out late at night. Their grades plummeted. They demanded to see their mother, though they knew full well she would give them no more than a weekend of her time. When they returned from a visit with her they were even more antagonistic toward Nora.

Nora realized before George that the love affair had reached a critical plateau. Familiarity had replaced the sensations of giddiness and excitement she used to feel when he walked in the door. They made love only once or twice a week. He was working longer hours. But the most dramatic change was the arguments, almost always about the children. She thought he was too lenient with them. He told her to stay out of it until she knew them better. She told him she'd be glad to stay out of it if he'd learn to control them. What they really meant was that they wanted to fall in love again. They wanted the rest of the world to vanish so they could continue drifting alone together indefinitely. The affair was over, and now it was time to choose: Were they going to start living their love, or were they going to cling to their romantic illusions?

The choice wasn't clear or easy. When Nora left, she blamed the children. George blamed himself. They realized they weren't giving the relationship a chance and suspected that if they were willing to accept the struggle, their love might ripen and mature. But neither was willing to make the concessions or commitments that such an effort would require. Nora was too in love with the subjective sensation of falling in love to put up any longer with the realities of George's family life. George was so attached to his image of Nora as lover that he couldn't relate to her in the more practical roles of stepmother and wife, and yet neither would he leave his children to be with her alone. Maybe with the next person, they thought, things would be different. Maybe next time the enchantment would last forever.

Infatuation is an even more intense experience than the illusion of love at first sight, but it is not necessarily more meaningful. While lust may be one-sided, infatuation is essentially a two-sided prelude to the real process of loving. The trouble is that by saying they are falling in love, many people confuse the warm-up exercise with the ultimate goal.

Infatuation produces feelings of closeness and ecstasy that are wonderful but dangerous. When you're in this state it's easy to believe that you actually have become part of your lover, that the two of you think the same thoughts and feel the same emotions. You can almost literally lose yourselves in each other. Yet in reality, this is not a shared experience at all. You may look into each other's eyes, touch each other's skin, and feel each other's heart pounding, but you cannot feel what's going on *within* each other's heart.

As a result, there's a great deal of self-delusion involved in infatuation. You may assume that you and your partner are equally excited because your own desire is so powerful that you can imagine nothing else. Actually, even if you both say you are falling in love, your separate perceptions can be extremely unequal. One of you may be head over heels, while the other views the relationship as a comfort. One may be ecstatic about the relationship, and the other ecstatic about the sex. When you're infatuated, it can be very difficult to subdue your own emotions enough to accurately read your partner's.

You also tend to think that your partner is perfect because, right now, you see only what appeals to you. Infatuation obscures many of the emotional and intellectual safeguards that normally would alert you to someone else's faults and shortcomings. Instead, your fantasies run wild with all the unknowns in the situation. Because your partner is naturally trying to impress you in the beginning, you tend to see only the best, which makes the relationship seem wonderful but intensifies your fantasies and creates impossible expectations. This is the greatest danger of infatuation and the first of the illusions to fade when the freefall ends. Suddenly, after weeks of rapture, he notices the irritating shrillness of her laughter. She discovers the heap of dirty shirts shoved under the bed. He wants to watch football, and she wants to listen to opera. They think they're no longer in love because they realize they're not one and the same person. In fact, this discovery is not the end, but the beginning of love — but first both partners must let go of their illusions about each other.

Unfortunately, once you convince yourself you've fallen in love, it's much easier to extend the illusion than to dismiss it. You willingly persuade yourself that the sensation will last forever and will eliminate all that's wrong in your life. This is natural to the extent that infatuation temporarily makes you *feel* all-powerful and distracts you from the world beyond your twosome. When you're together, you create your own world, an oasis of comfort and happiness where you become oblivious to everything but your own pleasure. However, romance doesn't transform anything else in your life. The more you expect it to, the more disappointed you will be when, inevitably, reality starts to come back into focus. Often, in fact, the more intense the infatuation, the more quickly the relationship burns out. This is partly because instant passions necessarily are based on superficial impressions, which can mask serious differences and conflicts. It's also due to the impossible standard this initial intensity sets up. As thrilling as it is to lose yourself in another person for a few moments, hours, or days, the oblivion can't last long. When you come out of the spell and regain your separate identity, there's an inevitable letdown. You may blame your partner or simply call the relationship a mistake. In fact, your mistake was to think that the feelings you experienced during infatuation would lead automatically to love.

Even if you understand the requirements for true love and are cautious about your partners, however, it's easy to be swept away by newfound passion. There is nothing wrong with riding this crest and enjoying it to the utmost — as long as you recognize that the high is temporary and keep your emotions in perspective. If this is as far as it goes, and you don't mistake it for true love, the experience can be quite beneficial. In general, the only way you can test your own needs and preferences in love is by experimenting with different partners. Few people can wholeheartedly commit themselves to true love without first playing the field for a few years. If you accept that this is what you're doing, it's innocent, fun, and very valuable.

But playing the field pits self-restraint against infatuation. Often, infatuation wins out. When this happens, you may be tempted to make certain sacrifices that not only are unnecessary but also can be downright threatening. How do you respond if your new sweetheart invites you to try cocaine, skip work for a week of reckless abandon — or elope? In that moment when you have temporarily lost yourself to passion, it's easy to fall for the bait and do things you'll later regret. A day, a week, a month later, your lover may be history, and you may be kicking yourself for being so submissive. Or the consequences could be far more serious.

Anticipate these kinds of seductions in new love. Expect to be excited and consumed with thoughts of the new person in your life. But unless you enjoy the risks, establish some protective boundaries to hold yourself in check. One man who had been burned a few too many times in his haste for love refused to date a woman for at least a week after first meeting her. This gave him a chance to cool down, think about her rationally, and overcome his first impression to decide whether he really wanted to pursue her. When he did go ahead with the date he was less susceptible to his own momentary desire and more responsive to her as an individual.

Try not to lose sight of your other priorities just because you're attracted to someone new. Unless you're fully prepared for a lot of inconvenience and the likelihood that nothing will come of the relationship, don't change your travel plans to tag along with someone who comes on to you in the airport lounge. If you're exhausted and have a full day of meetings the next day, don't stay up all night just so you can get to know someone you met at a cocktail party that evening. And don't ignore the best friend you *know* will still be there in a year so that you can spend every second with someone who may be old news by next month. Love has a better chance if you remain true to *yourself* and catch up with your partner when the time is right than if you throw yourself at the moment.

To achieve a secure relationship, both partners must get beyond the passive illusions of falling in love and begin *actively* loving each other. This means accepting and dealing with each other's problems, faults, and inadequacies. It means giving not just what you want to give but what the other person truly needs from you. It means combining forces so that you broaden and deepen each other's life instead of devouring each other.

Once you have passed beyond infatuation and are truly in love, you no longer feel lost in the other person. Rather, you are stronger and more aware of yourself as an individual. You come to see yourself through your lover's eyes, instead of drowning yourself in them. While infatuation tempts you to forget yourself, true love forces you to extend yourself. This is not a process that occurs overnight, as infatuation often does. To the contrary, it takes place gradually and continuously as long as the relationship endures. By allowing — and sometimes forcing — a romance to build gradually, you minimize the risks of infatuation, allow yourself the time to push past superficial impressions, and create a context in which the relationship has a chance. Starting slowly also gives you the time to safely withdraw or change the terms if you realize that what's developing is actually false love.

Learning to recognize the warning signs of false love, therefore, is an essential step toward achieving a successful, lasting relationship. The next four chapters will help you identify the red flags in the case histories of some of my patients and, perhaps, in your own relationships.

2

FALLING IN LUST

DRESSED IN TWEED and corduroy, with horn-rimmed glasses and tan oxfords, Jeremy fit the stereotype of a university professor. As he entered my office, however, his expression seemed more like that of an embarrassed little boy than a man of letters. Eager to get past the preliminaries, he perched awkwardly on the edge of his seat and quickly, guiltily, poured out his story.

"Two weeks ago, I was perfectly happy," he began. "My life was steady. After two months of dating, Laura and I finally had what I considered to be a good, solid relationship. Everything was on an even keel — just the way I like it." He took a deep breath. "Then I met Karen."

Jeremy had first spotted Karen in the back of the audience during his weekly lecture. He was talking about deviant sexual behavior among the ancient Romans, and every time he mentioned the word *intercourse* he noticed her blushing and smiling at him. He told himself that he was imagining things, that she was just another young history major embarrassed by talk of sex. At the end of class, the tide of students rose, and he assumed she'd vanish with the rest.

When, in fact, she did disappear, he was mostly relieved —

after all, he was in no position to take up with an undergraduate — but his ego had been punctured. Karen was one of those fresh-faced blondes — a real heartbreaker — and his heart was doing a marathon despite his efforts to put her out of his mind.

That night he and Laura went out to dinner with some friends and spent hours talking about everything from child development to the space race. There was good food, good talk, good wine, and good company. As an undergraduate he'd dreamed of becoming a history professor and having these stimulating evenings as a routine part of life. He'd also dreamed of having a bright, loving, attractive woman to share them with. Now those dreams were coming true. Academia was fulfilling most of his fantasies, and Laura was fulfilling the rest. When they got back to his house, she nestled into his arms as if she had always belonged there. He berated himself for even fantasizing about someone else.

That weekend Jeremy was home alone grading papers when the phone rang.

"You probably don't know who I am," she began. But he knew exactly who she was. His pulse already was off and running. "I'm in your Roman history class, and I was so fascinated by your lecture this week. . . . I wonder if you would share your source material with me." It was a flimsy pretext, but one he could hardly turn down.

"Actually, I drew most of the information from some rare books in my own collection," he told her. "I'm free this afternoon if you'd like to stop by."

Jeremy was, in fact, dangerously free. Laura was in New Mexico all weekend purchasing Indian artifacts for the university museum where she was a curator. She had left in a huff because he refused to go with her. He couldn't see why she was annoyed. He had a substantial pile of work that he'd set aside for this time, and he wasn't really interested in Indian art. Besides, their relationship was good, but it wasn't as if they had to spend every second together.

Waiting for Karen to arrive, Jeremy ran through a long list of excuses and rationalizations to tone down his excitement and allay his guilt for what he suspected was about to happen. "Laura and I aren't married," he reminded himself. "We don't even live together. We're allowed to see other people. She still has dinner with her old boyfriends, after all. I'm not ready to be tied down." Then, regarding Karen: "As soon as I see her and talk to her I'll realize this is all absurd. She's nothing but a college kid looking for a thesis idea. None of my students have ever come on to me before, so why should this sensational-looking girl be the first?"

As soon as he opened the door, he knew he was in serious trouble. She looked both older and much more ravishing than he remembered her. The eyes that had drawn him in initially were surrounded by long lashes which she lifted and dropped with irresistible timing. Her lips were full and soft, and she kept them parted in a kind of breathless invitation. As she moved past him into the hall, her hand grazed his and he felt as if he were being drawn by a magnetic force.

They pored over his books together for about an hour, each hesitating to make the first overture toward the real purpose of the visit. As she told him later, Karen had sensed from the way Jeremy talked about sex in his lecture that he had something "special" to offer. Languishing in a stale relationship with her boyfriend from high school, she wanted something new and exciting, and when Jeremy's eyes had met hers, and then had come back to hers repeatedly, she had known this was what she'd been waiting for. Now here she was, and the quiver in his voice, the tension in his body assured her that her assessments were accurate — but she didn't know how to release the spring.

In one of the texts they looked at a photograph of a frieze depicting a Roman emperor entwined with one of his concubines. "You didn't come here just to see this, did you?" Jeremy asked.

"No," she replied, her voice suddenly throaty.

He closed his eyes and tried to focus on what exactly was happening. His entire body was sizzling with desire. He had never before felt like this, never before even been tempted to be unfaithful, and that realization suddenly made him doubt his relationship with Laura. This feeling is so out of the ordinary and so strong, he told himself, that it must mean there's something meaningful here. If I turn it down, I'll always wonder if I've made a mistake. On the other hand, if I have sex with Karen and it leads to nothing, who's to know? This doesn't *have* to hurt anyone!

His conscience momentarily appeased, Jeremy took Karen by the hand and led her to his bedroom. Naked, her body was even more perfect than he had imagined, and she used it without inhibition, doing things that Laura would barely imagine. They made love for three hours. She was insatiable, and he had never felt as potent in his life. When they finally released each other and he pulled back to look at her from a distance, it occurred to him that Laura had never made him feel anything like this.

They ordered pizza for dinner so they wouldn't have to leave the house and then spent the next night and day in bed together. She made him feel as if he were seventeen instead of thirty, and a virile seventeen at that. In reality, he'd been a pimple-faced bookworm at seventeen and had never gone beyond French kissing. Had he known then that sex could feel like this, the entire scope of his life might have been different. In the throes of his infatuation, Jeremy was convinced that Karen was the woman he should marry.

Karen, meanwhile, was telling him that he made her feel like a goddess. With her boyfriend, she felt neglected and bored. She didn't love him anymore; he brought her down. But Jeremy was an entirely different story. "You're mature, cultured, brilliant," she said, "and a passionate, sensitive lover as well."

When Laura returned on Sunday evening, Jeremy kept his prearranged date with her for drinks, but the meeting didn't last long. "I've met someone," he blurted out. "I don't know yet what it's all about, but I know I can't just walk away from it."

At first Laura was speechless. Then her face darkened. She was terribly hurt, but the emotion that registered was outrage. "I don't know how I misread you so badly," she said through clenched teeth. "I thought you were decent and trustworthy. I thought you actually deserved my respect. You really had me going, Jeremy. I only hope you get what you deserve. May whoever she is do exactly to you what you've just done to me!" And with that she walked out.

At that moment, Jeremy had no idea what a mistake he was making, but by the time he arrived in my office, he understood all too well. As powerful and delicious as sex was with Karen, it was not enough to hold him. All his initial reservations were absolutely accurate: She was too young; they had no common goals or interests; she was the greatest sexual partner he'd ever had, but she was no companion for him. After just five nights together, the thrill already was fading. He felt empty. He found himself yearning for Laura's intellect and empathy.

"Can you tell me what happened?" he asked me. "How could I have been so desperately in love one minute and so indifferent the next?"

"Were you really in love, or was it lust?"

Jeremy looked sheepish. "Maybe that's a better word for it. But it was such an incredibly strong sensation! I turned my whole life upside down because of it!"

"It sounds as if you enjoyed how much Karen wanted you. Maybe it felt like compensation for all the experiences you missed when you were younger — when you were that pimple-faced seventeen-year-old."

"I never even dreamed of experiences like that when I was seventeen!"

"What do you dream of now?"

"Honestly?" he asked. "Honestly, I guess my fantasy is a woman who's a cross between Karen and Laura." He laughed. "A kind of pneumatic sex queen with a Ph.D. But realistically, I just want to put this all behind me and find some way to make Laura forgive me."

Although Jeremy thought he was back on track, it was clear he remained conflicted. He still seemed to believe that the sex he'd had with Karen was better than his sexual relationship with Laura. Until he understood the difference between his sexual feelings for the two women, and until he believed that his sex life with Laura could eventually become just as rewarding, he was not really ready for her forgiveness.

Through therapy, he gradually came to understand that what he'd had with Karen was an infatuation that appealed to his ego and his fantasies of his own virility. He also began to view true love as a much broader and deeper commitment than he had envisioned before. This new outlook on true love, far more than his repentance, ultimately persuaded Laura to give him another chance.

Lust versus Love

True love usually involves sexual intimacy, but powerful sex doesn't necessarily involve love. For many people, this is a brutal paradox. And the confusion it produces is one of the primary sources of false love.

The very words we use to talk about sex contribute to this confusion. We say "making love" when we mean nothing more than having sex. Is intercourse with a prostitute "making love"? Not often. Nor does your sexual partner truly become your "lover" simply by taking you to bed. When you say that someone is a "great lover," you probably mean that person is a great sexual mechanic, acrobat, or performer, not someone who actually loves you better or more than your other romantic partners.

The term "consummation" is also a gross misnomer. It implies that the first sexual act is the completion of the relationship — both the high point and the finish. While many false love relationships do end shortly after "consummation," the course of true love has virtually nothing to do with when — or, in rare cases, even whether — sexual intercourse takes place.

Some people recognize that these terms, as they are commonly used, are nothing more than euphemisms for the taboo "S" word, but others genuinely believe what the words say: that having sex is the same as making love, that sexual performance reflects a quality and degree of love, and that sex is the primary focus of a loving relationship. Women especially tend to blur the line between sex and love, grasping at fantasies that "if we sleep together, it means we're in love." When sex is unusually exciting in a relationship, both men and women can fall prey to the misconception that "great sex" equals true love. How could Jeremy *not* be in love with a woman who ignited his passion the way Karen did? How could he truly love Laura when the most accurate adjective he could find to describe their sex life was "comfortable"?

Similar contradictions plague every one of us in love, and our own lust is the culprit. Unfortunately, lust is a much more aggressive motivator than love, especially fledgling love. It produces all the physical sensations and pleasures we're taught not just to associate but to *equate* with love. The heart, supposedly the barometer of love, goes crazy. The skin becomes flushed and hot. A weakness in the knees and a dizziness set in with intense lust, accompanied by a feeling of giddiness that often comes with being desired. All this physical excitement is directed toward one objective, which is not love but sex.

Sex is a basic human drive, and lust is its tool. For many reasons, including basic physiology and conditioning, men generally are motivated more by lust than most women are. Male hormones are partly responsible. A man who goes without sex for an extended period will have a nocturnal emission and spontaneous erections, but women have no comparable physiological release. This imbalance between the sexes is greatest in youth, when male hormones are strongest and males tend to be most driven by lust. Young men are also more susceptible to pressure from their buddies — and perhaps even their fathers — to prove their virility by "scoring." (This male stan-

dard is retreating marginally in the face of AIDS and other ve-
nereal diseases, but even with the threat of death many young
heterosexual men are reluctant to so much as use condoms,
much less reduce their sexual activity.)

Many adult men who are insecure in other areas of their
lives adopt this same form of victory to boost their flagging
egos. Sex becomes entangled not with love but with issues of
self-esteem. Later, unfaithfulness may be a man's way of reaffirming his desirability. The midlife crisis descends, and the
husband who's been faithful to his wife for twenty years starts
chasing airline stewardesses on business trips. The middle management executive gets axed when his company falls prey to a
takeover, and he moves into the neighborhood singles bar and
begins seducing nineteen-year-olds. To these men, sex provides
a form of validation that partially compensates for the disappointments and failures they've experienced in other areas.

Men generally are less likely than women to confuse lust
with love. They are *more* likely, however, to fall in love with
exciting sex; and for some, the one type of sex that's reliably
exciting is adultery. The man who keeps a mistress for thirteen
years may feel addicted to her, in a sense, even though he never
considers leaving his wife to marry her. What actually has him
hooked is not his mistress but the ego gratification and the
physical thrill of the illicit situation.

While women are less susceptible than men to this kind of
sexual ego gratification, they're certainly not immune to it. A
single, fifty-year-old woman lawyer may be just as likely as a
man would be to seduce attractive clients and boast about it.
And a bored, neglected, middle-aged housewife may take secret
pride in luring a young boxboy from her local supermarket to
her bedroom. Once the deed is done, however, most of these
women have trouble accepting that their passion was based on
lust alone. Unlike men, women are taught to be ashamed of
their feelings of lust but to take pride in love. While men
"score" by sleeping with women, women "score" by persuading men to "fall in love" with them.

In these scenarios, of course, true love does not exist. Men who are more interested in sex and variety than commitment may dismiss or accept a woman purely on the basis of her body, sometimes on first glance and sometimes after the first night together. A woman with great wit, compassion, and intelligence may qualify as a best friend, but if she lacks a pretty shell, these men will reject her as a lover.

Sometimes lust is driven by nothing more than suggestion and the thrill of being pursued. One of my patients admitted that he'd become irrepressibly excited when a woman in his office accosted him in an empty conference room and overwhelmed him with blatant come-ons. He wasn't about to leave his beloved wife of fifteen years, but he did feel enticed enough for a roll on the floor. Afterward, he subdued his feelings of guilt by reminding himself that he had done nothing to invite the incident and that it had fed his pride and ego. He compensated by acting unusually passionate toward his wife for an entire month afterward.

For others, the suggestion can be far subtler. One young woman told me she became aroused every time she saw male ballet dancers in their tights or attractive men in snug bathing suits at the beach. Ironically, because lust requires some mystery, nude beaches tend to be less provocative for many people than other beaches. As long as the veil remains, we can imagine perfection, but when all is exposed, the flirtation with the unknown is over. Too much reality can ruin a fantasy. In lust, familiarity breeds indifference.

While lust plays to our appetite for change and uses the excitement of the unknown to bait us into temporary liaisons, true love plays to our need for one constant companion — a partner in life as well as in sex. True love is strengthened by familiarity and a host of individual qualities that no one would dream of calling seductive. When was the last time you heard anyone say, "He was so honest and loyal, I couldn't restrain myself" or "His understanding nature really turned me on"? While in and of themselves these characteristics are not particularly sexy, they contribute tremendously to the intensity and intimacy of a loving relationship in the long term.

Sex is just one of many components of true love, and it is possible to love someone without having sex at all. However, sexual intimacy is so powerful and so beneficial, both emotionally and physically, that it is a necessity for most loving couples. What is not necessary — or even feasible — is for sex to be wildly exhilarating each and every time. In true love, sex is the result of a progressive relationship, and as the relationship becomes deeper and more complex, sex improves as well. However, variations will naturally occur as the relationship changes. What makes for good sex after years of marriage is quite different from what makes the first night thrilling.

Good Sex, Bad Sex

What consitutes "good" sex? Contrary to popular belief, it has little to do with technique or physique. You don't have to "last" all night to be a good lover. You don't need a perfect body. You don't need to know every position in the Kamasutra. But you and your partner do have to care about pleasing each other and yourselves.

Good sex is neither a contest nor a performance, but a shared experience based on trust. It simultaneously involves several different forms of communication: verbal, emotional, and tactile. Ideally, both partners feel relaxed and open enough to talk honestly before and during sex about what they like and dislike and to experiment with different ways of pleasing each other. Neither feels embarrassed or reluctant. Instead, each treats the other as an equal, but with the understanding that each person has different sexual needs and preferences.

There is no ego in good sex. Accusations and comparisons are out of place. If your partner does something that feels wrong, you don't yell out, "You're hurting me!" or complain, "Nobody's ever pulled that on me before." By the same token, the object is not to impress or dominate each other. There's no reason to feel particularly proud of bringing your partner to orgasm or to feel guilty or humiliated if you don't. Unfortunately, most people assume that both responses are appropriate.

Despite the fact that many people blurt out "I love you" when they climax, love does not produce orgasm, and orgasm is not a measure of love or good sex. In true love, partners are more likely to be truthful and uninhibited and to know what the other likes. To this extent, love is conducive to orgasm, but it is no guarantee. Often, masturbation or mechanical stimulation produces "better" orgasms than intercourse does, but that certainly isn't "better sex." Few people would trade a loving sexual partner for a vibrator, even if they never climaxed during intercourse. The satisfaction of good sex has at least as much to do with human intimacy and emotional bonding as it does with physiological release.

So what about couples like Jeremy and Karen, who seem to have great sex without love? What they have, in fact, is great sexual excitement without the completeness or unity of sex in love. If two people enter a relationship purely out of sexual desire and mutual attraction, they can have a wonderful affair. True love may or may not follow, but one thing is certain: Exciting sex at the outset of the relationship is not a reliable predictor.

There are three conditions that make sex without love so compelling:

1. It is very low risk. With nothing at stake emotionally, many people find it easy to perform sexually.
2. Both partners are concerned about sexual prowess and will take great pains to prove themselves by pleasing the other. It's relatively easy to do this because physical performance is the only criterion; neither person expects intimacy on any other level.
3. Sexual flings are supercharged with lust. Everything is new and revealing. The attraction is intense. Moreover, there's often a tacit understanding that the relationship will last only as long as the mutual attraction is at its peak. When

either person begins to lose interest, it's over. If the relationship doesn't end at this point, the seemingly good sex quickly wanes unless the partners decide to plunge into the more complicated and demanding process of love.

The real trouble occurs when the unloving couple stays together, ignoring the warning signals and trying to revive the sex but refusing to invest any additional energy in building the rest of the relationship. Sometimes these situations can turn very ugly, as in the case of Marcella and Denis.

They met over dinner at the home of a mutual friend. At first they were unable to take their eyes off each other. Later, they were unable to take their hands off each other. But that was as far as their intimacy ever went. She was black, he white. She was a professional, he an artist. She was well educated, he never finished college. She had money and style, his income and wardrobe were uncertain. They had little in common but their initial attraction, which began to falter exactly two weeks after they started sleeping together.

Rather than accepting that this was the end, Denis began demanding more sex, often twice a day. He said it was because he loved her so much, which appealed to Marcella's need to be wanted. Most men, she'd found, were intimidated by her. So instead of walking out when she no longer was enjoying it, Marcella complied, often faking orgasm in the hope that she'd recover her enthusiasm. It had been a long time since she'd had a sexual relationship, and she wanted to trust that first lusty impulse that had brought them together.

But it never occurred to her to welcome Denis into any other part of her life or to become more involved in his world. She had struggled to lift herself out of lower-class beginnings. She'd worked her way through college and consciously made herself over as a modern success story, a model for other black women. On the one hand, she didn't want to detract from her image by being seen with a marginal white artist. On the other, she was genuinely fearful of social and professional repudiation if she was known to have crossed color and societal lines in her choice of a partner. Denis may be good enough for me, she told herself, but he would not be acceptable to the people who determine my success.

Denis never challenged her decision. The truth was, he didn't want any part of her life because it made him feel like a failure. With Marcella alone and naked, he could feel powerful and masculine, but with her corporate friends he would feel just the opposite. He came from the kind of background that should have groomed him for success: a wealthy family, private school upbringing, lots of pressure, and endless opportunity. He'd turned his back on it all when he got to college. For him, the pressure had been too great and the opportunities had all been channeled to meet his parents' needs, not his own. He chose to get away from his roots just as Marcella had chosen to get away from hers. At first, this common dynamic helped draw them together. Ultimately, it pitted them against each other.

Gradually, when the pleasure of sex failed to return, Denis's desire for dominance increased. He became jealous of the time Marcella spent away from him, time she was spending with "the other side," as he called it. He got rougher in bed. Once he held her so tightly that he bruised her. She was genuinely afraid and never saw him again after that night.

But the memory of that affair haunted her. She was so nervous that she changed her phone number and entered therapy soon afterward. It took many months for her to begin to unravel the confusion in her mind between false love's illusions and true love and between good sex and bad sex.

There's a big difference between bad sex and disappointing sex. Bad sex is dishonest, imbalanced, and sometimes abusive. When one person wants to have sex and the other doesn't or when one wants love and the other wants sex, bad sex is almost inevitable. When one person uses sex as a form of domination, the result is always bad sex.

Disappointing sex, on the other hand, can occur for a multitude of reasons, including indecisiveness and even wanting *too* much to please. This was precisely what happened to Sarah when she began having an affair with one man while trying to break up with another.

She had begun therapy several months earlier when she first realized how dissatisfied she was with her four-year-old relationship. At age twenty-six, she was starting to think about marriage, but her boyfriend refused to discuss it. Ultimately concluding that he was incapable of making the kind of commitment she wanted, Sarah granted herself permission to begin seeing other men.

When she met Mitch, a young law student with whom she felt an immediate affinity, she thought he was exactly the type of man she would like to marry. He was self-assured, stable, intelligent, and charming. She readily accepted his request for a date. The evening went even better than she'd hoped and led them back to Mitch's apartment, where he put some soft jazz on the stereo, poured wine, and in no time had Sarah in his arms. By the third cut on the album, he was gently undressing her, and to her surprise she was willing. He had aroused her sexual curiosity, and she intuited that she was safe with him. Yet soon after they began intercourse, she cried out in pain. She wasn't used to a man so well endowed, she explained. Although a little flattered, Mitch was concerned that he was hurting her and pulled away. Afterward, riding back to Sarah's apartment, they both were quiet, trying to understand what had happened.

Sarah was still perplexed when she arrived for her session the next day.

"You seem worried," I commented after she told me what had happened. "How do you feel about Mitch now?"

"I like him very much," Sarah said. "But I'm afraid he won't want to see me again."

"Why do you think he would feel that way?"

"Because I ruined the evening." Sarah looked at her hands. "And I lied to him. He wasn't really hurting me. I just said that because I didn't feel I could go through with it. He was so eager and excited, and I just didn't feel that way."

"How did you feel?"

"Guilty. I'm not really out of my other relationship and already I'm in bed with somebody else. That just doesn't feel right."

"Was Mitch pressuring you?"

"No, not really. I wanted to go to bed with him at first, but once we were there I felt uncomfortable and unsure. It all happened too fast."

"You're telling me you have many conflicting feelings," I said, trying to interpret Sarah's confusion. "You want him to want you. You like the idea of having sex with him, but the reality of it makes you nervous. You want to act like a single woman who's free to get involved with someone new, but you haven't been able to terminate your last relationship." She nodded, a little embarrassed.

"Perhaps you just need to give yourself some time," I reassured her. "You went too fast with Mitch, and now you feel you made a mistake. Try to stop blaming yourself, and work toward a decision. It's clear that being involved with two men at once is going to make you uncomfortable, so your first step is to face your old boyfriend. Do you want to try to revive that relationship or end it?"

"End it," she replied quickly. "Even if I never see Mitch again, I can't go on like this, and I can't go backward."

"Then you need to decide where to take your relationship with Mitch."

"But what if he doesn't call again?"

"That would probably mean that he just wanted sex, not a relationship." I smiled. "If what you've told me about him is accurate, he'll call."

Sarah's fears proved unfounded. Mitch had never had a woman complain of pain before. He always tried to be very sensitive to his partners' needs, and Sarah's reaction had hurt his ego. It had not dampened his enthusiasm for seeing her, however. He wanted to get to know her better anyway, and now he was additionally motivated to compensate for their first time. He called the next day.

Sarah took the time she needed to collect herself. Before she would agree to see Mitch again, she ended her previous relationship once and for all. Then she explained to Mitch that she wanted to go more slowly. By the time they had sex again, they'd had five dates and it was three weeks later. They were both more comfortable and relaxed. Though it wasn't perfect, it was good, and they now trusted each other enough to know it would get better.

Ideally, no relationship should ever be decided purely on sexual grounds. Sex is a barometer not of love but of the moment. Its quality changes dramatically with each individual's level of desire, other concerns and anxieties, health — and drugs and alcohol. The key is to enjoy sex when it's good, accept that there will be times when it's disappointing, but let your judgment and feelings for the person determine whether you get more seriously involved.

Starting with Sex

It's not always easy to tell when it's time to start having sex with someone new. If the only purpose of the relationship is sex, you may not want to wait at all, but if the goal is to develop love, then it can be a mistake to have sex on the first or second date. In any case, it can be dangerous, since the risk of sexually transmitted disease is much higher when you're not sure the other person is taking the necessary precautions. But whether you wait a week or a year, your timing will depend on common sense, trust, and desire.

Common sense tells you that you should have a certain level of emotional and intellectual intimacy with someone before becoming sexually intimate. Would you immediately reveal your most private thoughts and experiences, your most embarrassing moments and gravest mistakes to someone you've never met before? If not, why then would you be willing to strip yourself naked before a near-stranger and reveal the most private physical parts of yourself? The first time you go to bed with someone you naturally feel vulnerable, and you want to know that your partner won't take advantage of that vulnerability. To establish trust, you need to spend time collecting information and getting close to the *person* before you get physically close.

Although it's easy to forget in the heat of attraction, trust builds gradually in any relationship. You learn to trust by watching how a person treats you and others at different levels of intimacy and by discovering how he or she operates mentally and emotionally. This requires a lot of talk and a lot of shared experiences before you ever get near the bedroom. Ideally, you'll talk about your attitudes toward sex and love first, to make sure you accept each other's priorities. If you don't, at least you'll be able to make an informed decision whether to stay or leave — before you find yourselves in bed together.

Trust is especially critical now because of the threat of sexually transmitted diseases. Before the emergence of AIDS, sexual standards reflected the general social climate of the times. In the relatively puritanical fifties, it was still socially disgraceful to have sex outside of marriage, so couples tended to wait at least until they believed they were in love before sleeping together. In the sixties and early seventies, free expression and social experimentation made it acceptable to "love the one you're with," even if you'd known each other for only a few hours. Brief sexual encounters were considered healthy and positive. By the time AIDS and the return to conservatism arrived with the eighties, much of this sexual freewheeling had begun to reverse.

At first AIDS was considered a problem for homosexuals only and had little effect on sexual habits among heterosexuals. By 1985, however, it was clear that everyone was potentially at risk. The rapidly increasing number of AIDS victims and a media blitz advocating safe sex began to turn the tide of promiscuity and casual sex that had been rising for so long. Today, deciding to have sex with a new partner requires more than fondness and passion; you need to trust the body as well as the soul, because each time you have sex with a person, you are actually having intercourse with his or her entire sexual history. Unfortunately, even true love cannot protect you from AIDS, herpes, gonorrhea, or syphilis.

The best way to establish this trust is to go together for a blood test for the AIDS antibody before having sex *and* then use condoms until you've both had consistently negative tests over a period of a year and are willing to remain in a monogamous relationship. Unfortunately, in today's world, this is the only truly safe sex for people beginning a new relationship. The process may not sound very romantic, but it is a strong gauge of maturity and concern, since anyone who is willing to take these precautions is displaying a great deal of respect for you. And it removes a layer of anxiety that could destroy the relationship unnecessarily. If your partner is *not* willing to be tested and practice safe sex, you will be mistrustful and worried about the consequences of your liaison, and you may be exposing yourself to a life-threatening disease.

Practicing safe sex, however, does not mean that you necessarily must delay for weeks before sleeping with a new partner. In some cases, there's a real psychological value to getting past sex in order to clarify a relationship. Sometimes couples are so overwhelmed with infatuation that they cannot see each other on any other level. Hard as they may try, they cannot distinguish between that initial desire and more serious interest in each other. If both are equally willing to practice safe sex and risk the possibility that lust is all there is, there's no reason not to proceed. Unfortunately, new romances are rarely that evenly balanced, and lust tends to sway even the most sensible among us. In general, familiarity and companionship are a more reliable way to start a relationship than premature sex.

Of course, all these warnings presume that you and your partner feel a distinct attraction to each other, but it's quite possible to have a tremendous intellectual attraction or enjoy each other's company without feeling an urge to have sex.

Sometimes that urge will develop, sometimes not. In the meantime, there's no sense in pushing physical intimacy before both partners are ready and willing. Not only does it tend to produce bad sex, but it may create a wall of uncertainty, mistrust, and resentment that unfairly destroys the entire relationship. Had Mitch insisted that Sarah go through with intercourse on their first awkward evening together, for example, she probably would have felt hostile and abused the next day instead of merely confused. Even though he wanted a deeper relationship, she might never have been able to forgive or trust enough to give him another chance.

Physical attraction aside, lovers must be friends. If you and your partner get to know each other over a period of weeks or months *before* becoming romantically involved, you can develop trust and affection for each other as individuals without your vision being clouded by infatuation. Not only will this increase your chances of achieving true love, but it probably also will benefit your sexual relationship in the long run. From the start, your sex life will be enhanced by the tenderness and caring you've developed as friends. Furthermore, when you understand that physical attraction is just one of many bonds that hold you together, you can accept the highs and lows of sexual excitement as a normal part of true love.

3

THE IMAGE TRAP

"I'D LOVE TO MARRY a rich man," Pamela announced with conviction. "When I was little, I'd dream about what it would be like to lie around a pool all day, to dress up and go out every night. I decided way back then that I'd never have to struggle for money like my family did." She shook her short, straight blond hair and smoothed her skirt. "I know that sounds terrible, but at least I'm being honest," she added, lowering her dark eyes.

At twenty-four, Pamela was striking — tall and confident-looking despite her constant battle with the scale. She had street smarts and a quick tongue, though she had never finished college. In therapy, she frequently was sarcastic. But although her act was tough and supercilious, underneath she was struggling to measure up to an illusion that had been imposed on her when she was very young.

Originally from Iowa, Pamela was the youngest of four children. Her father owned a hardware store, and her brothers worked with him. Her older sister was bright, but not as pretty as Pamela, and had gotten a degree in accounting and married one of her classmates right out of college. Pamela was her parents' darling, and her mother in particular had always envisioned a different life for this favored daughter. She entered her in children's beauty pageants, which Pamela frequently won, but eventually her father put a stop to it because he said it made her look cheap. Then her mother began telling her that she could become rich and famous by marrying the right man.

Pamela listened and believed what her mother told her. She devoured news stories about small-town girls who went to New York or Hollywood or London or Paris and became famous socialites. By the time she was sixteen, she wanted desperately to be one of them.

While there were some very wealthy and eligible farmers in her hometown, agriculture could never buy her the status and glamour she envisioned for herself. Pamela might eventually settle for a professional, perhaps a doctor or a lawyer, but what she really wanted was someone powerful and exciting — a celebrity. At her father's insistence, she completed secretarial school so she could support herself "while husband hunting," but then she packed her bags and moved to California.

She knew she'd need to manipulate the odds in order to find the kind of man she wanted, and she did so aggressively. She rented a tiny apartment just off an alley. It wasn't much to look at, but it had a Beverly Hills address, and she believed that that helped her land a job as secretary to a top television executive at one of the major studios. Her boss was newly and apparently happily married, so *he* was not much of a prospect, but sitting in his outer office and being on the studio lot allowed her to meet a great many others who might be, including a slew of movie stars.

For several years Pamela's freshness and enthusiasm attracted a sizable following of struggling actors and aspiring directors. Everyone in Los Angeles seemed aimed toward the same targets of money, power, glamour, and status. It was not always easy for her to distinguish who would make it from who would fail, but one thing gradually became clear. None of the men who were on the success track had yet chosen her.

She had to be tougher on herself, she finally decided. The surest way to attract a successful man was to look like a successful woman, and that meant she'd have to lose about fifteen pounds, change her hair and clothes, and adopt a much more mature image. So she put herself on a strict diet and exercise regimen, invested her savings in a new wardrobe and car, and had her hair restyled. She worked at her appearance every bit as diligently as an actress grooming herself for a prize role. At the same time, however, she began to have gnawing doubts about her prospects for success, and she also worried that others might think her too shallow. She began therapy to try to deal with these concerns.

"Do you think I'm being unrealistic to think I could marry someone rich and famous?" she asked me, after describing her life to this point.

"Not if you work at it as hard as you seem to be," I commented. "The real question to consider is, what will it really do for you if you succeed?"

She looked bemused. "The obvious, I guess. I really believe it would make me happy." She giggled, a little embarrassed. "And rich, too. What could be more exciting than having a husband who's powerful, handsome, exciting, and stylish?" Then, almost as an afterthought: "And loving too, of course. . . . It's every girl's dream. Why not shoot for the top?"

"You're expecting a great deal," I commented. "What if you meet someone who's rich, handsome, but not a nice *person*?"

She laughed. "I'd use his money and my love to turn him around!"

Soon after this conversation, Pamela met George. The moment he caught her eye in the studio commissary, she felt her efforts to make herself over were finally paying off. Twice her age and ruggedly attractive, he was a well-known star and a serious traveler among the jet set.

Breathless, she watched him make his way across the crowded dining room to her table. "Mind if I sit here?" he asked. She shrugged, doing her best to look nonchalant. "I hate it when strangers plop down and ask to share my table, don't you?" he said, a twinkle in his eye. She burst out laughing. He was charming and attentive. It occurred to her that she was making herself an exceptionally easy mark, but she didn't care. When he asked if she was free to come to a party that night, she instantly accepted.

He had a pool, a Jaguar, a large home with an ocean view. His latest picture was going to be very successful, he told her, and he had three films lined up to do in the next two years. He'd been married twice and had two teenage daughters, but Pamela saw nothing unusual about that. Most of the men she dated had fractured pasts.

They started out fast. The party was extravagant. George's salt-and-pepper hair set off his Palm Springs tan. He held Pamela's hand comfortably. He offered cocaine, and though she ordinarily refused drugs, she accepted. After a couple of hours, they went back to his house, swam naked in the pool, and then stayed up all night having sex.

The next day, she was too tired and distracted to go to work. That afternoon, she arrived triumphant in my office. "This is it!" she cried. "My mother was right. I really can have it all!"

"You're very excited just now," I said, trying to inject some sense of perspective, "and it sounds great, but you've had only one date. In so short a time, can you really tell what attracted you? Was it his personality, his looks, his fame, or his possessions?"

"Everything," she answered confidently. "I'm thrilled with the whole package. I'm falling in love."

"Pamela, you badly *want* to be in love. Right now you feel as if you're finally getting what you've worked so hard for all this time. But what about your deeper personal expectations and needs? Can this man give you what you need *emotionally* as well as materially?"

"Of course," Pamela scoffed. "I wouldn't be with him if he couldn't."

"You need to get to know him and enjoy him as an individual apart from his public image before you decide whether to turn your life around for him," I suggested. "Try to take it slow."

For weeks Pamela refused to look beyond the surface of the relationship. At the end of her first month with George, she quit her job, stopped coming to therapy, and moved into the big house with the pool. They frequently stayed out all night and routinely got up at noon or later. She used so much cocaine that she no longer worried about her weight. But she also started to look and feel like a ghost. Her identity was becoming completely submerged in George's and, aside from allowing her to accompany and have sex with him, he was giving little in return.

Gradually, Pamela began to realize that her looks and youth were only part of the reason he was attracted to her. Just as important, she was noncompetitive and nonthreatening. She knew enough about the movie industry that he could talk to her, but she was not a serious player herself, and he could command her to do and say things that made him feel powerful. His previous wives had stood up to him and made him feel weak, even needy at times. They had left him. He wasn't about to see that happen again. With Pamela, he felt confident of his control.

But when George's film failed at the box office and his deal for the next three pictures fell through, his ego plummeted and his confidence shattered. One day Pamela asked him for some money to buy a new dress, and he pulled back and slapped her. "You'll get what I give you," he said. "If you want more, do something to earn it."

Later that day he caught her flirting with one of his friends over the phone and ripped the receiver from her hand. "As long as you live in this house, you're mine," he yelled at her. "Don't forget it!"

Still, his celebrity status, his image, and his power held her like a vise. Until she was literally bruised and battered, she couldn't give up her love affair with the "good life." She returned for therapy during this period and struggled to make sense of what was happening. She knew she should leave him, and yet every time she decided to get out, she'd feel guilty — as if she were betraying her dreams. Anyone who had so many of the superficial trappings that she had so long desired must be worth a certain amount of sacrifice: This was the thinking that kept her in his grip. If she just stood by him, she told herself, she could make him see how wonderful she was, and he'd start to treat her with love. It was almost as painful to face the loss of her illusions as it was to endure George's increasingly possessive brutality, but after several weeks she finally began to recognize that her dreams had become self-destructive and that the sacrifices she now was making far outweighed any potential benefits.

"I feel so abused!" she concluded after leaving him at last.

"You're hurt that he didn't love you," I said. She nodded emphatically. "But did you honestly love him?"

She looked as though I'd caught her with her hand in the till. "I gave up my job for him. I devoted myself to him. He used me!" she exclaimed, but she knew the truth. "No," she said, taking a deep breath. "I don't think I ever really loved him."

"You loved what you wanted him to be. You thought he could give you what you'd always wanted. You thought he could make you fit your fantasy image of yourself, and so you followed him. It's difficult to see past an illusion that runs so deep."

"I've learned my lesson!" She laughed.

Nevertheless, the illusions of wealth and power continued to entice Pamela. Over the next six years she had a succession of similar affairs, all of which ended with her feeling used and unloved. Not until she finally stopped chasing false love and lowered her materialistic expectations did she begin to penetrate the outer image of the men she dated. Only then did she stand a chance of finding true love.

The American dream can be a tough taskmaster, not only setting up unrealistic expectations but also pushing people to find shortcuts to achieve them. For people like Pamela, false love becomes an irresistible way to chase the dream. When she looked in the mirror, she wanted to see one of the Beautiful People who fill the nighttime soaps. She wanted to see a woman who not only looked great in an evening gown but had the money and lifestyle to wear one often. Instead, she saw a small-town girl whose only assets were a pretty face and optimism. Snaring a man who was wealthy, chic, and powerful seemed like the perfect ticket to happiness. She played right into the hands of George, who kept her as an attractive trinket, a playmate he could control when everything else was spinning out of control. He gave her the trappings of celebrity. She allowed him to feel powerful. Both were caught in the image trap.

As transparent as a couple like Pamela and George may seem to an outside observer, it's much more difficult to spot the red flags when you are the one falling into the image trap. And it happens to almost everyone at some point during the search for a partner in love. Maybe you're spellbound by beauty, status, or intelligence instead of wealth or power. Maybe the illusions are even more specific, as "I'm only attracted to blue-eyed blondes" or "I'll only marry a man who has completed graduate school." But sometimes you may be influenced by image on such a subtle scale that you don't consciously even recognize your preferences, much less how they may be distorting your selection process. This is why it's important to examine the role of superficial images in false love and discover just how dangerous these illusions can be.

The image trap uses your own insecurities to bait you into false love. There's bound to be a discrepancy between your ideal self and your actual self. Instead of improving yourself or accepting your own shortcomings, you may be tempted to try to use romance or marriage as a shortcut to your most distant, perhaps impossible goals. And naturally, you will use your own image assets — be they beauty, intelligence, money, or power — as bargaining chips to exchange for the illusions you desire.

Any relationship that ensues won't be based on love, or probably even on affection, but on a seemingly innocent form of deceit. You may be not only misleading the other person but lying about your true motivation to yourself as well. If the truth strikes you as too flagrant, you may convince yourself that passion alone is motivating you. "Of course I like it that he's a millionaire, but I love him because he's really a good person." I've heard this type of defense many, many times from my patients, and it often signals false love.

If a core of true love does develop apart from the attraction to image, the relationship may succeed, and you may indeed live happily ever after. But while it's true that people do sometimes become wealthier, more powerful, more cosmetically attractive, or better informed as a result of marriage, relationships that are motivated *primarily* by this desire rarely advance past the superficial attraction or produce true love. A few people are content to accept the lifestyle benefits in lieu of love, but most are not. Usually, as soon as one partner realizes that the attraction is limited to image, the relationship self-destructs.

One reason such relationships fail is that they are essentially anonymous. In focusing so hard on the surface, you can easily miss the person within. Many people resist any deeper insights for fear of being disappointed or of uncovering more emotional baggage than the relationship can handle. But it's only a matter of time before glimmers of the person beneath the facade start to appear. These may hint at qualities that are even more appealing than the surface characteristics that initially attracted you — or they may suggest less appealing, even downright disturbing personality traits. At the very least, they are bound to put your superhero into a more human light. You may begin to see many of the same frailties, needs, anxieties, and problems you were trying to escape in yourself. Or you may find additional, possibly even more serious, problems than your own. In either case, this probably is not the image that initially attracted you. To survive as a couple, you and your partner need to accept and learn to cope with these human complexities, to enjoy each other as people regardless of your surface characteristics.

The second reason relationships based on image tend to disintegrate is that they can intensify your own feelings of inadequacy. Often, what you really want is to take over the other person's image, to make it your own. But even true love can't make this happen, and false love certainly can't. For a while the game of make-believe may be quite convincing to the outside world, perhaps even to the other person, but you soon will realize that internally you still are exactly the same. Then you may start to resent the other person for having what you can't have. The very illusions that initially attracted you may now spark your anger because you can't acquire them by osmosis. The longer you live with the pretense, the more painful and obvious it may become that you alone can correct your own flaws. Self-improvement is *not* the primary goal of love, whether true or false love.

The third reason the image trap is so dangerous is that it plays on the grass-is-greener impulse that lies within all of us. From a distance you see someone rich, beautiful, powerful, or brilliant, and you honestly may believe if you could be just like that, all your problems would be solved. However, the closer you get to the person you admire, the more obvious it becomes that having these advantages doesn't necessarily make life all that rosy. Often, the price of these illusions is simply too high. As soon as you realize this, the whole basis for the relationship may start to crumble.

Even recognizing these dangers, it's easy to walk into the image trap because the images themselves are so compelling. Films, television, advertising — American culture in general pushes us to value the superficial. If you find someone you think can supply the right image, you may convince yourself that you'll overcome the odds, make the relationship a success *and* achieve your ideal existence. Or you may become so mesmerized by the image that you truly believe you're in love.

The Beauty Complex

Consciously or unconsciously, we all tend to judge people initially by their looks. To a certain extent, this is due to Madison Avenue programming, which teaches us that beautiful people are somehow more valuable, powerful, and desirable than the rest. The media spend fortunes to make us lust after faces and bodies that are nothing but images on page or screen, and many people comply without even questioning the shallowness of this desire. Anyone who looks great simply must be great. And anyone who does not look great has to be twice as appealing in other respects in order to measure up.

While this rule certainly affects both men and women, there is a double standard that judges women's looks much more harshly than men's and also makes men much more vulnerable to the romantic illusion of beauty. A man can trade romantically on his intelligence, professional achievements, and bank account, even if he doesn't look like Clark Gable. A woman has a much harder time winning a man's affection if she isn't attractive. While a man who's funny-looking, smart, and rich might easily be called "sexy," a woman with the same attributes is called "strange," if not "pushy" or "butch." Many men feel threatened by any woman who is bright and successful. If she's plain they see her as direct competition. If she's very attractive, they may reassure themselves that "she slept her way to the top." If it's obvious that she's their intellectual equal, they may simply steer clear of her. These men prefer a woman who is good-looking and not successful in her own right, one who will serve as an ornament, making them look good and giving them pleasure without challenging their self-image. If she is beautiful, in other words, she not only doesn't need much else, but to some men she may be even more appealing if she is *not* bright and skillful in other respects.

Women like Pamela play right into this double standard by evaluating *themselves* on the basis of their looks. If they like what they see in the mirror, they accept that this is all they need to attract a man. Once they've got him, they may think that preserving their looks is all they have to do to maintain the relationship. Furthermore, instead of challenging the criteria men use to judge beauty, they go to extreme, often expensive and painful, lengths to conform to almost impossible ideals.

In fact, few people, men or women, are very independent when it comes to measuring beauty. We're all conditioned by those mouth-watering cover shots to embrace the ideals they proclaim. We expect a "presentable" woman to have dark lashes, shadowed eyes, rouged cheeks, glossy lips, or whatever is "in." There's a tasteful medium in terms of amount, of course, but few women would dream of going out on a first date without some cosmetic front, and few men are as impressed by any woman's face naked as they are when she's made up (the young Ingrid Bergman having been the one possible exception). The mask of powder and color simultaneously attracts the opposite sex and keeps it at a protective distance. For some people this barrier is so necessary that years after marriage the wife still refuses to let her husband see her barefaced even at bedtime.

Most people show slightly more independence when it comes to judging the body beautiful, a game which for many men is even more important than rating the faces of prospective partners. Again, men tend to be much more critical and demanding of women's bodies than women are of men's. Most women are perfectly happy with a man who's relatively lean, strong, and taller than they. If he has other appealing qualities, they'll take his body as it comes. Men, on the other hand, are often self-proclaimed "breast men," "ass men," or "leg men." They may prefer their women tiny or big, narrow or wide, buxom or flat-chested. But whether the model is Audrey Hepburn, Marilyn Monroe, Grace Kelly, or Madonna, most men have a very specific image of their ideal female figure. And just as they use cosmetics to measure up to men's ideals in facial beauty, women take great pains to create the bodies men want.

Millions take diet pills, go to spas, mail away for bust develop-ment programs, or undergo plastic surgery. Each year, hun-dreds of thousands of women receive breast implants or have breast reduction in order to achieve the "ideal" feminine bust-line. While some women undergo these "improvements" to boost their self-esteem, for most the true purpose is to attract and please men.

Age is another important standard of beauty in women that is perpetuated by men. Despite the headway made by Jane Fonda, Linda Evans, Sophia Loren, and others in the "Women Can Be Beautiful over Forty" campaign, most men still prefer their women young. In an effort to keep the men they've got or attract new ones, aging women pile on wrinkle creams and concealers, spend hours in exercise classes, and take pills and elixirs that promise the restoration of youthfulness. Ironically, men put themselves through similar gyrations to attract and then, perhaps, keep up with the younger women they desire. More and more men as they get older join executive fitness clubs, have hair transplants, and substitute Perrier for their lunchtime cocktails. Some of these changes, of course, produce substantial health benefits, but that's rarely the underlying mo-tivation. The image trap is the real motivator, and false love is often the ultimate result.

If you're like most people, you probably assume that the bet-ter you look, the more desirable you become and the easier it will be for you to achieve true love. Up to a point, this is cor-rect. When you're in shape, well groomed, and stylishly dressed, you tend to feel good about yourself, and when you feel good about yourself you radiate a certain confidence and poise that make others enjoy being around you. This in turn boosts your self-esteem even further. How you look and care for yourself are also expressions of your personal style and self-discipline and, when you're in a relationship, your respect for your partner. But no love can survive on looks alone, and in fact beauty sometimes can be more of an obstacle than an in-centive for true love because it sets up artificial expectations and competition. The following cases illustrate some of the ways this can happen.

The Love Object

The first time he saw her, in a cabaret in Saigon, Don thought Susie was the most enchanting woman he'd ever seen. She was tiny, with flashing eyes and black silken hair that fell to her hips. Seventeen years old, she was a Vietnamese orphan who had been working behind her uncle's bar for three years. Other girls in the club danced and slept with the American soldiers, but not Susie. Her uncle was extremely protective of her and insisted that she not sell herself so cheaply. Any man who wanted Susie had to be prepared to marry her. Because he spoke her language, Don was able to get to know Susie during his last week in Saigon. He stayed each night until closing time and walked her home. The day before he was to ship out, he proposed and she accepted. They were married the next morning. Three months later, he sent for her to join him in the States.

She arrived in Minneapolis in February with nothing but a small satchel of summer clothes. Don bought her a coat at the airport so she could get home without freezing. She was astounded by the sight of snow, which she'd never seen before and which lay about in drifts eight feet high. "How can the markets stay open in this climate?" she asked, thinking of the open-air markets back home. Don laughed, enjoying the prospect of transforming his bride into an American housewife. And yet, he thought with satisfaction as he looked her over, she would never be an American woman, but always his Oriental doll.

For years they lived quite contentedly. Don provided well for Susie, taught her to drive and speak English, took her with him to his Thursday night bowling league. Susie wanted to have children, but Don didn't, so she dutifully took her birth control pills and filled her days with housework while he ran his plumbing supply business. He was — for the most part —

faithful to her and she was devoted to him. As long as she looked as she had that first night when she was seventeen, everything ran smoothly.

The problems started when she went off the birth control pill for a few days between prescriptions and became pregnant. He insisted she have an abortion. She resisted and then caved in. Afterward, she was resentful and unhappy about it and began to gain weight. Don ignored her unhappiness but was furious about her weight gain. Suddenly, for the first time, it dawned on him that she was not going to look seventeen forever. He had thought he'd found the perfect wife, one who was beautiful and totally in his control. But this new development made him realize she was not entirely under his thumb. He threatened to leave her if she didn't lose the weight, and she promised to diet, but he seemed to have lost his power over her. Weeks later she just looked fatter to him. He weighed her and found she had gained fifteen pounds — it was the only way she could find to protest his domination and express her discontent. Maybe if she got rid of the image that enchanted him so, she thought, he'd be forced to recognize the person underneath. Instead, he had an affair with an eighteen-year-old waitress. By the time Susie found out, the illusion of love between them had been smashed, and there was nothing but regret to take its place.

Mutual Narcissism

They looked like the perfect couple. Burton wore Izod shirts and Top-Siders and had a face that looked as if it had been chiseled by Rodin. Gayle shopped at Neiman-Marcus and was often mistaken for Ali MacGraw. Burton and Gayle went to the same health club, which was where they'd met, and ran several miles together each morning. At lunchtime they often met to go shopping together, and in the evenings they both preferred restaurants and nightspots to quiet dinners at home. They joked about their "mutual narcissism," but below the surface they were dead serious about it. Occasionally, at the health club, he'd stare pointedly at the lithe college women working out. She'd bristle and walk away. Later, while he was inspecting his newest $500 suit, she'd saunter over with a copy of *GQ*. "Now *there's* a well-dressed man!" she'd exclaim, pointing to the cover.

As long as they considered each other equals, the relationship sailed along on an even keel. They enjoyed looking at each other, sleeping together, and being seen together. They even enjoyed the perpetual fitness and beauty competition because they felt it made them both more attractive than they otherwise would be. But once she gained the edge over him, everything started to slide.

The trouble began when Gayle started running marathons and Burton broke his nose in a skiing fall. His nose set crooked, giving his perfect face a decidedly imperfect center. He would have it fixed, eventually, but he didn't have the money, time, or courage to go through the procedure now. Besides, he was reluctant to let his friends know how truly compulsive he was about his looks. Real men didn't have nose jobs, he thought. But while he was struggling to accept his new flaw, Gayle was becoming truly perfect. Her training regimen gave every muscle in her body beautiful definition. Her skin glowed and her eyes shone with pride and pleasure every time she glanced in the mirror. She expected Burton to be just as proud, but instead he tried to get her to give up running.

"Why don't you give yourself a break?" he'd mutter as she leaped out of bed at 5:30 A.M. to do her ritual seven miles.

"Why don't you come along?" she'd retort. "We could race each other."

But the fun of competition was over for Burton. He wouldn't admit it, even to himself, but he was jealous of Gayle's looks. Now, each time he looked at her she just made him more painfully aware of his own small flaws. He no longer had the energy or the confidence to go after her. So he let her go and soon afterward began a romance with Janice, who was pleasant but not nearly as stylish or stunning as Gayle. Moreover, she didn't think of herself as pretty and told him every day he was the most gorgeous man to walk the earth.

The Inferiority Complex

In fact, Burton's Janice had always been painfully aware of her plainness. She'd been a pimply, overweight adolescent and had never quite believed it when she blossomed into an attractive young woman during college. She had been struggling to secure her self-image through therapy for some time when Burton entered her life.

Like most other young women, she'd dreamed of finding her gorgeous white knight but never honestly thought she'd attract anyone who didn't wear glasses and have a receding hairline. When Burton started flirting with her, she was suspicious. When he took her out to dinner, she was flattered. When he wanted to sleep with her, she was terrified that he'd run screaming from the room as soon as she took her clothes off. He didn't. Instead, he said she made him feel warm and content. She also made him feel perfect again.

"I don't know what he sees in me, but he is very, *very* special," Janice reported during her next therapy session. As the relationship progressed, she also commented that her friends seemed to be treating her with newfound respect. They seemed to feel that if Burton was dating her there must be something special about *her* as well. Even strangers stared at her when she was with Burton, something that had never happened before. "They must think I'm rich, brilliant, or tremendously sexy to have caught a guy like Burton," she said with a laugh.

Much as she enjoyed this sudden elevation in status, however, it began to make her uneasy. It seemed obvious why she should be smitten with someone as good-looking as Burton, but she couldn't understand why he wanted her. Despite what others might conjecture, she *knew* she wasn't rich, brilliant, or unusually skillful in bed. And every time she looked at his perfect body she felt as though her own were made of cream cheese. "Why do you waste your time with me?" she'd ask, pretending to joke about it. "You could have anyone you want."

"I want you," he'd say on cue, knowing that this was what she wanted to hear. He was aware of the murmurs that surrounded them every time they went out. He knew people were curious, especially those who used to see him with Gayle. But he also felt that the contrast between Janice's appearance and his made him look even better. It was nice not having to compete for the limelight. He felt more at ease with her than he ever had with Gayle.

Yet the question kept gnawing away at Janice, and when she eventually saw pictures of Gayle, all her insecurities flooded to the surface. She was convinced that he'd soon tire of her and go after someone beautiful again. Then what would her friends think? How could she face another man? Instead of increasing her self-esteem, the net effect of this relationship was deflating.

"Honestly, what do you see in me?" she asked Burton one evening, this time without joking.

"Why?" he responded with a sigh of annoyance.

"Because I feel like I'm the ugly duckling, and you're the swan prince."

She'd hit the nail on the head, but in the process she was putting herself down yet again, and Burton was sick of it. "You know, I thought you were very attractive when we started dating," he said. "I didn't question why I was interested. I just knew you made me feel comfortable and secure. I would have been happy to go on like that for a long time, I think, but you won't let that happen. You're *convincing* me that you *are* ugly — you seem so sure that I'm a fool to waste a minute with you."

Janice struggled for a few weeks to build some confidence about the relationship, but ultimately she broke it off. As she analyzed her decision during therapy, she concluded that she had never felt truly comfortable with him. She was too busy being impressed by how beautiful he was and embarrassed by how plain she was.

•   •   •

Of all the illusions that contribute to false love, beauty is the most superficial. Some women buy into the beauty complex because it's an easy way to win attention. It requires no education, few skills, and little money. For the cost of makeup, an occasional haircut, and a flattering wardrobe, almost anyone who is relatively attractive can look beautiful. And the image trap lures us into believing that anyone who is beautiful will be loved.

Men buy into this illusion for similar reasons. Few are as obsessed as Burton with their own looks, but most men recognize that being with a beautiful woman brings them as much attention as it brings her. For the price of a dinner, their status momentarily rises a notch higher purely by association.

All these attitudes are understandable in light of the value that society assigns to appearance, but they become dangerous when they're confused with love. The illusion is that beauty can buy love, and love can buy beauty. For a while Gayle was convinced that her beauty had sealed Burton's love for her. For a while Don thought his love had bought him Susie's beauty forever. But what both men felt was really false love. Burton's was sheer narcissism, temporarily transferred to Gayle and later to Janice. Don's was domination.

One fundamental flaw in the beauty complex is that neither love nor money can make beauty last forever. As soon as you find someone you think is ideally beautiful, you start noticing imperfections — the subtle wrinkles, stretch marks, crooked teeth, or gray hairs. Ten, twenty years later, these flaws inevitably will be magnified, and what do you do then? Substitute a younger partner? That's precisely what many men and some women try, but what they usually get in exchange is another round of false love.

Most relationships based on this illusion never make it that far. Much earlier, sometimes just a few weeks into the courtship, satiation sets in. The face that at first looked ravishing gradually becomes attractive, then acceptable. Before it becomes flawed, it becomes boring, and unless there is some other strong basis for attraction, the relationship then takes a nosedive.

Unfortunately, most of us grow up being conditioned to believe that love is based on attractiveness. Ask a typical sixteen-year-old girl, "Why do you like him?" and she'll reply, "Because he's cute!" as if that's the only appropriate answer. Ask her boyfriend, "Why do you like her?" and he'll shrug and say, "Because she looks sexy." Adults may try to rationalize sexual attraction in more complex terms, but for many, looks are still the bottom line. The belief is that appearances are enough to hold a relationship together, when all they really provide is a spark of interest that will flicker briefly and die if deeper bonds don't soon develop.

The Money Market

Money rests at the core of the American dream. It represents security, comfort, luxury, and status. Especially in today's society, it is both a basic necessity and a measure of success. Every time you open a magazine, turn on the television, or walk down the street, you are hit with reminders to spend and buy. To some, it seems that no matter how much they have, it's not enough, yet they keep telling themselves if they just were *rich* their lives would be perfect. Given the rising cost of living, professional competition, and a highly uncertain economic horizon, even those who claim not to care about money inadvertently start to judge themselves and each other at least in part by their financial worth. Such attitudes inevitably influence behavior in the romantic market as well as in the world at large.

Some people are purely pragmatic in their quest for a partner with money. "I want a comfortable life," explained one of my patients. "Where I live, that means I need at least seventy thousand dollars a year. But I'm a high school teacher with a salary closer to forty thousand dollars. I don't want to give up my work, and I do want to get married, so why not marry someone who can make up the difference? It should be as easy to find someone with a decent income as someone who's penniless." Technically, he's right. He's not asking for an heiress to support him, but a woman who will share his values and contribute financially. As long as salary is not the sole criterion he uses in choosing a partner, it's a reasonable request.

Money can also be used as a measure of a person's character. Someone who has pushed his way up from poverty to a corporate boardroom shows a great deal of drive and determination. If he did it honestly, without leaving bodies in his wake, it shows that he also has moral and ethical strength. By the same token, someone who has backbitten, stolen, and lied his way to the top in business is probably just as ruthless and deceitful in the bedroom. And someone who has inherited and squandered fortunes may be totally out of touch with commonplace values and desires. Examining an individual's bankroll from this perspective could prevent a lot of heartbreak.

But it's one thing to search for someone who will be a decent and responsible partner and quite another to look for a free ride. People who are susceptible to the image trap don't really want to know about the underpinnings of wealth. They're seduced by the gloss on the surface. This is especially true of people who do not have the resources to make their own fortunes.

When Alice met her husband-to-be, it never occurred to her to probe into his business affairs. She had run away from home at seventeen to join the air force as a base secretary in Greenland, and while there she had had an intense affair with a married air force captain. When she returned to Seattle, her military career concluded, she began looking for someone to replace him. She found that someone — or so she thought — at an airport hotel bar. Frank was tall and muscular and had the face of a male model, which he said he had been in his younger days. He was a pilot, just as her captain had been, and he treated her like a queen. Each night he picked her up in his big shiny car and took her to expensive restaurants, nightclubs, and the track. Money was never an issue. He was determined to show her a good time, and in the process he swept her off her feet.

Frank intimated that he had had difficulties with women in the past. He'd always wanted women with class and worldliness, women who could make him feel superior just by associating with him. But he still was wrestling with feelings of inadequacy dating back to his childhood. Coming from a Polish working-class family, he had been the butt of ethnic jokes throughout his school years. As a youngster he'd been painfully shy and had had a tendency to sway from side to side when he stood in front of his class. As a teenager, he'd vowed to break the mold his classmates had carved for him. He became a bodybuilder, took acting lessons to cure his stage fright, and vowed someday to win over one of those prom princesses who'd snickered at him throughout his childhood. To Frank, Alice looked just like a grown-up prom princess, and he wanted her.

When Frank told Alice his story, she was touched and impressed by how dramatically he appeared to have succeeded in making himself over. To her, he was devastatingly attractive and seemed very self-assured. Moreover, he treated her like the lady he believed her to be. She certainly couldn't afford such a nightlife on her own meager secretarial salary, but she liked it a lot. She also liked the way he looked in his pilot's uniform and the vicarious thrill she got from hearing him tell of the cities to which he flew.

They'd been together for eight months when he proposed. Frank had helped her recover nicely from the heartbreak of her first affair. She was now nineteen. This seemed like the appropriate move, so she said yes.

After a simple civil ceremony, they moved into an apartment together, and life went on as usual. Each morning she went to work. When he had a flight, he'd leave and be gone for a couple of days. When he returned from those distant cities, he'd bring her expensive presents. On nights when he wasn't flying, they'd go out drinking and dancing, and he drank quite a lot.

But on nights before his flights he wouldn't touch a drop. Alice accepted that he needed to unwind a little between flights, so she tolerated the drinking without saying anything. He treated her better than any other man had, and she wasn't going to rock the boat.

Occasionally they would attend family gatherings at Frank's mother's house. He was one of eleven children, however, so Alice always felt a little lost at these events and never really got to know anyone very well. His mother, whom they all worshiped, didn't seem to like her, so Alice kept her distance. She didn't need to know any more about Frank's past — not if it meant asking his mother.

The only major excitement in their relationship occurred when Frank moved from a small, independent airline to a larger one. She heard all the details, the change in flight schedules, the upset with his supervisors. It was the major topic of conversation for several weeks. She was pleased that he chose to share his concerns about work with her and felt it proved how solid their marriage was.

But while her husband talked about his work and spent his income liberally, Alice never saw a single one of his paychecks. She paid all the household bills out of her own salary. If she ever questioned this arrangement, he accused her of being ungrateful and disrespectful, so she persuaded herself that he spent his money on other obligations that were unknown to her. As long as he kept acting like a success — and bringing her lavish gifts — she was satisfied.

The blow came completely unexpectedly. Frank's mother became ill one day while he was away on a trip. For the first time in three years of marriage, she needed to get in touch with him while he was working. So, also for the first time, she went to the airport to meet his plane. It arrived on schedule, the crew got out, and there was no sign of her husband. When she stopped them, the crew told her they'd never heard of Frank, so she went to the airline office where several different schedulers searched their computers in vain. Frank had never worked for this or any other airline.

Only when he turned up the next day and she confronted him did he admit that his career had been totally fabricated. He was actually a used-car salesman. On his "trip days" he'd stayed at a friend's house. "It was all to impress you," he confessed. "You're such a snob, you never would have gone out with me, and you certainly wouldn't have married me if you knew the truth."

Out of guilt and regret, Alice bought the line and stayed another year with Frank. But he drank continuously now, fully revealing his alcoholism. She discovered that he had been a male model, as he'd claimed, but for tawdry pornographic and muscle magazines. And when the bookies started calling, she realized that his flashy lifestyle was now financed primarily by gambling. She finally decided to get out when the dunning calls turned to personal threats.

Frank, too, threatened her when she said it was over. Then she ran, moving every few weeks to escape him. It took months to shake him for good, and it took many more months of therapy before Alice began to understand what had happened. She had been seduced, just as Frank had intended, by an image of money and flash that, to her, represented a desirable lifestyle. There was nothing truly loving about him or their relationship, and beneath the veneer, both were a fraud.

Most people are much more aware than Alice of the role money plays in attraction. Some, the classic gold diggers, care about little else in the relationship. Though they may never achieve true love, their hearts rarely get broken. Others assume that as long as the money is there, they'll make the romance work. But this means that both partners must eventually stop thinking about the money and start concentrating on love, something that is rarely possible in these kinds of relationships. Unless love *becomes* the main objective, the preoccupation with wealth will subvert it.

While men and women both can be attracted to wealth in the opposite sex, men generally are more likely to use this illusion to manipulate their partners than they are to fall prey to it themselves. Rich men know they can buy sex, if not necessarily love. Ideally, of course, a woman will be impressed by a man's fortune and also perceptive and sensitive enough to meet his emotional needs. If not, it's enough temporarily if she's very attractive and good in bed — but only temporarily. This is rarely sufficient to make a man open his heart or his bank account to her. In fact, some wealthy men who are seriously searching for true love are so afraid of being chased for their money that they refuse even to date anyone but equally affluent women.

By contrast, the vast majority of women — including those who themselves are successful — set their sights on wealthier men. Sometimes this preference is based on a realistic appraisal of their own independent financial prospects. One of my patients, whose first husband left her with two small children, no alimony, and no salable skills, felt the only solution was to find a man who could take care of her. "In this economy and with my high school education," she pointed out, "I can either get protection from a man or protection from the government — and that's called welfare. I'll take the man if I can find him!" It's true that even qualified women earn roughly one-third less than men with the same skills. Compound this situation with the conditioning that says men are "supposed" to provide for their families, and it's understandable that women look to men for financial security. As long as both partners agree on the roles each of them will play and the contributions each will make to the relationship, they should be able to achieve a financial balance that works for them. The illusions set in when women want men who will not just provide for them but surround them with luxury. That's when the relationship gets hopelessly tangled in dollar signs.

Even when these women "get" their men, they rarely comprehend the price they must pay for luxury. Sometimes they become just another bauble in the man's collection of expensive possessions. Sometimes they're expected to serve as slave labor — or sexual or emotional slaves. And sometimes they're expected to honestly give love when all they honestly feel is greed. Sooner or later, their original illusions will backfire and they'll become desperate to escape. "I don't care about the Rolls or the swimming pool or the Arabian horses," one distraught wife said to me. "I'll give it all up to get away from *him*."

Unfortunately, the confusion between money and love has been virtually institutionalized in the most basic rules of courtship. If a man is attracted to a lovely woman he knows has less money, he may bring her an expensive bouquet, take her to a chic restaurant, and expect her to sleep with him in return. Even today, many women still feel obligated to repay such favors sexually unless they have paid or shared the tab. But it's not an even trade. The man remains in power, and the woman is expected to remain submissive. Unless both partners can get past the surface posturing and start dealing with each other as human equals, the relationship will remain little more than an exchange of services for image.

The Power of Prestige

Occasionally, people seek therapy not because they are unhappy or in trouble but because they are confused or worried that they're not conforming to what they think are "normal" patterns of behavior. Mary was such a patient. Four years out of college, she was in her sixth year of a relationship with a man who seemed to have everything a woman could want — and she was intensely attracted to a man who fit none of her preconceptions of an ideal partner. What, she asked, was going on?

As she pieced together her feelings during therapy, it soon became apparent that she was caught in a contest between image and instinct. Mary's parents, themselves divorced, had been mightily proud of Mary's blond good looks and her crisp intellect, and they'd encouraged her to stretch and demand the best for herself. At the same time, they knew their divorce had been hard on her, and they didn't want her to suffer the same turmoil in her own adult life, so they urged her to be very cautious in love. Make sure the man you marry is good enough for you, they told her. Make sure he measures up.

But Mary didn't know what criteria to use in measuring her partners. All the men she dated were bright and ambitious; if they weren't, she wasn't interested. The trouble was that she attracted lots of men and so needed additional guidelines to help her choose the ones who were suitable. Quite naturally, she relied on the standard values held by her friends: looks, athletic prowess, leadership, popularity, career prospects, and reputation. On all counts, Jim was ideal. There was no question when Mary met him in college that he would become a successful surgeon like his father and that he would be a stable, reliable husband, as his blue-blooded family expected. He was captain of the lacrosse team, a leader in his fraternity, and a descendant of Thomas Jefferson. He graduated Phi Beta Kappa and had been accepted by one of the leading medical schools in the country. He was the handsomest man Mary had ever met, much less dated. To cap it off, he admired Mary's goals to become a novelist and political activist and promised to supply the income so that she could freely pursue her dreams.

"I know he sounds too good to be true," sighed Mary several years later. "My friends in college were all intensely jealous."

"It sounds like you were very happy with your choice at first," I remarked. "When did you start to change your mind?"

It was after Mary and Jim moved from college in Wisconsin to Baltimore and began living together that her doubts began to surface, she told me. He was so laid back, so nonconfrontational, and, well, smug about himself that she felt isolated from him. He never seemed to invest himself emotionally in anything he did, and even after five years she didn't feel they really understood each other. He was buried in work or on duty at the hospital most of the time. On his rare days off, he would collapse in front of a ball game on TV, or they'd visit his family homestead in Pennsylvania where his mother would instruct

Mary in the joys and responsibilities of being a doctor's wife. For a long time, Mary accepted the family pressure and the boredom, in the faith that she'd made the right choice. Jim was still the most attractive, promising man she knew, and his family's air of quasi-royalty remained damnably appealing, if a bit restrictive.

Mary's feelings didn't change dramatically until she became attracted to Stu. They met while working together on an urban litter campaign. She signed on to direct the project for the city government. He was the city council's legal representative. Both were politically active and committed to revitalizing the inner city. At first their relationship was purely professional and not altogether friendly. Although they shared the same goals, both were extremely opinionated and clashed frequently over the details of the campaign. The friction was refreshing for Mary, whose intellect, energy, and drive tended to overshadow most of the people in her life. Her associates at work all were a bit in awe of her, and Jim, while clearly her intellectual equal, rarely challenged her.

Quick-tempered, stubborn, and combative as Stu was, he fought hard out of conviction. If it's not worth defending, it's not worth much, he'd say. Neither arrogant nor reluctant, he gave his time, energy, and money to everything from free legal advice for the homeless to literacy projects for inner-city youths. His many friends were as fiercely loyal to him as he was to them. Although Mary was still living with Jim, she found herself increasingly drawn to Stu. He wasn't rich, didn't come from a socially prominent family, and wasn't especially handsome — her college girlfriends would never understand the attraction — but even after just a few weeks Mary felt that they somehow had more in common than she'd ever had with Jim. Stuart was intensely thoughtful and well read. They could discuss issues for hours, and he was willing to debate ideas, which Jim was not. Whereas Jim was supportive and perhaps mildly amused by her goals and interests, Stu actively shared many of them.

"My relationship with Jim never had the vitality that I now

realize I need," she concluded. "But still I feel so unsure of myself."

As she dealt with this situation in therapy, Mary was panic-stricken that she was making a terrible mistake. Everyone who knew her warned her that she would have trouble finding anyone as worthy as Jim. They told her she was just being seduced. What she realized when talking it through, however, was that all this outside advice was based on the illusions that had surrounded her life with Jim, but not its reality. Likewise, the opposition to Stu was based on the most superficial view of his position in her life. It did not reflect the substance that lay within their relationship.

As quickly as it had happened, theirs was not an irresponsible or superficial match. From casual conversation over coffee and between meetings, they knew they shared many goals. Both were activists with the same philosophical and political leanings. Both wanted children. Both had divorced parents and were determined to have a strong, close-knit family themselves. This would not be easy to attain, they realized, but each believed strongly in the power of commitment.

All this had been stated quite matter-of-factly, without any angling or deception. Stu and Mary both had wanted as much information as possible before either made the first direct advance. By the time they opened the door to love, both were ready to walk through.

"You've been relying on other people's values for a long time to guide your love life," I suggested after Mary realized where her thoughts were leading her. "It's difficult to disregard them all of a sudden. But it would seem that you've finally discovered your *own* standards. Possibly this is what your parents really meant when they told you to find a man who measures up. The test is for him to measure up not to your girlfriends' or family's criteria, but to your own."

Seven years later, Stuart and Mary have two children, two active political careers, a large, ramshackle home, and a volatile but thriving marriage. They've survived despite the warn-

ings from Mary's friends and family, because they were motivated by deeply felt convictions rather than by an impressive
résumé or pedigree.

While a pragmatic argument can be made for considering
money when searching for a partner, no such argument can be
made for chasing prestige. Strictly speaking, no one *needs* to
be socially prominent, influential, or highly regarded. These are
forms of status that a few people attain by luck, hard work, or
genius. For some they are apt rewards, but for many others
they are annoying and compromising. And in any case, neither
love nor sex can buy this status.

Unlike money, prestige cannot simply be handed over in the
form of greenbacks or credit cards, but that doesn't stop the
illusion that it can be achieved by osmosis. The thinking, particularly among women, is that if you rub shoulders with the
right people, sleep with the right people, and marry the right
people, one day you become one of the right people.

Families are sometimes responsible for planting this illusion.
Some youngsters are taught to admire university professors or
diplomats but disdain plumbers. Others may be encouraged to
hunt for a mate who is a surgeon or corporate executive or
whose family is listed in the social registry. But society may be
even more responsible, though the specific source of prestige
seems to vary from culture to culture. In America, success in
business tends to buy the most prestige. In Russia, success in
politics and the arts is more impressive. No matter how it's
earned or where you live, however, prestige itself is always
prized because it involves fame, influence, respect, and often
wealth. In almost every culture, young girls learn that they can
get ahead by marrying a prestigious man.

This illusion is perpetuated by the media, which often glorify
women who marry famous men. All over the world, women
watched in awe as Diana Spencer and Sarah Ferguson, two relatively unknown young women, became modern-day princesses in front of the television cameras. But however much

women may envy the two princesses, few would survive the constraints of royal life with their marriages intact. The price of marrying into prestige is much higher than most of us are willing to pay, and the rewards are far less enjoyable than most imagine. Prestige in itself is simply not a quality worthy of love. If your partner is a prominent public figure, his or her status may initially attract you, but it won't make it any easier to develop a loving relationship. More likely, as women such as Betty Ford and Joan Kennedy probably would agree, the public scrutiny that accompanies prestige often makes it even harder to build true love.

Relationships based on prestige are often plagued by stereotyping. The partner who has the status is supposed to be powerful inside as well as out, while the other partner is weak and vulnerable. One couple let these illusions dominate their marriage for ten years before they finally came for therapy. They had married when Adam was in his late twenties, just out of graduate school. Sheila was working as a medical technician at the time but quit when they married. She believed that Adam was going to become a successful politician, powerful enough to take care of her for life. She saw him as self-assured, wise, and protective, and she thought she'd be content to live in his shadow. At first, Adam enjoyed these roles. Sheila made him feel almost as omnipotent as she imagined him. She helped him launch his political career, produced two children, and generally became the model politician's wife. He provided the home, the security, and the attention she needed to feel secure.

But as Sheila became more comfortable in her new role in the public eye, she never became either more assertive or more giving with her husband. He, meanwhile, was starting to tire of the he-man image that had been vastly overblown from the start. It was one thing to seem invincible when on stage or in front of the television cameras; it was another to have to maintain the act when alone with his own wife. He had lost three times in his bid for Congress; his mother had died recently; he had just turned forty; in short, he was feeling vulnerable and a little needy himself, and he wanted his wife to help him. But every time Adam let the tough, capable facade slip and demanded attention, Sheila became defensive. "How can I give you attention on demand?" she'd ask. "It's like having a gun put to my head."

Fortunately, neither Adam nor Sheila wanted to sacrifice the marriage. Although their relationship had begun as false love, they had been well intentioned, they had a shared history and a family, and they were willing to get professional counseling to help them recognize and correct their mistakes. They agreed to give up their illusions instead of the relationship and to probe beneath the surface images. The process required several years of therapy and was extremely painful for them both. Had they been able to see past their illusions in the first place, they and their family might have been spared this trauma.

Avoiding the Image Trap

Because society trains you to envy surface images such as beauty, wealth, and prestige, you must be vigilant in separating these yearnings from the search for a partner in love. The following three steps will help you accomplish this.

1. Determine your own vulnerability to image. Consider how you were raised and what values were passed on by your family. Were you taught to value money, intelligence, beauty, status? Do you envy or resist the images of the rich and famous you see in the media? Are you satisfied with your own achievements, or do you long to be vastly more successful, attractive, or powerful? The more strongly you're affected by surface images and the more disenchanted you are with your own life, the more vulnerable you are likely to be to false love.
2. Understand your own image. Even if you are not particularly impressed by surface illusions in others, you may be

setting yourself up for the image trap by ignoring the way others perceive you or by misrepresenting yourself. Many exceptionally beautiful women don't see themselves as beautiful and are hurt and outraged when men chase them for their looks. Others work very hard at cultivating an attractive image and then are hurt when men are interested in them only for their looks. Men often have the same reaction when women chase them for their money, power, intelligence, or status. If you understand how others look at you, you can adjust either your image or your responses so that you encourage others to see beyond the outermost layer.

3. Look beneath the surface in your partner. This may be the most difficult step, especially if your partner is using the image trap to manipulate you. The trick is to strip away all the superficial things that attract you. Would you be as interested if he were unattractive and penniless or didn't drive that Jaguar? How much of her appeal is in the clothes she wears and the company she keeps, and how much is in her sense of humor and her ability to care and share her most intimate thoughts and feelings? Only by separating the human qualities from the surface appeal can you honestly determine whether you can build a loving relationship with this person.

If you accept that true love develops over time, you must also make room for the dramatic changes that your image and your partner's image will undergo during this time. No one remains youthfully stunning forever. There are no guarantees of continuing wealth or status, even among the very rich and powerful. But true love doesn't demand this. What it does demand is that *each partner* remain flexible and understanding in the face of changes. This means looking past the illusions to your partner's and your own enduring emotional and intellectual characteristics. Here is where you discover if you can truly honor and trust each other as you must in order to build true love.

4
ROMANTIC DECEPTIONS

THE EVENING HAD a frosty nip in the air and the skies threatened snow. Although it was only October, New England was bracing itself for winter. Julie shivered as she stood in her doorway awaiting her date. She'd just as soon be curled up in bed with a good book. It had been a long day at the bank, and she'd been at either her night classes or meetings every evening this week. Her date was a friend of a friend. He had gone to the same college and claimed he used to watch her across the dining hall, but she didn't remember that. He seemed amiable enough when their friend introduced them, and she willingly agreed to this date. It wasn't easy to meet eligible young men in this small town. But she had had such dismal luck with men for the last few years that she hardly dared hope for anything out of the ordinary.

As his headlights traced the path up Julie's driveway, Paul carefully smoothed his hair, adjusted his collar, and checked the arrangement of flowers on the seat next to him. He knew he hadn't captivated Julie at their first meeting, but he was confident he could sway her eventually. He had studied every romantic movie produced for the past fifty years, and he knew how to conduct a romance. Even if he didn't win her heart, he'd have a good time trying.

The flowers took her breath away. They were nòt the usual bouquet, but an array of birds of paradise, each one looking like a carefully crafted piece of art. "They're exquisite, Paul!" she exclaimed. "I've never seen anything like them." The delight on her face told him he was off to a good start.

"Come. Get your coat," he said. "This is going to be a very special evening."

They drove up the coast to an old whaler's inn which had been restored as a restaurant. He escorted her to a quiet table in the corner between the blazing fire and a window overlooking the ocean. Outside, the full moon cast a bewitching glow over the water. Inside, the dancing flames created a warm and cozy atmosphere. Already, this was the most romantic date Julie had ever had.

For the first time, she took a good look at the man who was responsible. He was olive-skinned with a thick shock of black hair and eyes as deep and dark as India ink. He held himself tall with beautiful posture and moved his hands gracefully, fingering his glass. His mouth curved in a quizzical smile as he stared back at her.

"Curious?" he asked.

"About you, yes," she replied.

So he told her a little of his childhood in Florida, his father who came to America as a shoemaker from Italy, his training as a furniture craftsman in Williamsburg, and, of course, his admiration of her from a distance during their college years. As he was talking he watched the way her auburn hair gleamed in the firelight, and the way her green eyes, like a cat's, darted here and there, then settled on him, motionless for long moments. Her pale skin was luminous against the deep brown velvet of her dress. She reminded him of Meryl Streep in *The French Lieutenant's Woman*.

Julie was entranced by his swarthy good looks. His imagination and the undertone of whimsy in his conversation made him quite enchanting. Even the name of his shop, Pinocchio's, reflected the sense of wonder he exuded.

After dinner he led her down to the beach for a walk on the sand. The clouds had cleared, opening the skies to a thousand brilliant stars. The surf made a gentle background roar as Julie revealed the salient details of her life, including her recently aborted relationship with her former boss. This had been particularly rough because it had threatened her career. Fortunately, her boss had been transferred out of town, but still, she warned, she wasn't in a hurry to get entangled again right away. Even as she said this, she was acutely conscious of Paul's warmth sheltering her from the chilly wind. She didn't want to let him go.

Paul kissed her good night but refused her invitation to come in. "Not yet," he said. "But when do you get up in the morning?" She told him. "Don't have breakfast," he said mysteriously.

The next day, as she stepped from the shower, he arrived with a picnic basket brimming with croissants, a carafe of coffee, and fresh fruit. "Breakfast, madame?" he said with a grin. He arranged the picnic on her living room floor. After they'd eaten, he cheerfully went off to his shop, leaving her, in a state of mild shock, to dress and make her way to the office.

Paul was elated by the way things were progressing. He loved setting up these romantic scenes and laboring over the details. The astonishment and pleasure in Julie's reaction thrilled him and gave him a sense of accomplishment that little else in his life could rival. In his shop, he labored to give his woodwork a soft, artistic touch, but he'd found that the responses of women to his romantic overtures in the past were generally much more rewarding than his customers' appreciation of his work. And to Paul, Julie had an ethereal quality that energized his dearest fantasies.

Over the next week, Julie received handwritten poems at work and surprise bouquets on her doorstep. Paul arrived for each date bearing ingenious little gifts. Then he took her to another charming restaurant where they dined and, as he put it, "courted."

By the end of the week, she was aching to sleep with him, but still he delayed. "I want you to spend the whole weekend with me," he said. "Our first time should be perfect." She agreed, and the next weekend he whisked her away to a small inn on a New Hampshire mountainside. It was only right that they should spend the entire weekend in bed, and so they did. He spent hours stroking her, searching for and finding her special pleasure points. At moments she felt as if it all was too much — he was too attentive, too inexhaustible. But how could she fault him for trying too hard? It was her own problem, she decided, certainly not his.

The romance continued over the next year. On the slightest pretext, Paul would proclaim a "celebration" and turn up with a gift, prepare a special dinner, or take Julie out. He orchestrated several more extravagant weekends, and when winter came he built a complete replica of a Swiss village in snow all around her house. There seemed no end to Paul's dramatic efforts to win her affection.

Unlike any other relationship she'd had, this one was never marred by any serious fights. Occasionally, she'd get irritable and criticize Paul for driving too fast or leaving dirty dishes in the sink. Once or twice, when she felt particularly ornery, she actually provoked an argument by bringing up religion. She'd been raised high Episcopalian and he Unitarian, and their views of spirituality were diametrically opposed. But although Paul would flare up momentarily — once, to her astonishment, even raising his hand as if to strike her — he seemed to be struggling against some inner restraint. And the next morning, there would always be breakfast in bed to secure the peace.

Appropriately, Paul proposed to her while standing under the Christmas mistletoe and suggested that they be married on Valentine's Day. Although he knew she'd consent, he held his breath until she actually spoke the word "yes." In his eyes, Julie had validated his belief that he could model his own storybook heroine. She was delicate and vulnerable, yet also strong-willed and beautiful in a unique, almost Gothic way. Together they were playing out fantasies that he'd dreamed for years. Even her name, so close to Juliet, cast him in the role of Romeo. He could almost see them riding off into the sunset together.

Once engaged, they became even more inseparable than before. Paul became jealous of Julie's girlfriends, business associates, even her work commitments and night school classes. He felt that all her attention should be directed toward the wedding, though as she kept pointing out, there would be only twenty people in attendance. "We'll be married at the church down the street and have a small reception right afterward. Why worry?" she asked. But Paul was determined that every detail be perfect. He wanted the reception to be at the restaurant where they'd had their first date. He wanted to be with her when she chose her dress. Most of all, he wanted her to care as much as he did.

Unfortunately, Julie simply did not care as much as Paul about these details — or, in fact, about any of the details he labored over. By the same token, he didn't particularly care about many of the issues that concerned her. He was content to spend every day perfecting minute inlays and hand-carved seat backs and then spend his income on romantic evenings and weekends. He never considered having what she called a "real" professional career, never worried about saving money for the future, and certainly never thought about larger issues such as politics or foreign affairs. He was charming, devoted, and sweet as a puppy dog, but he did not fit Julie's definition of a responsible citizen. These thoughts gnawed at her as she was fitted for her wedding dress, as she met her elderly parents arriving from Ohio for the ceremony, as she stated her vows and watched him place the specially selected antique ring on her finger. But Paul's relentless romanticism gave her doubts little chance to fester.

After a honeymoon in Bermuda, Paul and Julie settled down

to their unique version of married life. For months he continued to dote on her, making her feel more and more guilty over her increasing restlessness. Occasionally she would try to engage him in serious discussions about the future — his and theirs. Somehow he always managed to wiggle away, either by blindly agreeing with her or distracting her with a tickling game or passionate kiss. When she said she wanted children, he said sure, but when she asked how he would raise kids, he had no response. Nor did he have any concrete suggestions when she asked how they'd finance a family. "Everything will work out," he'd say with a quick grin, turning the television dial to yet another romantic old movie. "Sure," she'd mutter and change the channel to MacNeil-Lehrer.

Everything was not working out, and Julie knew it. When she was offered a position at her bank's headquarters in New York, she realized the showdown had come. They had visited New York twice together. She had loved it. He had hated it. She saw it as the global hub of finance and culture. He saw it as a magnet for the immoral and destitute. At the time she was amused by what she considered his naive reaction. Now she was concerned.

At Julie's insistence, they tried marital counseling, but so much of their relationship was based on false love and their individual expectations of the marriage were so far apart that it was virtually impossible to make any progress. The more their illusions of each other faded, the less they liked each other. It soon became apparent that neither was willing to make the personal sacrifices their marriage demanded.

Nevertheless, Julie's eventual announcement that she intended to accept the job offer devastated Paul. The image of Julie as a Manhattan executive clashed violently with his romantic fantasy of her and forced him, once and for all, to confront the inherent differences between them. They both knew that Manhattan would devour Paul. He simply didn't have the drive or the toughness to survive there, either professionally or socially. Julie, on the other hand, was bored with small-town life. Paul had charmed and distracted her, filling many months with his irresistible magic, but she now realized that she had fallen in love with his concept of love, just as he had fallen in love with his idealized concept of her. Unfortunately, they did not truly love *each other*.

Falling in Love with Love

Romance can be dangerously seductive. A moonlit night, a crackling fire, a bearskin rug, and the mood is complete. Add an attractive partner and some soft background music, and who can help but feel "in love"? This, after all, is what the magazine ads say love is supposed to look like. If you find a partner who provides this setting, including all the appropriate props, and invites you in, it's natural to think of love.

Unfortunately, romance can be just as illusory as exciting sex, beauty, or any of the other superficial images that contribute to false love. It's all too easy to fall in love with love, even when you barely know — maybe don't even really like — your partner. Sometimes, as with Paul and Julie, romance can lure you into relationships that never have a chance of becoming more than false love. At other times, the inappropriate expectations created by romance may prevent a promising relationship from developing into true love.

Romance is both an atmosphere and a state of mind. It's easy to bask in it and, at least temporarily, feel great. However, no long-term relationship can remain continuously romantic. And even if it were possible, the aura that seemed so appealing at the outset would soon become stifling and tedious when the elements of spontaneity and surprise were gone. Ideally, romance will be woven through a loving relationship, and reviving it periodically is an excellent way to express affection and commitment. But romance on demand and romance that is taken for granted are not really romantic. If you insist that your relationship be in a constant state of heightened romance, not only are you asking the impossible but this pressure may end up destroying your chances for success as a truly loving couple.

One reason romance seems so important is that years of conditioning have taught you to believe in it. In a society that uses this illusion to sell everything from cognac to pickup trucks, you're surrounded by reminders of the "right" way to conduct a love affair. Add the influence of fairy tales, romance novels, soap operas, and movies, and there's no question that love is made out of moonbeams and tropical beaches. Especially among young adults who are new to the search, these images are extremely powerful.

An even more compelling reason for the power of romance, however, is that it momentarily satisfies one's yearnings to be adored and to escape from the humdrum of routine. Everyone wants to be placed on a pedestal and prized from time to time — to feel special and privileged and to be reassured that others recognize these qualities. When someone voluntarily goes to a great deal of trouble (or what seems a great deal of trouble) to set just the right mood, give you just what you want, and treat you as if you were special, you naturally are flattered and pleased — and, understandably, you may confuse this pleasure with love.

Romance, in this sense, is a courtship ritual orchestrated by one partner to impress or please the other. By definition, it is an unnatural setup. This does not necessarily make it bad. There's no question that romance can generate a great deal of vitality and pleasure throughout a relationship. Between loving partners, it demonstrates affection, caring, and the desire to please. It's also just plain fun. But it's not a replacement for or even a measure of true love.

Unfortunately, many people don't understand this, and they easily fall prey to partners whose motivation is not purely to please but to seduce. Then romance turns to deception. Sometimes it's used as a ploy to win sex, sometimes to attract attention, sometimes to gain money. Often it's used in a misguided quest, like Paul's, for a relationship that is pure romance. What he wanted, and what he briefly persuaded Julie to want, was not genuine love but an illusion. As enticing as this play-acting was in courtship, it could never sustain a marriage.

Even among those who intellectually know better, romance is a tough illusion to shake. The conditioning is strong and continuous. The gratification it provides can be addictive. In short, you may not *want* to disbelieve it. But you have to put it in perspective in order to build true love. This means understanding how the game of romance is played and learning how to deal with romantic deception.

Romantic Gifts

You naturally want to believe that a gift from someone reflects genuine affection. You want to believe that thought and care went into the choice of the present and that the final selection was made especially to please you. Yet all you really know is that someone hands you a package, perhaps nicely wrapped, perhaps accompanied by a hug and a kiss. If you like the gift, you're thrilled and you compliment the giver on knowing your taste so very well. If you don't like it, you may pretend you do or tell yourself that it's the thought that counts. But how much thought — and what kind of thought — actually goes into the gifts of romance?

One of my patients had been dating a man exclusively for four months when Christmas arrived. She shopped for a week before selecting just the right combination of shirt and sweater to match his eyes. On Christmas day she was overwhelmed when he presented her with an array of gifts, including a negligee, a vintage camera, and a bottle of expensive perfume. None of these gifts really suited her, but the number and quality of them told her that he cared very much for her.

The one gift she did like was the negligee, but it was too

large. Since the tags were still on it, she assumed it would be a simple matter to exchange it. Shortly after Christmas she went to the department store named on the tag and presented it at the credit office. The woman behind the counter examined the garment without recognizing it. She scanned the tags, still with a puzzled look on her face. She searched in her computer for a few minutes and then her face fell. "Dear," she said, "I'm sorry, but we used this code three years ago. I'm afraid this is too old to be exchanged."

Stunned, the young woman went home and debated what to do. She felt betrayed. This gift certainly hadn't been bought with her in mind. Finally, she decided to confront her man. He was unhappy to be caught, but when she pressed he confessed. In his bedroom he had a closet full of gifts, mostly items his widowed mother received from her admirers and then rejected. For years he'd used this cache to supply his girlfriends. None had ever complained before. For this girlfriend, however, complaint was not enough. If he didn't care enough to invest in a personal gift, how much could he possibly have invested emotionally in the relationship as a whole? She broke up with him shortly thereafter.

There's nothing wrong with enjoying a gift, but it is a mistake to misinterpret a material offering as an emotional investment. Some gifts are offered only because they are expected. Men probably do this more than women, primarily because this is the way the conventional game of romance is played. Initially at least, it's the man who's supposed to send the flowers and arrange the enchanted evenings. The game gets much more sophisticated, of course, if the man has money. Then there's no sacrifice whatsoever in supplying a woman with strawberries and champagne in bed, five-pound bars of Krön chocolate, sapphire earrings from Cartier, silk lingerie — perhaps even a penthouse suite or a high-paying job. But often, ironically, the more expensive the gifts the less they represent true affection and the more they function as bribes. Some extremely wealthy men manipulate the game of romance simply to keep women at their disposal. And the women who fall for their ploys are duped not so much by the men as by their own romantic illusions.

Romantic Posturing

Romantic posturing is a slightly different aspect of the game. Men and women both use a certain amount of posturing to lure prospective partners. This is only natural. You dress to look your best, or perhaps your most provocative. You modulate your voice to make it clear that you're romantically interested in the other person. You may wash the car and clean up the house to make a good impression on the first few dates. And then, once the relationship begins, you may go into high gear with phone calls "just to say I love you," with love notes, and with promises of nightly ecstasy. This all seems fairly innocent and fun. But behind romantic posturing is the attempt to appear perfect, both as an individual and as a mate. There is no place for conflict, stress, or problems — only harmony and agreement. Everything from sex to housework is supposed to be easy and companionable. In the game of romance, all this seems appropriate. In the game of love, it's absurd.

Establishing a precedent of perfection is more risky than setting a precedent of gift giving. When the courtship phase is over, a wealthy and devoted partner might conceivably continue to give presents, but no relationship can continue for very long without exposing some flaws. The strength of the relationship is determined not by its ability to ignore or mask these blemishes but by its facility in accepting and accommodating them. To pretend that such imperfections don't exist is to court disaster.

Often, the more romantic the gesture the more trouble lies beneath the surface. One patient, in the early months of marriage, found love notes from his wife every morning on his car.

At first he was touched by this gesture of affection, but as time went on, the notes lost their impact. Then they became irritating because they made him feel as if she was following him. His wife, however, kept leaving them on the car because she believed they would prevent him from cheating on her. They didn't. The notes were not a symbol of the relationship's perfection but of its failings. There was neither trust nor honesty between these two people, and no amount of romantic game playing would compensate.

Even in brand-new relationships, there's little redeeming value in pretense, yet many people automatically misrepresent themselves in an attempt to hide or downplay conflict. Ultimately, this only intensifies the conflict, turning what may be a very minor disagreement into a major issue and a source of resentment. A friend once told me how he'd asked a young woman out for Chinese food on their first date, and she accepted the invitation without telling him she actually hated Chinese food. As the relationship progressed, they went back to the same Chinese restaurant often, and he came to think of it as "their place." Finally one night, she was tired and irritable and he, trying to cheer her up, suggested going to "their place" for dinner. She cried out, "I hate Chinese food!" and he was hurt and astonished that she could have sustained this pointless ruse for so many months. A slight difference of opinion, which could have been overcome in seconds, had become a major issue in the relationship because she had chosen to deceive him.

The theory behind such deceptions is that the simple truth up front will destroy the relationship while simple lies will do no harm. What actually happens is that the lies quickly overshadow the issue being concealed. However inconvenient the original truth may have been, the act of lying is almost always more distasteful. In any case, the other person deserves to have the bad news up front in order to make an informed decision whether to continue the relationship. Delaying disclosure only increases the danger of a breakup and intensifies the antagonism that will occur when the truth comes out.

Dealing with Deception

Although most of us want to believe that romantic behavior is a sincere expression of affection, we are all prone, particularly in new relationships, to use romance for ulterior motives. When you give a gift to a child, the motivation is usually genuine affection and the desire to please. The same is usually true when you give gifts anonymously. When you extend the same favors to a new love interest, however, the objective usually is to get something in return. This may be sex, affection, attention, or more specific declarations of love. If both partners understand and accept the real purposes of the game, no harm is done, or at least both deserve what they get. But usually the person on the receiving end is so distracted by the aura of romance that the motivation is obscured. Then that person falls prey to deception.

To break through the deception, try to accept romance for what it is and consider the other person's behavior when you are not distracted by an impressive present or atmospheric candlelight. Actions in everyday life speak far louder than gifts or staged performances. If your partner is no longer appealing when stripped of the romantic trappings, then true love doesn't have a fighting chance.

It's not always easy to see through these kinds of romantic deceptions. When you're in a new, exciting relationship you naturally want it to be romantic, almost supernatural, and you probably are in no rush to tarnish the illusion by interjecting real life. Unfortunately, that's sometimes precisely what is necessary. You may well learn more about each other by doing the laundry together than by picnicking on wine and cheese. In addition to gazing longingly into each other's eyes, you need to ask how each of you feels about marital roles and having children. Instead of allowing yourself to be overwhelmed by lavish presents, you need to understand the motives of the person giving the gifts and ask yourself whether you'd like him or her as much without these offerings. It's essential to explore what life will be like after the romance fades, because sooner or later real life will intrude, no matter how hard you try to stave it off. Better to prepare for that day than to establish romantic expectations that are impossible to meet.

Romance without Love, Romance with Love

All of this does not mean that romantic behavior automatically should be suspect. It's natural to expect and strive to achieve some level of romance in a new relationship. That's part of what makes a relationship fun and exciting. But it's essential that both partners understand the role that romance is playing.

Some relationships are destined to be pure romance and nothing more. A friend once told me of just such a liaison he'd had while studying in Florence, Italy, during his college years. Carl met Lisa, a young Canadian tourist, in the middle of the Piazza della Signoria as Lisa and her two companions were attempting to communicate in broken Italian with a street vendor. Carl, pretending to be Italian, interceded on their behalf. He chatted with them for several minutes before admitting his true identity and then offered to show them the city. Along with two of Carl's friends, they spent the day together, exploring by motorbike all the secret sights that only the cognoscenti would know. Come nightfall, they wound their way to a rustic country restaurant where they dined by candlelight on stone tables surrounded by a field of fragrant wildflowers. They talked and laughed late into the evening — so late that the girls had to climb over the wall to get back into their youth hostel after curfew.

By now Carl had taken a special liking to Lisa, so as he hoisted her over the wall he whispered, "Meet me tomorrow at noon at the Duomo." The next day they met as planned, and Carl showed Lisa some of the most romantic spots Florence had to offer. At the end of the afternoon they found themselves alone, drinking champagne on a rooftop garden overlooking the Arno. They still knew next to nothing about each other, but the aura of romance was palpable between them. It held them together in a kind of a trance as arm in arm they surveyed the ancient city below. The evening unfolded effortlessly, leading them down to the darkened streets and on to a riverbank café. The first time Carl looked at his watch, it was hours past the hostel's curfew.

"Come stay with me tonight," he urged.

"I couldn't!" she protested, but not with a great deal of conviction.

"We won't do anything if you don't want to," he assured her. "It will be so much easier than trying to get you back into the hostel now."

So she stayed, and they held each other in an embrace that seemed to last hours. Predictably, they went to bed together, and the sex was sweet, tentative, and strangely innocent. The next morning Carl begged Lisa to let her friends go ahead, leaving her with him. Sadly, she told him she couldn't and left.

Though he had no serious desire for anything more than a few extra days with Lisa, Carl felt inexplicably depressed in her absence. That morning he walked the streets of Florence for hours nursing his bruised ego. When he returned to his *pensione* the concierge told him Lisa had come looking for him. In a panic, he ran back out to scour the city for a trace of her. Unearthing no clue, he came back to news that she had appeared a second time, but though Carl waited and searched through the afternoon, she never returned again.

That evening, back in the piazza, he spied a beautiful young American woman with her parents. "Excuse me," he said, introducing himself, and with that, Lisa became history, lost but never forgotten.

A week or two later Carl sent a letter for her to American Express in Greece. It was a long, soul-searching review of their "all too brief romance," ending with an anguished plea for an explanation of her disappearance. "I was tempted by you and by our day together," came Lisa's reply, "but when you still

were gone the second time I returned to your *pensione*, I decided not to quarrel with fate. It was a beautiful romantic adventure but probably would never be anything more. To try to
make it more would only have tarnished an exquisite memory
for both of us."

Lisa was absolutely right, as Carl well knew. In a matter of
weeks he could hardly remember Lisa as an individual. She was
nothing more than an apparition in a romantic dream. The romance had been delicious — an experience neither of them
regretted — but it probably could never have led to love. Had
the relationship continued, testing the bounds of romance, no
doubt they quickly would have discovered more about each
other than they wanted to know. Ultimately, their delight with
each other would have led to resentment and disappointment.

Pure romance free of love can be fun. It creates wonderful
memories and poignant feelings, and as long as both you and
your partner fully accept its limitations, it can remain innocent
illusion. But when the romance — the circumstances and gestures of an affair — lures you into deeper territory, the result
may not live up to your expectations. Then, when you discover
each other's deeper personal qualities, ideas, and histories, you
may even find that you actively dislike each other. Possibly, because the romance has been so enjoyable, you'll be reluctant to
delve into areas where you suspect disagreement and conflict.
You might postpone the inevitable until after you're married,
perhaps even after you have children in an attempt to preserve
or recapture the illusion of romance. But few couples can
maintain such evasion forever. Eventually, the differences between you will emerge, and you will have to either resolve
them or surrender to them.

When romance encompasses and reflects the unique characteristics of each partner, it may contribute to true love, but if
you both are unwilling to devote the effort and commitment
to take the relationship beyond the romance stage, your love
probably won't mature. As evidence of this, a great many
failed marriages begin with an outpouring of high romance,

while a great many successful marriages start with very little, if any, romance. These trappings are like icing on a cake; they make the relationship more attractive and enjoyable, but they do not provide substance.

Even when romance is a natural expression of true love, it is often most satisfying when unpredictable. If it's expected or taken for granted, it may lose some of its meaning. A candlelit dinner, for example, is compellingly romantic only when it's a special event. Candlelight every night quickly becomes ordinary. This is because we're all most susceptible to random conditioning. In experiments, birds will peck less enthusiastically when the seed drops after every third peck than when it drops after five, then ten, then two, then twenty pecks. Human beings are much the same. If our rewards take us somewhat by surprise, we remain more alert and responsive. We also tend to believe that romantic gestures are more heartfelt and meaningful if they are impulsive. Flowers brought home daily are soon taken for granted, but the man who surprises his wife with a bouquet every now and then, "just to say I love you," can count on a delighted hug and a kiss in return. Romance is, and should be, a special treat and not a requirement.

In true love, the purpose of romance is not to deceive or manipulate but to express genuine affection and enrich an ongoing relationship. It is heartfelt and relatively spontaneous. It pleases both partners and rejuvenates their commitment to each other. It gives them a brief release from the daily grind, an opportunity to focus, even if just momentarily, on each other and the relationship in a purely positive way. Romantic interludes can be very valuable. They certainly add to the pleasure of true love, and they can have a healing effect on a relationship during periods of stress. But they can never provide or replace the substantive bonds that develop through open, ongoing communication and genuine caring. These are the bonds that form the core of true love.

THE PARENT TRAP

White, college-educated women born in the mid-'50s
who are still single at 30 have only a 20 percent chance
of marrying.
— *Newsweek*, June 2, 1986

THE ARTICLE CONTAINING this statement lay in Vanessa's
lap throughout our first meeting. Although she was attractive,
smart, professionally successful — and only twenty-nine — the
statistics had her worried sick. She had tried to reassure herself
that they couldn't possibly be accurate, but they haunted her
nevertheless, just as they did millions of other women that
summer and for many months to come. Even after many of the
conclusions of the study that produced this shock wave were
formally discredited, the dilemma it had pinpointed remained:
Because of the post–World War II baby boom, there are fewer
men over age thirty-five than there are women age thirty-five
or younger. Since women tend to marry older men, this means
there is an excess of eligible women for the available pool of
men. Furthermore, by the time a woman reaches age thirty or
thirty-five, many men her age or older are attracted to younger
women.

Vanessa concluded that her chances of marrying were about
to start shrinking rapidly. Her chances of having a child would
shrink even faster, she calculated, given her biological age limit
and the chance that her marriage might fail or that she'd fall

for a man who didn't want children. For a young woman who had always taken for granted her future as a wife and mother, it was a moment of sober reckoning and dread that sent her charging into my office for counseling.

Vanessa had worked hard to become independent. She grew up in a Detroit tenement, the youngest of three sisters. Her mother was just nineteen when the eldest was born. Her father was an alcoholic who deserted the family when Vanessa was two. Both her sisters had shotgun marriages in their late teens which quickly ended in divorce. Instead of following in their footsteps, Vanessa left home right after high school and worked her way through college. It required tremendous strength for her to break the pattern of premature marriage that she felt had pulled down her mother and sisters, but she did it; she landed a good job with a Fortune 500 corporation and was dependent on no one. Once she was established professionally, she assured herself, there would be plenty of time to have a family. That would give her the means to provide her children with the comfort and security she never had growing up.

Vanessa was just starting to think that she had everything under control when she picked up that magazine and felt her life go into a tailspin. Suddenly, she had a vision of herself at forty, alone, childless, and miserable, her career nothing but a source of frustration and disappointment. Fortunately, she was willing to be persuaded that this vision was far-fetched. She had too much energy and assertiveness and enjoyed her professional accomplishments too much to ever fit this pitiable portrait. Nevertheless, she was not going to take any chances. She decided to overcome the odds against her having a family in the same way she had overcome the odds of her having a good career. She wanted a husband and she wanted children, and so far in life she'd managed to have everything she wanted. This, she decided, should be no exception.

For the next two years her social life became a frenzied round of dates and brief affairs: business acquaintances, computer dating service selections, friends of friends. She was, in effect, auditioning one man after another. There was little of the relaxed fun and romance that had characterized her earlier relationships. She was on a mission! Though Vanessa tried to be subtle, men quickly detected the undercurrent of desperation that was driving her. When they fled after the first few dates, she told herself it was okay: If they're so frightened by the idea of settling down and raising a family, they're not right for me, she rationalized. The trouble was that none of the men she met who did seem ready for domesticity were attractive to her. While she was touched by their warmth and maternal nature, she found them boring and passive as sexual partners.

By the time Vanessa turned thirty-two, her biological clock was ticking so loudly that the noise obscured almost everything else in her life. Her standards for men changed accordingly, and even those boring, maternal men began to look more appealing. She had less interest now in romance and friendship. She just wanted a man who would have children with her.

One of the reasons Vanessa became so obsessed with having children was that many of her friends suddenly were having babies. For years, her women friends had been too busy building careers and "finding themselves" to contemplate family life. Many, concerned about the world population explosion and the nuclear threat, had vowed to remain childless. Now in their thirties, however, they were suddenly aware of their own mortality and wanted to have children who would survive them. Some claimed to feel a strong "biological urge" to procreate. Others simply did not want to miss having the experience of nurturing and loving a child of their own. Their urges were validated by the many celebrities, such as Meryl Streep, Jane Seymour, Amy Irving, and even renegade rock stars like Pat Benatar and Chrissie Hyndes, who were starting families. Members of the fifties baby boom seemed almost universally to be reevaluating their careers and independent lifestyles and deciding that the time had come to start a "boomlet" of their own.

A few of Vanessa's friends were even choosing to have children without a husband, sometimes by having unprotected sex with an unwitting boyfriend. In rare cases, the pregnancies ended in marriage, but in most cases the women became single mothers. That was not what Vanessa had in mind. Several of the men she dated would gladly sire children and then walk away. She wanted a *family*, and to her that meant having a husband who would be a good father. He had to be responsible and caring. He had to agree with her on issues like discipline and religion. He had to have good genes. He was probably nonexistent, she chided herself.

Then her cousin set her up with Kurt. A blind date. The ultimate act of desperation, Vanessa thought. To her amazement, it was a success.

Kurt was different from the men she usually dated. For openers, he was a year younger than she and had been on the police force for ten years. Having burnt out on police work, he now was in business school. When he finished, he wanted to land a management position with a major corporation and someday start his own company.

"What about the rest of your life?" asked Vanessa.

"How do you mean?"

She hesitated and then, trying to sound offhanded, took the plunge. "Oh. You know. Personal goals. Like climbing a mountain or having a family."

"I want children," he said thoughtfully. Vanessa's heart started racing. "I come from a big family, you see. I was the youngest, and my older brothers and sisters were already starting to have kids of their own when I was still in grade school. I grew up envying them. Besides, kids are a lot of fun!"

Vanessa suddenly understood what it is to swoon. He sounded so casual, as if every man on earth should feel this way. He clearly didn't know how rare he was.

From that moment on, she was determined to marry him. If he wanted children, she convinced herself, he would make a good father. If he made a good father, he would make a good husband. Above all, he seemed to be willing and available now, before it was too late for her.

Vanessa didn't say a great deal about *her* desire for children, except to let him know in no uncertain terms that she too wanted a family "someday." She knew from experience that pressure would get her nowhere. She would be much more attractive to him if she seemed nonchalant, available but not too eager. What she failed to realize was that Kurt wasn't interested in games. He wanted a truly loving relationship.

Kurt saw in Vanessa a woman who had achieved the kind of success against all odds that he hoped to duplicate himself. Although he was fortunate to have a very close, loving family, in his eyes he still had to conquer almost insurmountable obstacles to escape his working-class roots. Here, he thought, was a soul mate, someone who could understand and help him confront these obstacles.

So began a courtship polarized between blind determination and cautious optimism. Vanessa spent every free moment scheming to make herself irresistible to Kurt. She started by losing ten pounds and having herself professionally "made over" from head to toe. When that met with his approval, she began taking cooking lessons and tempting him with delicacies from her kitchen. She gave him a key to her home. It should be, she said, "a place of refuge" for him.

Kurt was amused and flattered by her obvious efforts to please and entice him. As far as he was concerned, it wasn't necessary. He liked her just as she was, but if she wanted to turn somersaults for him, he certainly wouldn't stand in her way! It was true that he was overwhelmed by the volume of work he had to do for business school, and Vanessa did give him a welcome retreat from it all.

What he didn't know was that four weeks after their first date, Vanessa took a thousand dollars of the money she'd been saving over the last three years for her wedding and bought a wedding gown, complete with veil and train. The week after, she bought a book of baby names and began searching for a name that would combine well with both her and Kurt's last names. She never told Kurt of the dress or the book. They had not yet discussed marriage.

About two months into their courtship, Kurt took Vanessa to his family reunion, a picnic for more than thirty people. It was the first time she had seen him with children, and he passed the test with flying colors. He played ball with his nephews, tossed the babies comfortably on his knee, and teased his giggling nieces.

Kurt's mother caught her staring at him. "What do you think of my boy?" she asked, smiling.

"I think he will make a wonderful father," said Vanessa.

Kurt's mother nodded calmly. "Someday," she said. "But he's in no rush."

Maybe not, thought Vanessa. But I am.

They had been dating for about six months and had been dancing around the "M" word for weeks when they had their first serious discussion about making a commitment. Vanessa tried to bring up the issue nonchalantly, but Kurt, as usual, deftly sidestepped it. Finally, in frustration, she blurted out, "Are we going to get married or not?" Kurt stared at her, speechless. She continued, "Because if that's not where we're headed, I'm gone." She took his hands. "Kurt, I'm *sorry*. But I want a husband. I want a family. And I just don't have time to work on the relationship for years and then have it fall apart."

"You'd rather race into it, have a bunch of kids, and *then* have it fall apart?" he countered.

"You know that's not what I mean. I just don't see why we should wait."

"Okay," he said, taking a deep breath. "Let me tell you how *I* feel about this baby business. For openers, I would like to have kids someday, but *not* now. I have another year of school, Vanessa. I'm still young, and I'm just not ready for the responsibility of a family. Second, I'm not interested in having a family without a wife, and I don't think you're ready to be my wife. In fact, I'm not sure now how interested you are in being a wife at all. It sounds as if marriage to you is nothing more than a ticket you get punched on the way to motherhood — "

"No!" cried Vanessa.

"Let me finish. I have too many friends who are divorced

and paying alimony and child support, and I'm not going to walk into the same trap if I can help it. I know from my own family how great kids are and how beautifully they can complement a marriage. But, Vanessa, it only works if the marriage is strong and loving to start with. And you can't establish that strength if you've got to contend with pregnancy, childbirth, and childrearing — all when the relationship is barely off the ground."

"So," said Vanessa. "Is that it?"

"I don't know," he replied. "I guess that's up to you. Personally, I'm still very interested. I'd like to try living together, maybe do some traveling together, and see what happens after I finish school."

"You're talking years, Kurt!"

"I know. I'm sorry, but I think that's what we'd need. Besides, you're still young. There's no reason for you to be so clutchy about it."

"I just can't risk the time. If we play by your rules and it doesn't work out, I probably never will have a child!"

"Then I guess it is over," he said.

Vanessa was devastated. Shortly afterward, she tearfully described the breakup to me.

"You're very disappointed," I said. "Does that mean you love him?"

She hesitated. "Yes."

"That didn't sound entirely convincing. Do you think he loves you?"

She hesitated again. "I thought so."

"Did he tell you he does?"

"Not exactly. He would say we don't know each other well enough yet, but I know if we spent the time together — if we had children together — he would realize he loves me."

"And you think getting married and starting a family *before* he reaches this conclusion is the best way to guarantee it?"

She looked a little sheepish. "Maybe."

"You wish it were, but you know that would mean taking a big risk, even if he were willing to go along with you."

"Honestly?" she said. "Honestly, what I know is that I want to have a child more than anything else in the world. It's a physical feeling, a hunger. I can see that Kurt would make a great husband and father. We would be terrific together. I don't understand why he's so afraid."

"Maybe he's not afraid at all. Maybe he just has other priorities that you've ignored because they didn't suit *your* priorities. What he's been trying to tell you is exactly what your own family history tells you. It's easy to make babies. It's much harder to make a marriage. And it's much, much harder to make a marriage *after* you've made a baby. Look at your mother and sisters!"

"But we're different. I'm older. I've got a steady income. He's not an alcoholic like my father or a dropout like my sisters' husbands. There's no comparison."

"But you're not truly committed *to each other*. Try to imagine what kind of family life you'd have."

Vanessa left the office frustrated but beginning to recognize the truth. She and Kurt tried for several weeks to start anew, but they couldn't reconcile their goals for the relationship. He wanted a partner in love, while she wanted a partner in parenthood. Neither was willing to make the adjustments necessary to continue. When they had completed the breakup, Vanessa remained disappointed, but she now accepted that what she missed most was not love, but the father she'd imagined Kurt could be.

Men, Women, and the Biological Clock

Single women in their thirties today are painfully aware of the lopsided marriage statistics. Men in their age group, it seems, can always find younger women to marry and bear their children. The male biological clock never runs out. Women, however, must find a partner before they turn forty if they're going to have children. They may still find a husband after this age, but the biological risks of childbearing become, for many women, prohibitive. Single parenthood is an alternative that attracts only a few. Most want bona fide families, including both husband and offspring. What they may be willing to compromise, consciously or unconsciously, is true love. This willingness makes women easy prey for the parent trap: the temptation to accept what is, in fact, false love in order to produce a family.

For men, the desire to have children seems to arise at a later age and with considerably less anguish. While women start to become nervous about parenthood as they enter their thirties, men can postpone the issue until well into their thirties, or even forties, and then consider it as a matter of progeny rather than a deeply wrenching need. For many men, having a child is proof of virility and a hedge against mortality. A child revives memories of youth and offers some protection against the loneliness of old age. Becoming a father can change a man from bachelor or husband to head of a household, a position of authority he may enjoy. But fatherhood is generally more of an intellectual than a visceral desire. Though their attitudes often change after becoming fathers, men initially tend to be attracted to the *fact* of paternity.

Some women view motherhood in much the same way. These are often very successful professionals who work six days a week, twelve hours a day, and plan to return to work within a month after they have the baby. Most women, however, have a much more encompassing view of parenthood. Whether it's instinctual, hormonal, emotional, or intellectual, women seem to have a greater drive to bear and nurture children than do men. They want the *experience* of motherhood.

Some women are so driven that, like Vanessa, they are more worried about their prospective mates' skills as parents than as husbands or even lovers. This reversal of the traditional order of priorities has created, primarily among women, a whole new set of illusions about love as well as a revised myth of true romance as a kind of adventure in parenthood. These illusions — the bait for the parent trap — can contribute as much to false love as do the illusions of pleasing a parent through marriage, finding eternal sexual satisfaction through love, or falling in love at first sight.

The Truth about Love and Parenthood

Until you become a parent yourself, it's virtually impossible to know what the experience is like. Some people imagine that it's pure drudgery and frustration. Others fantasize that it's all fun, games, and baby talk. Still others believe that they can skim the joy for themselves and assign the routine annoyances to the other parent or to a housekeeper or au pair. While most do recognize that raising children can be both a blessing and a curse, the exact ratio remains in doubt until the child arrives. Your personal aptitude for parenthood also is difficult to determine beforehand. Many people who seem extremely aloof and self-centered become avid nurturers as parents, while others who are very sympathetic and concerned for the welfare of their adult friends and family seem unable to connect emotionally with children. Simply wanting to have children does not in itself make anyone a good parent.

The reality of parenthood is affected by a great many factors that cannot be foreseen, the child being chief among them. Even as a newborn, a baby's sex, health, and temperament will dramatically influence your responses as a parent. If you've always dreamed of having a bouncing, active baby, you might feel disappointed and detached if your infant turns out to have a quiet, passive temperament. And try to imagine how you would cope if your child should have serious health problems or if you should be confronted by severe financial or marital difficulties while trying to raise your child.

Facing and accepting all these unknowns is an important part of becoming a parent. Couples who truly love each other and choose to have a baby as an extension of that love understand that they are taking a gamble and that their life will change considerably after the child arrives. They may not anticipate just how dramatic the changes will be, but they have the core of love and trust to hold their family together whatever the outcome.

The illusions that make up the parent trap, however, do not suggest the countless variables in parenthood. Rather, they reflect unrealistically idealized versions of the experience. Take a moment to imagine yourself as a parent. Even if you have a very fast-paced, spontaneous lifestyle, you probably have quite traditional expectations of family life. You may envision a perfect Gerber baby; a comfortable home with a safe, shady back yard, and a family with all the warmth and ease of *Father Knows Best*. But even among strong, healthy families, few fit such a picture-perfect ideal. It is natural to have disagreements and disappointments, especially when it comes to childrearing, and it is important to be prepared for these stresses *before* undertaking family life. Couples who fall into the parent trap are often completely unprepared to meet its challenges. For them, the realities of parenthood are obscured by the following illusions.

Illusion 1: A loving parent equals a loving partner.

There is a vast difference between romantic love and parental love. A parent must assume authority over a child, while partners in love must treat each other as equals. A parent must give love unconditionally, while true love is based on the condition of mutuality. Even qualities such as respect, honesty, and trust, which characterize both relationships, are communicated very differently between lovers than between parents and children. But the key difference lies in the goals of the two relationships. The experience of parenthood begins with absolute unity and devotion and graduates to separation. Your ultimate goal as a good parent is to teach your child to be independent. By contrast, true love begins with separation and graduates to unity. Your objective in true love is to form a strong and permanent union as a couple.

If you are susceptible to the illusion that a parent and partner are one and the same, you are missing these key distinctions. If you assume that someone who is great with children automatically will be a great spouse, you may be sorely disappointed. Consider the stereotypical criteria for a good parent. A prospective father should have "good genes," which means that he's relatively attractive and intelligent and has no family history of hereditary illness. He should earn a good enough living to support a family or be very nurturing or both. He should enjoy being around children, which means he should be tolerant of noise, clutter, and interruptions. And he should be willing to give the time and energy that raising a child demands. A prospective mother is expected to be warm, nurturing, and openhearted. She too must have "good genes" and should be physically and emotionally healthy enough to withstand the rigors of pregnancy, childbirth, and childrearing. Finally, she should be willing to sacrifice some of her own personal ambitions, if necessary, for the sake of her children.

While these may be reasonable ideals for parents, they have little to do with an individual's capacity for true love. I have seen many couples who make wonderful, devoted parents and yet are unable to sustain a marriage. Bobbi and Sam are a good example. They appeared in therapy on their first wedding anniversary, and it soon became clear that they would not be together for a second. The current of their discontent ran so deep that they hardly could stand to look at each other, yet they both doted on their six-month-old son, who lay in an infant seat at our feet throughout the session. When it came to the baby, their hostility seemed to melt. In a way, this was understandable, since the child was the sole purpose of their union, their only common interest.

Bobbi had spent several years searching for a man who was ready and willing to start a family. Sam seemed the answer to her prayers. He was blond, slender, and cherub-faced. His voice and demeanor were gentle, his lifestyle apparently calm and steady. He had money in the bank and worked as a CPA.

Adopted himself, Sam was very eager to have a family of his own, but until he met Bobbi, most of the women he dated seemed reluctant. He was attracted to career women, whom he perceived as bright, capable, and assertive — good role models for his children. But at the same time, he thought they should be willing to give up their careers when they had children. Not only did his past girlfriends disagree, but most took the mere idea as a frontal assault. Bobbi, however, saw things his way. At thirty-four, she was disenchanted with her job in advertising. She had no use for the incessant office politics, and she no longer knew what she was working for. Her ideas all seemed stale and her career prospects limited. She would welcome a chance to break free and devote herself fully to motherhood.

Almost from the first date, Bobbi and Sam spent most of their time either talking about children or playing with children. They would go to the park, and Sam would join the kids playing on the baseball diamond. Or they would fly kites together, an activity that always attracted little ones. Eager to please, they both exuded warmth and affection in these situations. They were not exactly posing; rather they were exaggerating their natural enthusiasm for each other's benefit.

The truth was that neither one had much experience caring for children. Sam's adoptive parents had a daughter, but she was eight years older. Bobbi was an only child. Neither had ever diapered a baby or spent more than a few hours around any one child. As a result, they both viewed parenthood as an extended playtime.

Barely three months after they met, Bobbi became pregnant. While they hadn't planned this, they had been sloppy with birth control, as if to test each other's fertility before they tied the knot. They married quietly soon thereafter and pooled their savings to buy a small house in a quiet residential neighborhood. In their free time, they shopped for baby equipment and decorated the nursery.

They stopped having sex shortly after Bobbi became pregnant. At first it was because of her morning sickness and because she simply lost her sex drive. Sam was understanding at first. This was, after all, his baby she was carrying. He could survive a few weeks of abstinence. Eventually, though, the balance tipped. Bobbi's appetite for sex returned just as her body began to take on whalelike proportions. Now it was Sam's turn to say no. "I don't want to disturb the baby," he'd protest, but in fact he simply didn't want to touch Bobbi. By the seventh month, he was having an affair with a young woman in his office. It's purely physical, he told himself by way of justification. It would be over as soon as the baby was born.

Bobbi suspected nothing. Though she was hurt by his rejection in bed, she was touched by his continuing devotion to the baby. He loved to feel it moving and listen to its heartbeat. He was constantly bringing home presents for "the kid," which he was convinced would be a boy.

They had differing views about childbirth. Sam, vehemently against all medication, felt Bobbi should have absolutely natural childbirth so that the baby wouldn't be subjected to drugs. She was afraid of the whole process and wanted the reassurance that drugs would be available if she needed them. When the time came and she was fifteen hours into labor, she pleaded for relief, but Sam intervened, persuading her not to give up. After twenty-one hours, she delivered a healthy baby boy. Despite her exhaustion and accumulated rage at Sam for having put her through such pain, she was as ecstatic as he about their son, whom they named Andrew.

Over the next few weeks, Sam proved himself to be an exemplary father. He walked the baby in the middle of the night, changed diapers willingly, and sang Andrew lullabies. Watching them together, Bobbi felt blessed that Sam was such a perfect father. Unfortunately, she felt far less happy when she and Sam were alone together. She still carried nearly thirty pounds of extra weight, about which she felt intensely self-conscious. An affectionate kiss or an occasional hug would have made her feel much better about herself, but Sam rarely volunteered. He talked to her only about Andrew and never asked how she was feeling. It was as though she had performed her services and now could be ignored.

Bobbi didn't want to fight with Sam over their increasing estrangement. For one thing, she felt so fat and ugly that she could understand his indifference. For another, she had quit her job and was now financially dependent on him to support the family. And finally, she told herself, thanks to Sam she had what she'd desperately wanted — a baby. They were both so overwhelmed by Andrew that it probably was natural for them to drift apart. When they got used to his presence, she told herself, their relationship would return to normal.

What Bobbi refused to admit was that their relationship had never been normal. Before or after he was born, Andrew always had been the focus. They had talked exhaustively about childbearing issues but knew surprisingly little else about each other. They each secretly had been afraid that if they delved too deep they would find things they disliked, possibly things that would tear the relationship apart and destroy their chances for having a child. So instead, they limited their relationship — and their commitment — to the single objective of having a baby.

Unlike Bobbi, Sam was well aware of the flaws in their marriage. As much as he had wanted Bobbi to become a full-time mother, he had never imagined the physical and emotional changes she would undergo in the process. To him it seemed that she'd been transformed from a voluptuously attractive and intelligent woman to an obese housewife who never thought about anything other than diaper rash and shopping lists. He was delighted to pitch in with Andrew when he was home, but Bobbi seemed to think that was *all* he cared about. Throughout the period when he was longing for a son and then anticipating Andrew's arrival, he had contributed to this illusion, partly because he too was preoccupied by the prospect and partly because he hadn't wanted to rock the boat. Now he felt that the time had come to restore some sense of balance to his life, but Bobbi seemed so immersed in motherhood that she was virtually untouchable.

Exactly five months after Andrew was born, Bobbi stopped by Sam's office to find him locked in a passionate kiss with his receptionist. It was clear that this was more than a casual friendship. It was also clear that the affair was Sam's way of rejecting their marriage. All Bobbi's illusions about this "perfect husband and father" evaporated in that instant. Before she stormed out of the office, she told him not to bother coming home to her or to Andrew. He would have to beg her to see his son, she decided.

And beg he did. Despite his infidelity, Sam remained devoted to Andrew. Once her initial fury had passed, Bobbi realized that Andrew would be the real victim if she and Sam didn't somehow reach a truce. This was what brought them in for marital therapy. But Sam had no genuine desire to be, as he put it, "restricted" by marriage, and Bobbi was so hurt and disappointed in Sam that there was no hope for a future together.

Despite all the animosity, however, they respected each other's abilities and rights as a parent to their son. Even before the divorce was final, they agreed on the terms for shared custody. At least until their son reached school age, his time would be divided equally between his parents. Sam bought a house in the same neighborhood so his son could have his own room and a back yard at both homes, and over time Bobbi and Sam learned to be amicable in their negotiations regarding Andrew's welfare. By the time she remarried, Bobbi had forgiven Sam. He did not remarry — he never found a woman who "completely" satisfied him — but otherwise he remained a model father.

Illusion 2: A true lover equals a willing parent.

If being a good parent does not necessarily make someone a good lover, neither does being a good lover qualify anyone as a parent. Many people who are in genuinely loving relationships are physically, financially, or emotionally unable to handle the job of raising a child. Some simply do not want children. Others have children from a previous marriage and are unwilling to have more. Not wanting or being unable to have children does not make these people unfit for an adult love relationship. To the contrary, in some cases it means they are so committed to an adult partnership that they don't want to burden it with the stresses and problems of parenthood.

Cheryl and David were both ambivalent about having a family. When they met in their early twenties, they thought they might have children, but they weren't sure they really wanted a family. Cheryl, a nurse, was the oldest of six children and had spent most of her childhood diapering and tending her younger siblings. She'd watched her parents compromise their own lives to educate the children. They'd never taken a vacation without the children, they rarely went out to dinner, and they never even seemed to talk to each other without someone interrupting them. Her father died at age fifty-nine, and in Cheryl's opinion he had never enjoyed a day of real freedom in his entire adult life. Her mother was now struggling alone to raise Cheryl's teenage brothers. While she recognized the joys of life in a large family, Cheryl was also painfully aware of the sacrifices parents are expected to make, not only of themselves but of their marriage.

David, by contrast, was an only child who had virtually no experience with infants, but he taught sixth grade in the inner city. He was dedicated to his job both because he believed it was necessary and because he felt he was succeeding in getting through to at least a few of the children in his class. But emotionally it was grueling. When he came home to Cheryl, he wanted calm, adult companionship, not more children to nurture and discipline. It was enough for him to play with Cheryl's young brothers and her baby niece and nephew. He and Cheryl were the family's favorite aunt and uncle. They lavished gifts and attention on the youngsters, took them to the beach and movies, spent the time and money on them that their own parents could ill afford. These youngsters would always be there for him and he for them, and he still had the breathing room his job and marriage required.

Cheryl and David were devoted to each other and to their life together. They both read the same books and discussed them at length. They had an assortment of pets, most of which they'd taken in off the street, and they worked together to remodel their old Victorian home. Their career demands left relatively little time for togetherness, but they made a conscious effort to spend a portion of each day just relaxing and talking quietly.

For the first years of their marriage they debated the pros and cons of having a child, at one point turning to counseling to help them reach a decision. David had suspected that Cheryl might acquire more maternal impulses after she turned thirty, and he was prepared to concede if she decided she strongly wanted a child, but these impulses never occurred. Pressure from their families about when they were going to "get started" seemed to crystallize the feelings she'd suspected all along. She didn't want to be a Mommy, and she didn't want to subject their marriage to the strains of parenthood. Besides, David agreed, they already had a large and loving family of close relatives, cats, dogs, fish, and rabbits — and each other. This was all the family they needed.

While neither Cheryl nor David was surprised by this decision, both were astonished by the feelings of guilt and anxiety it unleashed. These feelings quickly became the focus of our sessions together.

David felt the guilt more than Cheryl. If he did not have a child, his family name would die with him. His parents, who had always wanted more children themselves, would be disappointed. And he did wonder if it was a mistake to "waste" all the childrearing skills he'd acquired during his years as a teacher. His students at school came and went each year. Would he regret not having children who would remain part of his life?

Cheryl feared that she might regret the decision later, when it was too late. She also worried about growing old without children. What would fill their lives when they both stopped working? Would they be able to sustain their love for each other? What if David died before she did?

Through our discussions, Cheryl and David came to realize that most of their misgivings could be traced to outsiders who were trying to influence them. It was true that David's parents would be very disappointed, and they were trying to use guilt to make him change his mind. Cheryl, meanwhile, was listening to all the young mothers in her circle of friends. They were all so thrilled with their new babies that they couldn't understand why she wouldn't choose to have one too. A few, it seemed, felt threatened by her resistance. Perhaps, Cheryl suggested, they hadn't really been sure about having children themselves and now needed her to get pregnant so they would feel validated.

Ultimately, what allowed David and Cheryl to overcome their fears was the realization that there are no guarantees either way. Their old age could just as easily find them lonely and disappointed with children as without. The one certainty was their devotion to each other and the lifestyle they had carved together. It would be a mistake, they reasonably concluded, to jeopardize this security solely to satisfy the needs of family and friends.

People who fall into the parent trap may be baffled by a couple like David and Cheryl, for they believe that a child is not only a product of love, but a measure of love. "If you love me enough," the thinking goes, "you'll want to have a child with me." As Kurt tried to tell Vanessa, however, committing to a relationship is an entirely separate decision from committing to have a child. The first choice can be tested over a period of time and revoked if necessary, the second is irreversible. The first involves a couple, the second a family.

This last point may be the most important, yet it is most often overlooked by those who believe that true love goes hand in hand with the desire for children. The dynamics of a couple are entirely different from those of a family — not necessarily better or worse, but very different. Most couples without children lead fairly flexible lives and thrive on spontaneity and a degree of independence. Usually the partners have separate work lives and both shared and separate interests, hobbies, and friends. Their relationship is an important part of their lives, but it is not necessarily the focus. To keep developing and growing within the relationship, most childless couples have to create joint projects that provide a common focus. Like Cheryl and David, they might read the same books, collect pets, or develop a "surrogate family" of relatives and friends. They might build a home, plan frequent vacation trips, take up ballroom dancing, or go into business together. Through such projects, they create shared goals and experiences that unify them as a couple. Without these experiences, childless couples may grow apart over time and one day discover they have nothing in common anymore and no mutual purpose to hold them together.

Families, by contrast, have a strong, built-in focus in the children. Parents do not need to manufacture additional outside projects, because the children are their project. In a healthy family, the partners' love for the children becomes a common bond. As parents, they share the same satisfactions, worries, and responsibilities, and these often become central issues in their relationship, especially while the children are young. But no couple will succeed if the children are *all* that is holding them together. They must make a dual commitment — to each other as lovers and as parents. This means allocating enough time and energy to satisfy each other in addition to juggling the demands of children, work, and outsiders. Over the long run, most committed parents agree that families are well worth this added effort, but no one pretends it's easy. Succeeding in these dual roles requires attention, patience, and understanding. If both partners are united, a baby can fit beautifully into a master plan for love, but trying to force a love affair into one person's master plan to have a baby rarely serves anyone's best interests.

Unfortunately, because having a child is such a momentous decision and is often so fraught with emotion, many couples sidestep the issue until well into the relationship. Some actually get married without ever having discussed it. But parenthood should never be left to chance simply because it's hard to talk about. You need to discuss this issue early in any relationship, *before* you become emotionally attached. If you deeply want to have a family and your partner is unable or unwilling to have children, there are only three solutions: agreeing not to have children, agreeing to have children, and breaking up.

Agreeing not to have children means that one of you must make a major, and perhaps very painful, sacrifice for love. It's a potentially dangerous solution if it is reached without due consideration, because it leaves one of you open to a later change of heart. In a stepfamily, for example, the new step-mother might initially believe that caring for her husband's children will quell her desire for a baby of her own. So she tells him it's okay that he doesn't want more children. Eventually, she recognizes that stepparenting is significantly different from parenting and begins yearning for her own child, but by then her husband is several years older and even more opposed to enlarging his family. This kind of stalemate, with its attendant regrets and resentments, can be disastrous even in strong, loving relationships, and it is particularly hard on the woman. A man who changes his mind after ten or even twenty years and is willing to remarry usually can find a younger woman to bear his child, but a woman doesn't have that kind of leeway.

Agreeing to have children entails dramatically different responses from couple to couple. For some it's as simple as discontinuing birth control pills. For others it means infertility treatment or trying to reverse a vasectomy. For still others it may mean adoption. Each situation requires a different degree of commitment and preparation initially, but the ultimate result is the same: a child to raise, feed, educate, and love. Sometimes couples try to compromise to make the agreement palatable to the reluctant partner: If you agree to have this child, you'll never have to change a diaper or get up in the middle of the night, we'll get a sitter so our social life won't change a bit, and I'll do all the Little League coaching myself. Such promises not only miss the point but are almost impossible to keep. The reluctant parent's sleep and social life inevitably will be disrupted, no matter how hard the other parent tries to prevent it, and the reluctant parent's lack of enthusiasm for being a parent probably will remain unchanged. It's true that some hesitant partners are happily surprised by the experience of parenting, but there is no way to be sure that this will happen. When it doesn't happen, the disenchanted parent may walk out on both the marriage and the child.

While many single parents succeed in raising healthy, well-rounded children, no one, least of all these single parents and their children, would argue that this is the *desirable* way to raise a family. Every child deserves two devoted and enthusiastic parents. If one parent is resentful or indifferent, both the child and the family as a whole will suffer.

In many cases, breaking up is the only realistic solution. It doesn't necessarily mean that the love is false. It just means that you and your partner have incompatible goals. For example, if a young woman who desperately wants children becomes involved with a man who's had a vasectomy, she might persuade him to try to have the surgery reversed, but there is no guarantee that this will succeed. If it doesn't, they could adopt or use artificial insemination, but this requires a tremendous commitment from the man and means a complete reversal of the convictions that made him have the vasectomy in the first place. And in the end they still would not have a child who was biologically their own. Given the time, emotional distress, and risk of failure that such a process requires, it would be perfectly reasonable for the couple to seek different partners. Even true love cannot conquer conflicts that affect us on such a fundamental level.

Illusion 3: Having a baby is a key to love.

This was the theory that, in addition to her own personal desire for a child, drove Vanessa to pressure Kurt to the breaking point. She genuinely believed that becoming parents would bring them closer as lovers. Kurt didn't disagree, but he rightly felt that their relationship as lovers should be firmly established first.

This illusion also is responsible for many "shotgun" engagements and marriages. When Darla and Steve came in for marital counseling, both acknowledged that their problems started the day Darla announced she was pregnant.

They had been college sweethearts, but by the end of their senior year they were on the verge of breaking up. Darla wanted to marry Steve. He thought they should have a year or two of independence before making this decision. She was afraid he was rejecting her.

Both were Catholic. Darla knew that Steve loved children, and she assumed she would have a family sooner or later. So when she found she could persuade Steve no other way, she decided to use pregnancy. She went off the pill without telling him and charted her menstrual periods until she knew she was ovulating. Then she invited him to her room for a "reconciliation chat." Instead of begging or fighting with him, she was on her best behavior. They drank some wine and talked about everything but the future. When they went to bed there was no hint of hostility or mistrust between them.

Five weeks later, when Darla told Steve she was pregnant, he exploded. "It was all a setup! Three years without a problem, and now you turn up pregnant. You went off the pill without telling me!"

"I couldn't bear to lose you," she replied, drawing back slightly in the face of his rage.

"This is one hell of a way to show it! So now you think I'm going to marry you and the three of us will ride off into the sunset together. Right?"

"Well . . . we don't have much choice, do we?"

"I could just dump you and let you deal with this mess on your own," he fumed. But Steve was too honorable and his family was too religious for him to do such a thing. Despite his anger, he felt trapped. Abortion was out of the question. He couldn't agree to adoption because he'd have to give up all claim of paternity and would never see the child. Leaving Darla in the lurch was tempting, since he didn't think he could ever respect or trust her again, but the baby didn't deserve that. Besides, he wouldn't respect himself.

So immediately following graduation they had a small wedding ceremony and moved into the apartment above his parents' garage. He got a job as a shipping clerk and took classes in computer science at night. Darla worked in a nearby stationery store until the baby came. When she and Steve were together she tried to make amends, but nothing she did seemed to melt his resentment. Mostly, he avoided her. He left early and returned late, working extra hours on weekends. Whenever she complained about his working too much, he turned on her. "I wouldn't have to work so much if you hadn't gotten yourself knocked up!" To which she'd reply, "I didn't get pregnant by myself. You helped!" But usually he would be gone by the time she completed this observation.

She told herself the relationship would improve after the baby arrived, but instead it got worse. Darla delivered prematurely, and their little girl, Annie, had to stay in the hospital for several weeks. They had no insurance to cover the costs. Now Steve blamed Darla not only for trapping him but for saddling him with a mountain of debts and producing a sick child.

Fortunately, Annie's condition improved rapidly once she was home, but her presence only drove them further apart. Darla was completely unprepared for the work of raising a child, and Steve gave her no help whatsoever. He played with the baby when she was happy but immediately handed her back to Darla as soon as she got cranky or needed a diaper change. He claimed he'd kept his part of the bargain and was paying the bills. If Darla wanted this child so badly, said Steve, she should be able to care for her. Darla did her best, but she was overwhelmed and lonely. Much as she loved Annie, she felt that this child had cost her Steve's love. Instead of cementing their marriage, the baby seemed to have ruined any chance they ever had.

Far too late, Darla realized that Steve's request for a year or two of freedom was perfectly reasonable and probably would have been good for her too. They might well have gotten back together — and stayed together — after this breathing period. Even if they hadn't, they probably would have found other loving partners. Now they both felt trapped.

The marriage lasted four years, sustained only by their mutual sense of duty to Annie. By the time she was in nursery school, they could keep up the pretext no longer. As a concession to their families, they came for counseling, but there was no way to restore their trust and respect for each other. The daily emotional rejection had become too much for Darla, and Steve felt suffocated in the relationship. Divorce was a relief for them both. Only Annie was devastated and wanted them to stay together. She was the real casualty of Darla's illusions.

If maturity and responsibility are the prerequisites of true love, they are even more essential to parenthood. Few experiences are as stressful as having a baby, and your marriage must absorb the bulk of this stress. If the foundation of love is shaky, as it was between Darla and Steve, this added pressure may drive you apart. At first a newborn baby may distract you from the real problems in the relationship, but the distraction is only temporary — you could build a house or move across the country and produce the same effect. Nothing is really resolved, and when the illusion wears off, you must face the same old problems. One big difference between building a house and having a baby, however, is that the child will absorb the worst of the situation. A baby is not a toy that can be used to buy or blackmail a partner into love. Whether you and your partner break up or stay together, the child will remain your joint responsibility for years to come and will be deeply affected by any discord. Furthermore, unless you eventually establish a genuinely loving relationship, with each other or with subsequent partners, the child may have no realistic models of true love and therefore be that much more vulnerable to false love when he or she grows up.

Paving the Way for Love and Parenthood

There are many reasons why you may want to have children, and it's important to separate the valid from the not so valid ones. Pressure from family and friends, for example, may be persuasive, but it's not a good reason to have a child. Nor is fear of loneliness or old age, the desire to experience pregnancy, or the desire to "culminate" a relationship. We're all curious to see how our children will resemble us, but that's not a responsible motivation either. The only truly valid reason to become a parent is the desire to nurture, teach, and learn from another human being, from birth through maturity. This does not automatically accompany true love.

While you and your partner may want both a love relationship and a family, these goals probably do not hold equal priority. If forced to choose, chances are you would rather have love, but it's difficult to think in these terms — it's much easier to assume you'll be able to have both. That can be a mistake, for unless you stop to consider which goal truly comes first for you, you can easily get your priorities backward. This is what happens to so many single women as they enter their thirties and the biological clock starts ticking louder and louder. They don't honestly want babies more than love, but they've never sorted out these two very separate agendas.

The degree of commitment to parenthood also varies from one person to the next. Some people dream of having a large family and will not be satisfied with anything less. Others are flexible — they'd be happy with one child, stepchildren, or adopted children. These are not "hard issues." They are natural goals and aspirations that two people should know about each other before deciding to pursue a relationship. If you and your partner share similar views of the future in this and in other respects *and* are ready to commit to true love, you have the makings of a strong family and a secure future as a couple. Explore the issue of children early in the relationship, so you know where you stand.

PART II

THE SOURCES
OF ILLUSION

6

CONDITIONED RESPONSES: OUR EARLIEST IMPRESSIONS OF LOVE

YOU AND YOUR BELOVED have adored each other from the first time you met. You spend every day together and consume each other's thoughts. Your loved one tends to all your needs, comforting you when you're unhappy, providing you with a place to live and scores of gifts, showering you with attention and praise, and demanding nothing in return. Whenever the two of you are apart, you worry and miss each other desperately, and when you reunite you both feel a rush of pleasure. Sometimes, if the separation is too long, you feel rejected and angry, but you never hold a grudge because deep in your heart you know this is a love affair that will last forever.

If this sounds familiar, it may be because you've read about it in a romantic novel, seen it played out in a movie, or heard it described in a wishful love song. Or it may be because you recognize it in your own memories. The fact is that most of us experienced this overwhelmingly "perfect" love affair while still in the cradle.

Looking back to infancy is not just an exercise in nostalgia, for our first illusions about relationships began to form in early childhood. From the vantage point of twenty or more years, many longstanding misconceptions can suddenly become very clear — but we first must give ourselves permission to face them. It's not always easy to search the past, especially when it contains the roots of unhappiness, but once we start, we have a foundation for change. And once we have a clearer perspective on old illusions, we can bring new insight to our present relationships.

On one level, that first intense bond between parent and infant is nature's practical way of ensuring that we'll be protected and nurtured as babies. On another, however, this love creates an irresistible model we all wish we could re-create to some extent in our adult love affairs. Unconditional, permanent, overwhelmingly gratifying, intimate and absolutely trusting — who wouldn't jump for a relationship with all these qualities? From early childhood you've probably been conditioned to think of this ideal as "true love," and no matter how independent and mature you may be, it's still easy to be seduced by the notion of a loving partner who will nurture and comfort you without asking anything in return. Why shouldn't a loving partner wait on you hand and foot when you're sick and bring you special treats just as Mama did? "You had it once," the subconscious voice whispers. "Why shouldn't you have it again?" Unfortunately, what is a perfectly reasonable reality in infancy becomes a dangerous fantasy in adulthood.

The relationship between infant and parent is predicated on dependency and a biological bond, and so it cannot be a relationship between equals. No matter how positive your family relationships or how hard you work at them, you have no control over your role as "child" and very little over your responses to your parents. You never chose your parents, yet as a newborn you depended on them for everything and loved them no matter how they treated you. They, in return, saw you as a reflection of themselves and loved you in large part because of this.

Parents naturally hope that their children will become "improved" versions of themselves. A mother who is a librarian fantasizes that her newborn son eventually will love books as much as she does and, perhaps, will become a successful author. A father who is a midlevel insurance salesman envisions that his baby daughter will grow up to become the top corporate executive he always wanted to be. In healthy families these fantasies subside as the children get older and develop goals of their own, but parents rarely let go of their dreams entirely. Their love contains a strong dose of possessiveness which you, as the child, never feel in the same way for them. Your love contains an equally strong measure of ambivalence, that tug between devotion to them and your own need for autonomy, which many parents wrongly interpret as a slap in the face. While the love between parent and child is mutual, it's never perfectly balanced.

Even as an independent adult, you remain aware of your parents' hopes for you. Because of the deep emotional connection dating back to infancy, you naturally are torn between the desire to please them and the need to chart your own separate future. You may be more successful, better educated, and more widely traveled than your parents, yet you probably never will feel that you've satisfied them one hundred percent. Those who do generally feel that they have relinquished their own needs or dreams in the process.

Most of us ultimately learn to live with this stalemate through a variety of compromises. For example, one young man appeased his parents by working in the family business but married a woman he loved even though they disapproved of her. He was trying to establish his independence without losing their approval. Others might run from their parents and challenge all authority, but this is usually a sign of despair rather than rejection. Young children who are denied affection, attention, and approval naturally become defensive as they grow up. This doesn't mean that they don't long for their parents' love and acceptance but that they have given up hope of ever getting it.

Behind all such conflicts, however, is the bond of blind trust and dependence that forms during infancy and develops into a kind of possession. Your parents have an emotional authority over you that you never have over them. They are entitled to place their hope in you, take pride in your achievements, and rebuke you for your failings. It is natural for them to live vicariously through you to some extent, but not vice versa. Either you live by their rules or you ignore them, but you do not have similar expectations for them. Even if your parents grow too old and weak to look after themselves and you become their caregiver, the emotional tables still don't turn. In your heart, you remain their child, not their equal.

These dynamics are both inevitable and appropriate in the love between parent and child, but they are incompatible with true love between a man and a woman, because true love requires relative equality. In a healthy family, you gradually come to accept this distinction as, in the natural process of separating from your parents, you prepare yourself to take on a more responsible and demanding role within your adult relationships. This acceptance doesn't completely dispel the yearning for that protective, unconditional, infantile brand of love, but you learn that such love is a fantasy. If, however, you are not permitted to achieve a healthy separation from your parents, you may look to romantic love either as an extension of or a substitute for their love. The young woman who never knew her father may expect her lover to serve as a stand-in. The man whose mother constantly criticized him as a young child may search for a wife who will place him on a pedestal. Such conflicts, dating all the way back to the cradle, lay the foundation for false love.

Learning about Love

One of the reasons your first love affair with your parents is so misleading is that no one ever explains it adequately. As a small child you probably heard "I love you" tens of times a day and quickly learned to parrot the phrase back to your parents. It was an easy way to win approval, but it didn't really mean anything to you. A hug or a cuddle — now *that* was a meaningful way to show affection. *Love* was just another word.

Eventually, you got around to asking *why* your parents loved you. The responses were either simplistic or misleading. "I love you because you're mine" was a typically obtuse answer. "I love you because you're so pretty and bright" was one of the more treacherous, leaving the impression that they would stop loving you if you lost these qualities. Your parents weren't intentionally stupid or cruel, of course, but they probably didn't really understand their feelings themselves, so how could they help you understand? Besides, the relationship is not the same for both sides. The pride, possessiveness, and expectations your parents feel for you will always be very different from what you feel for them.

As frustrating as this situation may have been for you as a youngster, you had no choice but to accept it. Eventually, you probably came to think of love as unequal and mysterious and applied this notion to your later relationships. If you never were given a rational definition of love, it would seem logical that love should strike "like lightning," that you should be "swept off your feet" or "bowled over." And if you happened to fall for someone who was much more — or less — powerful, wealthy, attractive, intelligent, older, or younger than you, then you'd have no reason to question it, because the only love you'd ever known was even *more* unbalanced. You'd naturally expect either to be taken care of or to take care of the other person because this was the way it worked with your first true love. No wonder love is so confusing!

The picture is not all bad, however. Children *can* learn many of the skills required for love if they grow up in healthy, well-adjusted families. The first and most important lesson concerns separating from parents, learning to function independently and responsibly. Most children begin this process of separation by the end of the first year, as their original dependent love for their parents begins to develop into much more complex and realistic relationships that incorporate respect, discipline, and guidance in addition to love. Through these interactions, children learn to love and respect themselves and gradually acquire the self-esteem they need to feel like equal partners in their relationships.

In families with open, honest communication young people learn to express their needs, feelings, and expectations in a positive way. When parents show children respect and concern, the children learn that this is how they should behave toward others, particularly people they care for. The way families handle disagreements and disappointments trains the children to deal with their own hard knocks without taking them out on the people around them. This early conditioning doesn't necessarily dispel the illusion of being babied in love, but it gives children the tools that will help them function in mature relationships.

In many ways, it's difficult to separate training for love from training for life, because living well and loving well require so many of the same skills and strengths. People who are happy with their lives tend to have happy marriages, while people who in general are dissatisfied often have trouble maintaining successful relationships. And although it is true that some of us are born with sunnier dispositions than others, we all need encouragement and guidance from our families in order to develop a strong sense of self-worth and self-acceptance. People who have successful careers and marriages tend to remember being treated with respect and appreciation from early childhood. Their parents accepted their failures as well as their successes, praised them liberally, and taught them not to be ashamed of their flaws. As a result, later in life they didn't feel compelled to strive for perfection to please their parents, and they weren't afraid to compromise or to be happy. In love, this relaxed attitude gave them the freedom to commit to a relationship and enjoy it without demanding the moon. Even when parents can't keep their own marriages together, children who are given this kind of nurturing have a far greater chance of making a success of love themselves.

Unfortunately, not all parents are successful at navigating the line between closeness and separation from their children. Even those who mean well may cling to their children too long and too hard, reinforcing the youngsters' impression that love is based on possession and dependence. Because they are not allowed to separate and discover their own needs and goals, the children may mistrust their own inclinations, becoming fearful and insecure. As they get older, they will experience the same internal need for separation that all young people feel, but because they've been given so little preparation for autonomy, they probably will be very ambivalent. This ambivalence may keep them so close to their families that they never venture into romantic love at all, or it may propel them toward a type of false love that mimics their bonds with their parents. In this case, instead of establishing healthy, mature relationships as adults, they bring to each new partner a subconscious expectation of the same interdependence and possessiveness that characterized their relationships with their parents. Even if they find partners who are willing to satisfy this expectation at first, it won't sustain the union for long. Ultimately, both partners must develop a more balanced view of love, or they will smother each other.

Child abuse generates quite different and much more ominous distortions of love. If parents mistreat a child, either emotionally or physically, the child doesn't necessarily stop loving them, nor does he blame them. Instead, he usually blames himself and submits to their demands in an effort to win their favor. Without any other cues to go by, he assumes that violence is a requirement for love. Most abused children can't even muster illusions of romantic love, and they have no idea what's involved in a truly loving reciprocal relationship. Abused children's self-esteem often is so low that it may never occur to them that they are worthy of true love. Even if an offer of gen-

uine love is extended, they will either sabotage it or run from
it, for fear that they'll never live up to it.

As they grow up, victims of abuse tend to seek out relationships that will perpetuate the cycle. By the time Gayle entered
therapy in her mid-twenties, this pattern was firmly established. She knew she was in trouble but had always subconsciously resisted tracing her unhappiness in love to her unhappiness as a young child. As we reviewed her upbringing, it was
clear where her problems had started. She'd been molested by
her father throughout her youth. Her mother had apparently
known about it but had never intervened, so Gayle assumed
that somehow it was her fault: She must not deserve any better. Trying to win her father's favor (that unconditional love of
a child again), she had never fought him or complained, and
occasionally he would do something nice, like taking her to the
circus or buying her pink hair ribbons. These treats told her
that things were okay after all. But things were really not okay,
and Gayle never developed the self-esteem to stand up to her
parents or defend her own rights. She left home at seventeen
and moved in with a girlfriend, but it was an act of defeat
rather than defiance. Any dreams of happiness she'd had as a
young child had long since been pounded out of her.

One day several months after leaving home, Gayle met Ben
in the supermarket checkout line. He asked where she lived,
and she confided that she was looking for a place. "Why don't
you move in with me?" he said without missing a beat. "I have
plenty of room." She was so overwhelmed by this sudden outpouring of kindness — and so desperate (her girlfriend was
threatening to throw her out) — that she turned up on the
stranger's doorstep that afternoon. He let her sleep on the sofa
the first night, but by the next night she was in bed with him.
He didn't have to pressure her much since this was what she
expected. She had no money. How else could she pay him?

Ben, too, had been abused by his parents, not sexually but
physically. In his loveless household dominated by alcoholic
parents, the children were routinely given beatings and kicked

out of the house. Ben had dropped out of school at fifteen and had gotten a job pumping gas. Now, at thirty-six, he was a mechanic. He was neither attractive nor particularly successful with women, but he got by. He drank occasionally, but not as much as his parents. His life was okay except that he needed a regular woman. When Gayle dropped into his lap, it seemed logical to ask her to marry him, so he did.

It wasn't much of a marriage, even by Gayle's standards. Ben was sexually aggressive, but not at all affectionate. He worked long hours and often went out drinking afterward. She was expected to be waiting for him whenever he got home. She cooked and cleaned for him, never asking questions, though she knew he had girlfriends. When he drank, he often beat her — just as his parents had done to him. But she was grateful for whatever scraps of kindness or attention he threw her way. Occasionally he would let her go see her mother, and once in a while he'd take her to a movie. She believed she loved him. He believed this was what married life was supposed to be like. They were sharing an existence dictated by childhood conditioning.

Once she understood the roots of her choices and saw that there were other options open to her, Gayle had the courage to break free of Ben and the specter of her father. With the help of therapy and a support group, her self-esteem gradually developed to the point where she no longer felt she had to apologize continually or ask a man's permission to be herself. She opened her eyes to men who did not mistreat her or look down on her, including many she previously would have considered either "too good" or "too nice" for her. One, a teaching assistant in the community college where she was enrolled in night school, courted her for over a year and then asked her to marry him. At last, Gayle's pattern of false love was broken.

If you are a woman with a background like Gayle's, the unresolved conflicts and pain you experienced in youth can become lethal baggage that you carry with you into adult relationships. Unable to come to terms with the past in any other way, you may unconsciously look to your sexual partners to explain and compensate for the shattered relationship with your parents. You find a man who treats you as you were treated in childhood and then struggle to make him give you the love and attention your parents denied you. When your efforts fail, you tell yourself you deserve no better and resign yourself to suffering until you can stand the pain no longer. While you may believe that what you feel for your partner is love, true love doesn't even enter into the bargain. Domination is the name of the game. Unless you receive counseling, you may fall into a spiral of false love that pushes your self-esteem lower and lower, making it increasingly impossible to establish mature emotional connections.

Women who have been mistreated in childhood play right into the hands of men who were also abused in youth. Unlike the women, many of whom become passive in defeat, men are likely to grow into hostile and aggressive adults. Unable to heal or overcome the wounds of their youth, most of them seem hell-bent on revenge. Ironclad walls surround their feelings. They take out their anger on their women, as if to get even for the pain they kept bottled up as children. Often they are conflicted between this uncontrollable anger and genuine remorse. A passionate plea for forgiveness follows each cycle of abusiveness, but they rarely have the inner strength to change the pattern for good. Most are unable to sustain any long-term commitment, for they have grown up with the belief that fidelity and compromise in a relationship are signs of weakness. And since they have been humiliated and made to feel weak all their lives, they're damned if they'll tolerate weakness in this one arena in which they feel powerful.

Women who have been abused can break the cycle if they get appropriate help. Psychotherapy, group therapy, and consciousness-raising groups all send the message "You're worth something. You don't have to suffer to be loved." This message, once it's finally received, is so powerful that it can catapult women out of disastrous marriages and into entirely new lives. At last they realize that they're not responsible for what happened to them in the past but that they are responsible for their future. They can remake their destiny.

Men who have a history of abuse, unfortunately, tend not to respond to professional help as well as women. Because our whole society discourages men from revealing and analyzing their feelings, they tend to have more defenses and be less trusting of anyone who tries to penetrate their emotional core. Sometimes their anger is so intense that they cannot hear reason, and their egos are so fragile that they may not admit there is any problem at all. Getting them into therapy and persuading them to come back until it does some good is often very difficult. If they can be convinced to listen and accept the truth, many of these men will eventually change their attitudes and behavior, but those are two very big hurdles. All too often, the legacy of childhood abuse in men becomes a lifelong pattern of fear, anger, and resistance to anything remotely resembling true love.

First Came Love, Then Came Marriage . . .

Your earliest notions of love came not only from your own relationship with your parents but also from your impressions of their marriage. Watching them, you learned how men and women should treat each other, the roles they should assume, the posturing that is permissible between the sexes, and how sexuality plays out in a relationship. Chances are that you learned that women are allowed to show affection, while men are supposed to appear powerful. Perhaps you also concluded that women usually have the real control in most households and the men are largely absent. Through a child's eyes, at least during the fifties and sixties, there was no such thing as feminine mystique, but masculine mystique was pervasive.

Sex itself was a real mystery, though. If you happened to glimpse your parents "in the act," you may have been horrified by the violence and physicality. More likely, you never saw even the vaguest signs of sexuality. From your perspective, your parents may have seemed almost neuter, their marriage a platonic friendship. Even after the sex act was explained to you, it was probably a dark mystery how *you* were ever conceived. Rumors of adoption abound in early childhood, not only because of the suspicion that they might be true but also because most youngsters cannot imagine their parents as sexual individuals. After all, the closest thing to physical contact many of us ever saw was a peck on the cheek or a quick squeeze. The "not in front of the children" rule left us in total ignorance about this essential element of love. If the only time you ever saw your parents kiss was at weddings and funerals, it's no wonder if the intimacy of your own earliest relationship with them seemed more appealing than the model of marriage they presented.

More than anything else about love, parents teach children what it's like to live day in and day out as a couple or, in the case of divorced parents, what mistakes can be made in love. The lesson depends on the family. If parents discuss problems openly and resolve them through mutual compromise, children learn how valuable communication, trust, and respect can be in sustaining a relationship. Partners in successful marriages often have strong memories of their parents conferring with each other, holding family meetings, accepting comments and criticisms, and working together to make responsible decisions and resolve difficulties. The memories may concern relatively minor childhood issues, such as whether or not the kids would go to summer camp or whether the family would adopt a dog, but the lessons in communication learned in youth translate directly to the more pressing business of maintaining a marriage in adulthood.

When parents fail to communicate honestly with each other or when they abdicate every decision to the other parent, children learn to sidestep confrontation. Of course, they also do their best to test any unity that does exist by playing one parent against the other. "May I go to Sally's house tonight?" the little girl asks. If Dad says no, she goes directly to Mom, who says sure. The child will identify with either the dominant or the submissive parent, depending on who appears to be favoring her most often. That parent then becomes a model for the child's own behavior in future relationships. The result is an extremely lopsided image of love: One person is controlling, the other weak.

If you grew up in a home where nothing short of all-out war would resolve a dispute, you may wage similar battles in your own relationships. Perhaps you remember that problems were allowed to stew for days or sometimes weeks and months and then inevitably exploded in a firestorm of yelling, slamming doors, and breaking plates, with one parent ultimately walking out. The message you got was that this is how couples communicate. When Shirley turned up for marital counseling, such violent outbursts were the only way she knew to express herself, just as it had been her mother's way of making herself heard. Shirley had inherited her mother's temperament, so perhaps she was predisposed to violent flashes of anger, but she never saw any indication that problems could be resolved otherwise. Shirley's father had been an extremely withdrawn, noncommunicative man who had virtually ignored everything her mother said unless she screamed. So her mother never even bothered trying to talk things out rationally. For better or worse, Shirley's parents survived this pattern for more than fifty years, but Shirley married a man who was very different from her father. He liked to talk about feelings and problems, and he detested battles. Not only was fighting unnecessary in their household, it was tearing their marriage apart. To salvage the relationship, Shirley had to reverse a lifelong pattern of jumping to conclusions, allowing grievances to build to the boiling point, and blaming everyone but herself when things went even slightly wrong. She also had to accept the fact that conflicts are a normal and even necessary part of love and that they needn't turn into frontal assaults to be resolved.

Some parents present a model of marriage based on the husband's total domination over his wife (or, in a few families, vice versa). He decides how she will dress, where and what she'll eat, whom they will entertain, and where they will take their vacations. She gives up any friends he doesn't approve of, reads books he chooses, and subscribes wholly to his political and lifestyle choices. In the process, she becomes incapable of making independent decisions. This is fine if she relinquishes her authority willingly, perhaps in exchange for security, comfort, or luxury. Right or wrong, it is her decision to make. Children growing up in such a household, however, generally miss this key point. Youngsters rarely understand the choices and compromises that are made in marriage. If they see inequality, they assume it is part of the package called love. Girls coming out of such a family often decide they want no part of it and may experiment purposefully to find an alternative marriage contract. Boys, on the other hand, may very well decide they want a marriage just like Dad's.

When Jerry Jr. entered therapy at twenty, he was determined to live up to his father's example of the powerful husband. Jerry Sr. had made his fortune by age twenty-one. He met Jerry's mother ten years later, when she was just eighteen, and swept her off her feet. She was pretty but not cultured, bright but not educated. In her Jerry Sr. saw an opportunity to create his ideal wife. He outfitted her in the latest fashions, introduced her to his friends, taught her social graces, and put her through college. He welcomed her into a world of luxury that would otherwise have been closed to her. In return, she became completely dependent on him. They were committed to each other and, what's more, they both believed they had made a fair exchange. But what young Jerry Jr. saw in his father was the quintessential MAN, master not only of his own destiny but of everyone else's as well. If you don't sweep a woman off her feet and dominate her, Jerry Jr. thought, you aren't really masculine. Domination in love, for him, became a prerequisite for the lifestyle he coveted.

So while still in high school he began searching for his candidate, a woman who was beautiful but uncultured, who would slide into his illusion and, not incidentally, boost his self-esteem and ensure his father's respect for him. But the truth is, Jerry was not his father and the circumstances of his life were radically different from his parents'. Born into wealth, he had never worked hard for anything. He dropped out of college and had neither the talent nor the drive to generate his father's brand of success. So instead he became obsessed with building a facade to disguise these differences. And finding a woman to "remake" was as important to this facade as wearing the right clothes, driving a Jaguar, flying on his father's company jet, and frequenting classy hotels and restaurants. Jerry was looking not for true love but for a miracle to transform him into his father's image.

What prompted him to enter therapy was his lack of success with women. Despite all the trappings his family supplied, inside Jerry was not a grown man but a small boy, and all the women to whom he was attracted saw right through him. To his dismay, he discovered that even the women he targeted to "remake" refused to take him seriously. He was so obsessed with imitating his father — and in such superficial ways — that he had no idea who he was as an individual. Until he came to terms with the fact that neither his life nor his marriage could possibly resemble his father's, he continued to strike out with women. As soon as he achieved this understanding, however, he began to release the more sensitive, sympathetic side of his own nature, and his luck with women improved. At last he was able to have friendships, even romances, with women without viewing them as conquests.

At the other end of the spectrum are the parents who seem to coexist in a kind of emotional limbo, if not outright alienation. Mom is wrapped up in the kids and the PTA, perhaps in her own career, and Dad is "at the office" or "on the road" ninety percent of the time. Any excuse will do to keep them apart, it seems, even in times of need. When Mom goes into the hospital, her young son visits her every day, but Dad is too caught up in boardroom battles to find the time to visit. Watching such scenes from the sidelines, children assume either that their parents aren't really in love (how could they be when they never see each other?) or that love simply has no impact on independence and requires no sacrifice or compromise whatsoever. This second assumption may seem to fit neatly into the "me" ethic of the late seventies and early eighties, but it will create serious problems in an ongoing relationship. The interlocking effect of mutual effort, sharing, and negotiation serves to strengthen love. Without a certain amount of give and take, and certainly without a substantial amount of togetherness, a couple almost inevitably will pull apart.

Youngsters whose parents are divorced or separated often develop a defeatist view of love and are particularly wary of marriage. Most feel initially that the breakup is their fault, a punishment for something they did. They also view it as a sign that their parents are rejecting them. "If they really loved me like they say they do, they'd be together because that's what I want," thinks the child. Divorce intensifies the confusion for the child between parental and marital love and in the process creates new illusions of love.

Helen was twelve when her parents were divorced, ending a twenty-five-year marriage that had produced four children. She was shocked and deeply disturbed by the breakup. At first she held the pain inside, blaming her father but lacking the courage to confront him. Not until she was fourteen, seeing her mother still unable to cope with life as a divorcée, did she realize her anger. "As far as I'm concerned I can never have a relationship with you," she told her father. "You left the family, something you always taught me to value. You hurt Mother. You hurt me. You've gone against everything you said you believed in." When her father tried to explain how unhappy he and her mother had been, how communication had broken down between them, she cut him off. "You should have stayed and stuck it out. That's what love is about, isn't it? True love is total sacrifice." It never occurred to Helen that the love she'd always taken for granted between her parents might never have existed. She was not ready to accept the idea that love had to be mutual in order to work, so instead of facing the situation squarely, she made up a definition of love that suited her desire for reconciliation.

As a grown woman Helen had tremendous difficulty regaining her trust in men and in love. Her anger at her father engulfed her relationships with all men. She yearned for commitment and felt she would be devoted as a wife, but she didn't believe any man who said he loved her. Eventually, this became a self-fulfilling prophecy. She was promiscuous but slightly contemptuous of her partners, and few were willing to endure such treatment for very long. Most walked out after a few weeks, adding "proof" to substantiate her claim that "men are bastards." Not until she'd been in therapy for several months did she begin to understand that she was sabotaging herself by taking revenge against innocents.

Divorce teaches children that love is painful, temporary, and closely linked to hatred. These lessons can drive them deeper into the illusions that produce false love so that they later leapfrog from one unsatisfying relationship to another. Much as they wish to avoid repeating their parents' mistakes, they may feel that they have no hope of ever achieving a successful marriage. As they begin to look for partners of their own, they may find it particularly difficult to place their trust in a mate, to take that chance. Even as they seek intimacy, love, and commitment, they may find themselves grappling with long-suppressed anger and anxiety, emotions that they must deal with before they can lay strong foundations for their own adult relationships.

First Rehearsals

Many of your early impressions of love were tested while you were still in the sandbox. Among other games, you played house, rehearsing for the roles of "Mommy," "Daddy," "Darling," and "Dear" and experimenting with much of the programming you'd already received. If your parents were demonstrative with their affection for each other, you probably kissed and said "I love you" to your playmates. If they argued, you probably mimicked their disputes. Although children don't understand the entire message behind these gestures and dynamics, they unquestioningly accept them as standard parts of the ritual they view as love. Even if they never question the words or motions, they probably will play out the same rituals in their own future love affairs. If all the gestures in a child's play are negative, it could mean that he has no positive models for love in his home life — not even superficial ones.

If displays of affection were absent in your family, you had no basis for interpreting them in your later relationships. An innocent squeeze or hug from an admirer may make you uncomfortable, perhaps even scared, because you were never taught to distinguish between personal affection and sexual advances. Even if you recognize the affection in the gesture, you may not feel you deserve it if you never received it at home. "I'm not that way," you might say to your partner by way of explanation, but unless you're able, together, to trace the sources of your hesitation, your partner may view your restraint as rejection. Sometimes you must break through such early conditioning to prevent it from becoming a barrier to true love.

Of course, your parents were not the only ones responsible for your early conditioning. Especially after you entered school, your playmates and teachers became at least as influential. Suddenly you realized that neither you nor your parents were the center of the universe, as you had always assumed. Instead you discovered that the universe is peopled by a vast assortment of individuals, each with needs and expectations every bit as urgent as your own. How smoothly you made this transition directly affected your ability to make and keep friends, which in turn was your first practice outside the family in giving and receiving love.

Many adults who are troubled in love recall feeling like "misfits" from the time they started school. Look back to kindergarten or nursery school. Remember the bullies who would pull all the girls' hair and refuse to take orders from anyone, including the teachers? And what about the kids who would give away their lunches and toys, virtually enslaving themselves to their playmates in an attempt to be well liked? If the other students and teachers let such children get away with being too abusive or too passive, these traits can become ingrained and lead to chronic social difficulties. On the other hand, many youngsters who come to the playground with bad attitudes and uncertain egos are quickly nudged into shape by their peers. The lesson is that relationships flow two ways, and we sometimes have to adjust our actions and desires to stay in the flow.

These playground encounters may have provided the first indication that you could feel affection for people who were your equal, who didn't take care of you and had no authority over you. Moreover, this new kind of friendship and love involved choice. You could choose whom you wanted as friends, and they could choose whether or not to return your interest. You had to struggle a lot harder to generate and maintain these friendships than you did your family relationships. You had to actively share belongings, thoughts, and feelings. You had to respect someone else's boundaries, both physical and emotional. You had to compromise your own impulses at times or risk the disapproval of your friends. "I don't like you anymore!" was a devastating pronouncement that made you realize this new kind of love was not permanent and secure like the love of your parents. Instead it was tenuous, vulnerable to uncertainties and mistakes on both sides of the relationship.

For the first time in your life, you had to become actively aware of what someone besides you was thinking and feeling. This was the beginning of empathy, that cornerstone of true love that so often is absent in false love. Some children view empathy as a positive challenge, while others either lash out in frustration or hold themselves aloof, conserving their affections for the families they *know* understand them. Some try to turn it into a game of manipulation and mental one-upmanship. Others become genuinely concerned about their friends and begin testing the feelings and skills that will later help them in romance. These tendencies, obvious as early as kindergarten, provide some of the first subtle indications of where problems might crop up in future relationships. They become even more pronounced with maturity as you move out into the world and actively begin the quest for true love.

7

CONFLICTING IMAGES

GRADE SCHOOL. That magical time when you were no longer a baby but were now "a kid," still innocent but insatiably curious. Fascinated by the world of "grown-ups," you were also mystified and a little afraid of it and rarely asked questions directly. Instead, you extracted bits of knowledge and pieced them together into complicated, if often radically incorrect, theories about the workings of the universe, life, love, and, eventually, sex. As you got older you continually measured and tested these theories against the behavior of adults and older brothers and sisters. You also filtered them through your own immature relationships to probe your capacity for friendship, trust, respect, and affection. These relationships were the first rehearsals for what you would one day know as love.

While your family remained the nucleus of your life, you were becoming increasingly independent from your parents and looked more to your friends for approval and companionship. When your classmates invited you home or praised your latest fashion ensemble, you were elated. When they ignored or teased you, you probably "wanted to die." Too uncertain and inexperienced to judge your own merits, you relied heavily on your friends to tell you what you were worth. The impact on your self-esteem was considerable. Between the ages of six and thirteen, it mattered much less what your parents thought of you; if the kids at school labeled you "misfit" (or any of the other endearing terms children use to put each other down), you probably were convinced you'd be scarred for life.

At the same time, the bonds of friendship you formed with your grade school playmates served as a kind of insulation against a universe that seemed increasingly forbidding. You were aware of many of the harsh realities of life, such as illness, old age, death, divorce, and poverty, yet you naturally resisted the notion that these disasters could ever happen to you. You longed for the independence and privileges that you imagined all adults possess, but probably not the curse of responsibility or mortality. Surrounding yourself with others who were equally innocent and full of illusions made you feel protected. There was power in numbers and in friendship. You probably believed that these friends would stay with you for life and that, together, you would take control of your destinies. If you did not have complete faith in the world outside, at least you believed in your companions.

These early friendships, for the most part, were with children of the same sex. Boys and girls might mix at school or camp, but they rarely chose to do so during free time. This division between the sexes helped solidify male and female identities. Children learn to accept themselves by spending time with others who are alike in body and mind. As their reflections collide and blend, the core personalities with which they were born and which their parents have polished acquire many of the flourishes that later will distinguish their individual adult behavior. Your peers during the elementary school years taught you how to dress and talk. They rounded out your self-image and sharpened many of your strengths and sensitivities. You trusted each other all the more because you were so much alike, and even when you treated each other callously or cruelly, you thirsted for each other's company. Although to a large extent it is a case of the blind leading the blind, youngsters naturally rely on each other for this support and guidance in growing up.

But the natural separation of boys and girls destroys much of the familiarity and trust established during the preschool years between the sexes. Where once children played together as equals and unabashedly kissed or hugged, by first or second grade they suspiciously eye each other across the classroom or school yard. The unisex games, toys, fashions, and conversations that dominated the early years are replaced by distinctly "masculine" or "feminine" preoccupations. Many boys drift toward war games, erector sets, and team sports, many girls toward doll play, romantic stories, and music and dance lessons. By the time interest in each other is rekindled at the end of grade school, they have relatively little in common. The same faces distantly recalled as nursery school playmates become mysterious strangers engendering awkwardness and insecurity.

You may remember that beginning around the third or fourth grade, boys began telling dirty jokes. They found them uproariously funny, even if they had no idea what they were laughing at. The jokes often dealt with issues such as oral and anal sex, bestiality, incest, and sadomasochism — all well beyond the purview of the average nine-year-old. They did not answer any questions and often raised new ones, but telling and laughing at such jokes made boys of this age feel brave and worldly. For both boys and girls, laughter was a defense against confusion and uncertainty about their future roles as sexual adults.

The intensity of same-sex friendships, the distance that develops between the sexes during mid-childhood, and the general embarrassment about sexuality at this age all contribute to illusions of love. No future relationship could ever fully measure up to those professions of undying devotion made between "blood brothers" and "best friends" in second, third, and fourth grades. Predicated on innocence and openness, those first close friendships are impossible models for later love affairs. It is almost inevitable that you look back nostalgically to your youth and try to find a mate who would bond with you as closely as your young soul mates once did. But just as most of those early relationships evaporate during the transition of puberty, so does your capacity for that kind of devotion. As you grow up, you are forced to become more protective of your feelings and your trust. You learn that people, especially members of the opposite sex, are rarely as accessible as they perhaps once seemed. Many of the emotional and experiential barriers that separate young boys and girls become ingrained, although you might later try to overcome them in your sexual relationships. Having been strangers for all this time, it is often very difficult to view each other as partners later in life.

Puzzling Out Love

Reviewing the early years when you were starting to form your first opinions about relationships, romantic mythology, and sexuality can teach you a great deal about your current expectations of love and how you became caught in the false love syndrome. As nostalgic as you may feel looking back to those days of "innocence," it's important to consider the people, experiences, and attitudes that influenced you then. If you examine your past closely enough, you will begin to see how you were able to develop such strong illusions about love and never actually learn *how to love.*

While the friendships experienced during grade school are the closest some people ever get to true love, few of us think of them in these terms. Think back to your own definition of love at age nine or ten. Love was what you felt for your family. Love was what your parents felt for each other. If you said you loved your playmates, your parents probably would correct you, saying, "No, you don't love her, you like her. She's your friend." While you may not yet have had a completely satisfactory definition of love, you understood that it was not the same as friendship.

All the standard descriptions of "true love" supported this impression. By age five, you probably knew by heart the stories of Snow White and her prince, Cinderella and her prince, and Sleeping Beauty and *her* prince. If so, there could be no doubt in your mind that love was something magical and instantaneous that happened to beautiful women and handsome, powerful men and that possessing this magic was the key to living happily ever after. It was assumed, of course, that you would grow up to become just like the beauties and their princes and then you, too, would be eligible for love. Even today, girls tend to take these tales more seriously than boys, at least in part because the stakes seem higher for them. According to these first potent myths, any girl who grows up ugly will become a loveless spinster like Cinderella's stepsisters or the various wicked witches. A boy who grows up ugly, however, still has a chance of succeeding in love — if "Beauty and the Beast" and "The Frog Prince" are any indication.

The double standards and illusions became far more confusing once you were exposed to movies and television. The media offered a profusion of romantic models, many of them at odds with each other. In the fifties and sixties, television presented plenty of affectionate marriages: Dick Van Dyke and Mary Tyler Moore, Lucy and Desi, Roy Rogers and Dale Evans, Ozzie and Harriet, and Ward and June Cleaver, to name just a few. But children viewed these marriages as they viewed their parents'. TV couples always slept in separate beds; if they kissed at all it was on the cheek; and their conversations almost always concerned their children or their work, but never their feelings for each other. They didn't say "I love you" or ride off into the sunset together, and it was impossible to think of them as lovers — certainly not lovers in keeping with the fairy tale models. Television sitcoms presented a sanitized, but not at all romantic, version of love.

The romantic movies of the era, on the other hand, were like updated fairy tales. Even before you understood the real meaning of sexuality, you could feel the sizzle of desire in those looks exchanged between Lauren Bacall and Humphrey Bogart, Annette Funicello and Frankie Avalon, or Omar Sharif and Julie Christie. Given all those framed close-ups of longing faces, the lovers' sweeping embraces, and the throbbing music, you knew immediately that these couples embodied true love. They were brought together by chemistry, magic, and destiny — and it went without saying that they would remain together in exactly the same trance of love for the rest of time. You never actually saw this happen, however. Like the fairy tales, these movies dealt solely with the inception of love, never the process of living love. While passion was taken for granted between couples who were "falling in love," you rarely saw longing embraces between couples who'd been married twenty years or had three children.

Just about the only movie stars who did portray happily married couples were Doris Day and Rock Hudson, the feature film equivalent of Ozzie and Harriet. Attractive and affectionate though they were, they were much too wholesome to qualify as romantic. Despite the standard assumption that couples truly in love would live happily (and that meant romantically) ever after, Hollywood warned that there was a catch-22: True love was restricted to single lovers and newlyweds. As soon as the honeymoon was over, so was romance. That's when love turned to marriage.

Except for the increasing explicitness of sex scenes, Hollywood's image of love and marriage really hasn't changed much in intervening years. Romance still seems to be based more on electricity and stirring music than on understanding or trust. Though much of the physical mystery is gone now that couples are shown naked and in bed, the motivations and attitudes behind relationships remain largely indecipherable. Movies about teen romance, in particular, tend to exaggerate the classic myths about love: Opposites always attract, the girls often go for the boys who mistreat them, and there's usually a single moment when a boy and a girl realize they've fallen in love. Just as the old-fashioned chemistry seemed to freeze after the trip to the altar, so does this new version. Most prime-time programming and G or PG rated movies continue to show married couples as either saccharine and asexual or on the verge of divorce. A few long-running series, such as *Family*, *Family Ties*, and *The Cosby Show*, have presented a balanced view of married couples making mutual concessions and confronting family problems in a unified way, but even these couples are not given the romantic appeal that would make them compelling models for young people. They are portrayed as parents and affectionate friends, but rarely as lovers. TV programs and movies that reveal the true complexities and intensity of love in long-term relationships are not considered appropriate for children and are usually moved into late-night slots or rated R. Meanwhile, images of gratuitous sex flicker across the screen (particularly on cable TV) at all hours. So while today's youths have a more detailed image of what couples do when they're in bed, they're exposed to just as many fallacies about the *development* of true love as their parents were.

Learning about Sex

For many, if not most of us, sneak peeks at girlie magazines provided our first intimations that sex involved more than just kissing. Stealing down to the basement or into the closet with one of Dad's *Playboy*s, we were awed by the shots of naked ladies flaunting their anatomies in a weird kind of invitation. These were not like any women we'd ever seen, and we were as fascinated by them as by pictures of monsters, dinosaurs, and demons. They seemed equally unreal to us. Their faces were like those of the women in fashion magazines, yet their bodies looked as if they were made of plastic — airbrushed, hairless, perfect. At a time when we were being taught to keep our clothes on in public, here were these grown-ups proudly and very publicly naked. They were adults, yet they were doing things we'd never seen any adults doing.

These pictures offered a glimpse of human behavior that we intuitively knew was secret and forbidden, at least to children. Were these models the only ones who behaved like this? We certainly couldn't imagine our mothers in such poses, but we knew if our fathers bought these magazines they must find something attractive about the pictures. What was the connection? Since there were never any pictures of men, we couldn't tell how men were supposed to respond. There was the come-on, but never the conclusion — the sexual act. As a result, these sneak peeks gave us the lopsided and incomplete view of sex as a relatively anonymous act enjoyed by men but provoked by women — at least a certain kind of women. Love had nothing to do with it.

Trying to imitate Dad, little boys feasted on these images. Boys had little sexual interest before the age of nine or ten, but it was clear that men were "supposed" to enjoy looking at the female body naked. Collecting these magazines, therefore, became a way for boys to prove to each other how masculine they were, and they'd cluster around a single picture, snickering with embarrassment, titillation, and apprehension about their own sexual futures. Apparently, there were some women who didn't mind taking off their clothes to please men. Few little boys dreamed of marrying such women, but almost all were eager to meet some. Once they began to suspect what was involved in the sexual act, they fantasized about "practicing" on girls just like the ones in the magazines, and by age eleven or twelve many boys secretly took the pictures to bed to help them masturbate. They still might not know the exact mechanics of "doing it" with a partner, but they learned early that naked women could be used as objects to give them pleasure. For young boys, this — not love — was what sex was about.

Pictures of naked women could be as bewildering for little girls as they were titillating for little boys. Although a third grade girl couldn't identify with a centerfold model, there was always the possibility that she might eventually acquire these same anatomical parts. Would she then be expected to display her body this way? Clearly, this was not a question to broach with Mom or Dad, so most little girls either debated it among themselves or tried to ignore it. Although the pinups were a source of endless curiosity, not many little girls wanted to grow up and be like them. Most found the mere possibility scary and disgusting. If this was what sex was about, they decided, they would have nothing to do with it. Later, when their parents assured them that "sex is something you do when you fall in love," some girls decided that they'd rather go without love than stoop so low. Others rationalized that sex might be an acceptable price to pay for Prince Charming, but why didn't the fairy tales ever mention this part? For most, however, the central question raised by the girlie magazines remained unanswered: If sex was supposed to be part of love, why were all those women exposing themselves for the total strangers who read the magazines? The only acceptable answer was that those women and the men who bought the magazines were fast, loose, cheap, and part of another world. Good girls would never do that, nor would they end up with men who expected them to. Good girls would never be asked to have sex unless the man loved them. No wonder we're all confused!

Early impressions like these, in combination with parental conditioning, can sometimes leave permanent scars. When Merle was twelve, one of her girlfriends showed her a copy of *Penthouse*. Merle vividly remembers how the two of them secretly took the magazine from the bottom of a pile in the basement and hid inside an empty cabinet with a flashlight to look at it. Her friend giggled and joked about the pictures, but Merle was mortified. Brought up in a strict Eastern European family, she had never been told anything about sex; if she even mentioned a boy's name in a friendly way, her father would glower at her. She'd been taught that her body was private and should be clothed at all times, and she took this so seriously that she didn't even dare examine herself in the mirror. The sight of naked women in a magazine was utterly shocking and baffling to her. She stared in fascination, mostly because she had no idea that this was what women looked like under their clothes, but she could not understand her friend's casual amusement. She was ashamed for the models and for herself.

When she got home, without revealing that she'd actually seen the magazine, Merle asked her mother who bought publications like *Playboy* and *Penthouse*. Immediately, the answer came back: "Sick, sadistic men, that's who!" Her mother said these men would look at the magazines to get themselves excited and then would go out to "take advantage" of some poor unsuspecting girl. Merle asked what "take advantage" meant. Her mother answered, "It means they use women. They do things to young girls that are only right for married people to do. They use the girls and then they throw them away. Ugh! I can't stand to talk about it anymore. Just don't ever let any boy sweet-talk you unless he's willing to marry you!"

This conversation unnerved her mother, who described it to Merle's father that evening. Merle's brewing interest in sex sealed her parents' decision to send her to a girls' school to protect her from boys. When the time came, they thought, they would set her up with the son of a family friend. Until then, she should remain innocent.

Another child might have decided at that point to find out as much as possible about sex, but Merle had been extremely sheltered throughout her childhood, and she didn't dare defy her parents. If they said she must wait until she married to be intimate with a man, then she would wait.

But inevitably, Merle picked up information about sex in bits and pieces. One day in study hall the girls passed around an illustrated copy of the Kamasutra. Merle was terrified by what looked to her like torture. Her mother's words "Sick, sadistic men" rang in her ears. As she got older, she noticed that the covers of the girlie magazines on newsstands were becoming more and more provocative and explicit. To her horror, some even contained pictures of nude men. Now she was sure her mother was right. But what could marriage do to make sex different? She would gladly remain a virgin until marriage. The question was, how would she ever have the courage to have sex with her husband?

Dutifully, Merle lived at home after graduating from high school and worked in her father's business. It wasn't long before her mother started matchmaking. Now that Merle was "of age," she should get married and start producing grandchildren. She couldn't understand why Merle acted so sullen every time she invited an eligible young man to dinner.

Merle was angered and frightened by her parents' turnabout. They who had convinced her men were demons were now trying to sell her off to the first bidder. They who had forbidden her even to mention the word *sex* all these years were now pushing her toward it so that they could have grandchildren. For the first time in her life, she began to feel rebellious.

She found a sympathetic ear in a young Egyptian man, Samir, who sometimes sat with her in the cafeteria at lunchtime. Raised in a traditional Middle Eastern family, he had always felt sorry for his sisters, who faced the same conflicts Merle was struggling with. He could see that mixing the Old World expectations with American culture made it very difficult for a woman to discover what true love was all about.

Merle chatted with Samir for weeks before it dawned on her that he was the first man who had welcomed her as a friend without making even the slightest sexual advance. In the past she had found that most men, including the ones her parents invited to dinner, regarded her with a kind of interest that made her skin crawl and her stomach turn. Her response to them was to shut down and withdraw into herself. Samir, somehow, brought her out. She felt neither self-conscious nor threatened by him. She wondered if she might be falling in love.

Samir was equally taken with Merle's gentleness and timidity. She was the most feminine woman he'd ever met, and her sheltered past made her all the more attractive to him. He could see just how inexperienced she was with men, and he loved the idea of educating her. Although he'd been raised to believe he should marry a virgin, he'd never actually dated one. The notion of being Merle's first man appealed strongly to his ego.

They had known each other for more than four months when they began to date formally. Merle's parents protested, irritated at Merle's defiance in selecting her own suitor over their hand-picked candidates, but their resistance was short-lived. Her father checked Samir's background and found him to be well educated, honorable, and from an aristocratic family. If he was not their ideal, he was better than no son-in-law at all, which was where Merle otherwise seemed to be heading. So they gave their seal of approval and subtly nudged the couple toward engagement.

The relationship developed gradually over the next few months until Merle was convinced she loved Samir. She dreamed of marrying him, setting up a home together, even raising children together. The one thing she could not imagine was having sex with him. It would be expected of her, she knew, and she supposed she would do it as a good wife, but she found the prospect disgusting. Sometimes when he was kissing her he would start to grope with his hands, and a wave of panic would sweep over her. She felt trapped, as if she couldn't breathe. At these moments she would push him away and gasp for air. Even these mild overtures made her feel filthy and cheap.

At first Samir was understanding. He could only guess how deeply frightened she was, but he blamed it all on her rigid childhood. His sisters told him they had grown up believing that sex was dirty but had changed their minds when they broke free of their parents and began dating freely. Samir trusted that if he was just patient and tender with her, Merle too would break out of this spell. He was worried enough about it, however, that he refused to consider marriage before they slept together. He knew she wanted to wait until they were married before having sex, but for him it was too great a risk. What if she still couldn't bring herself to have sex even after they were married? What if she was frigid? What if they were sexually incompatible?

The contest of wills persisted for nearly a year and ultimately destroyed the relationship. Merle simply couldn't understand Samir's need for physical intimacy, and eventually she began to resent and mistrust him because of it. The gentle man who made no demands on her had become just another sexually obsessed male. The yearning that she had thought was love suddenly turned cold. Samir had no choice. Though he loved Merle and felt sorry that he couldn't be the one to lift her out of her shell, he was not prepared to sacrifice himself for so little in return. The burden of her childhood conditioning was simply too great for him to overcome.

Several weeks later, Merle began therapy to deal with the rage, resentment, and fear that she was feeling as a result of this episode. She needed long-term counseling so that she could go back through her past and present attitudes about her sexuality, men, marriage, family, and love. At this point she could no longer trust anyone — not men, not her family, and especially not herself. Until she recovered her ability to trust and began to accept her own sexuality as natural and normal, she would continue equating physical intimacy with exploitation, and true love would remain beyond her reach.

While pornography offered early lessons about sexually provocative women, televised performances of early rock-and-roll stars gave many of us our first exposure to sexually provocative men. From the vantage point of second or third grade, Elvis Presley and his many successors looked pretty funny grinding their hips before audiences of swooning girls, but even to a child there was more than humor to the movements. Parents wouldn't look so horrified and disgusted otherwise, nor would teenage girls weep and grab for these performers so desperately. These men were singers, but their power seemed to emanate from their eyes and bodies. Their clothes were skin tight, and their gyrations accentuated parts of the male body that were foreign territory to most young girls. Not many other adult men behaved like that! Nor did teenage boys seem to be excited by these performances. All that thrusting and preening was obviously for the exclusive benefit of females, just as the pictures of nude women were for the benefit of males.

The fact that the performers sang of love made their performances all the more confusing for those raised on fairy tales and romantic movies. Though they sang the words, these men did not seem either loving or particularly lovable. Sometimes they seemed silly, sometimes aggressive and a little frightening. These were no knights in shining armor, so why were they America's heartthrobs? The answer lay in that mysterious link between men and women — sex.

As rock-and-roll got more daring, the hit lyrics became more explicit in describing this link. Stars like Mick Jagger and Jimi Hendrix thrusted not only with their bodies but with the words of their songs. They described sensations, positions, motions, even tastes. While not all of the words were decipherable, youngsters got the general idea. The picture was complete when female vocalists like Donna Summer and the Pointer Sisters started recording the female view of sex — complete with moaning, touching, and the allure of "muscles." Some of the records were like audio pornography. For young people who had never experienced sex, it was difficult to imagine what all this panting and groaning had to do with love.

Such vicarious previews of sexuality made it even more difficult to accept the basic clinical facts described in "hygiene" classes, parental instruction, or school yard word of mouth. Those fortunate enough to receive formal sex education usually were shown diagrams of intercourse and of male and female genitalia. Girls were instructed in the "miracle of menstruation," and boys sometimes were advised about nocturnal emissions. And that was usually as far as instruction went. Sex education before the late seventies and eighties never explained the role of sex in love or of love in sex. There was no discussion about the emotional and physical drive for sex or the critical differences between male and female attitudes toward sex. Classes were not coed, and boys and girls never discussed the information with one another afterward.

Those who did not have sex education in school had to rely largely on innuendo and hearsay. Even when parents tried to be forthcoming, somehow, embarrassment on both sides clouded the information. Few families were comfortable or direct in discussing sex. Most parents became flustered when asked about genitalia and waited until their children were sexually mature before even broaching the subject. By then, much of what they said was automatically rejected. Teenagers, after all, are just as willing to believe outrageous fictions about sex from friends as they are the tentative — and sometimes just as inaccurate — explanations offered at home. It's not surprising that notions like these become school yard "facts":

- To get a girl ready, you tap twice on the outside of the vagina.
- There are teeth inside the vagina.
- You can avoid getting pregnant if you douche with Coke after sex.
- You never get pregnant the first time you have sex.
- You can't get pregnant if you don't have an orgasm.
- Oral sex means talking during intercourse.
- Penises are always erect.

The myths that pose the most immediate danger are the ones about getting pregnant, as the thousands of teenagers who become pregnant each year can testify, but the ones that contribute most to false love are those that shape a child's expectations of sex: for girls, the notion that having sex is always "making love," even if it hurts or the boy disappears for good the next morning; for boys, the idea that having sex means "screwing," "balling," or "getting laid." As a child you didn't discuss the feelings aroused during sex or the emotional and physical motivation to have sex. Though you knew this was something older people chose to do, it was almost impossible to understand why, much less to imagine yourself doing it. Until you reached puberty and began to feel true sexual urges, there seemed no compelling reason to have sex, other than to prove that you were grown up.

Learning the Game of Love

As youngsters mature, male and female stereotypes become increasingly important in determining social patterns. The typical adolescent struggle to fit in goes hand in hand with the internal urge to establish a sexual identity. How well a boy or girl plays the accepted role as male or female often determines the adolescent's popularity and desirability. Unfortunately, the stereotypes tend to exaggerate the differences between the sexes rather than promote common interests and goals. As a result, the more susceptible youngsters are to the standard roles, the more likely they are to fall for false love later when they begin dating.

Prior to the seventies, most adolescent girls were encouraged to concentrate on fashion and makeup and to downplay any interest in team sports or rugged athletics. By the time they entered junior high, they were preoccupied with appearances and with dieting. Their goal was to be popular with the boys — and that meant being dainty, petite, perfectly groomed, and beautiful. It did not necessarily mean being smart, getting top grades, or aspiring to a career in business, politics, or science. To the contrary, if a girl was very bright, even if she was pretty, she might be shunned by any boy who was not clearly more intelligent. If she was athletic, she might come to be accepted as a "girl jock" or a "tomboy," but she was nobody's pick for the perfect date.

Boys seemed to accelerate academically and athletically beginning in junior high. Having generally lagged behind girls in classwork throughout grade school, they suddenly surged ahead in math and the sciences. In sports, they began the drive to "make the team" — football, soccer, basketball, baseball, or hockey. Math, science, and sports were all associated with masculinity, which distinctly separated the boys from the girls. Boys who preferred music, art, or English might be labeled "sissy" or "fag" by the other boys and would find it difficult to attract popular girls.

It was a curious theory. If a boy and girl shared the same interests or competed on each other's turf, they were deemed incompatible. In fact, a boy and a girl who considered themselves friends were thought to have no interest in each other as boyfriend and girlfriend! The assumption was that friends knew each other too well, shared too much, were too honest — in short, there was not enough mystery between them. But if they played the stereotypical masculine and feminine game, which essentially meant they had nothing in common, they made a "perfect match." For youngsters, this formula crystallized the illusions that opposites attract and that lovers cannot be friends. The great irony, of course, is that feelings of friendship and common interests provide a far better foundation for love than does sexual fascination.

Couples who "went steady" in sixth or seventh grade rarely did anything more provocative than holding hands, dancing to slow music, and exchanging ID bracelets. For all their fantasies of love (girls) and sex (boys), they were still really children, and the act of voluntarily spending time with a single member of the opposite sex was in itself an enormous step toward maturity. The motivation usually was not any particular affection for the partner, but a desire to be popular. Making a "good catch" was a guaranteed way to boost self-esteem and earn the respect of peers. It proved that a young person was wanted and valued. It also seemed a very grown-up thing to do, and acting grown up was *very* important at that age.

The downside was the built-in impermanence of such relationships. The average life span of an adolescent couple was about two weeks. Members of the class "in" group would rotate partners like interchangeable parts. Each breakup produced heartbreak and crushed egos, but as long as the jilted partner stayed within the group, a new partner was sure to come along, perhaps for a second round. The superficial emotional roller coaster created by short-lived pairings was a preview of the false love cycle for which everyone was rehearsing.

There were always a few in the group who went a little further than just holding hands. Kissing games like spin the bottle or seven minutes in heaven seemed deliciously naughty at the time, but they actually represented a compromise between the needs of girls and boys. Limited to kissing on the lips and perhaps an embrace, the games seemed romantic to the girls. The boys considered them a brief preview of sex. Getting so close gave boys a sense of how a girl's body felt, boosting their fledgling fantasies. There may not have been any passion, but it was a great thrill to act in a way that seemed sexy and mature. Within the confines of the games, boys and girls were both willing partners, and that made these experiments fun as well.

Fantasies about romance and sex consumed a lot of attention during this early adolescent period. Boys began eyeing "older women" — from high school cheerleaders to their teachers — trying to imagine what they would look like naked, what it would be like to be in bed with them, and — yes! — what it would be like to have intercourse with them. They dreamed of being seduced by a beautiful, experienced woman who would make them experts in sex before they turned fifteen. The affair would last perhaps a day, perhaps a few weeks, but never longer. It was for sex only, and the word *love* would never come up.

The girls' fantasies were just as strong, but much more romantic than the boys'. They imagined love with older men whom they considered glamorous and alluring but who were also securely unattainable — celebrity rock stars or movie stars. The focus was not on sex, of course, but on true love. While the boys were fantasizing about sex with experienced older women, the girls saw themselves walking hand in hand with, maybe kissing, the man of their dreams. Some went to concerts and stared desperately at the stage in the hope that the lead singer would return their gaze and fall hopelessly in love. "I'll make him love me," they told themselves. Though they never succeeded, this didn't stop them from papering their bedrooms with wall-sized posters of their beloved's face or from joining his fan club. Group infatuations gave young girls a unique chance to share the experience — and the drama — of unrequited love. For perhaps the only time in their lives, several girls could share their love for one man without becoming competitive or catty. Unfortunately, they also supported and reinforced one another's illusions of love. In these dream love affairs, they had nothing in common with their beloved; he was vastly rich and powerful; the attraction was instantaneous and electric; if sex were to occur at all, it would be innocent and safe; the passion and romance would last forever and remain bigger than life. In short, their idealistic vision of true love was actually false. Yet even if most young girls eventually realized that the idea of marrying a rock star or a leading man was far-fetched, many clung to this illusion of love long after they'd given up group infatuations.

Mixing Sex and Love

As puberty arrived, the motivation for sex started to become clearer. By age eleven or twelve, boys and girls were much more aware of both the opposite sex and the dramatic changes in their own sexual equipment. The first of these changes for girls was the sudden sprouting of breasts. Embarrassed perhaps, but driven to keep up with the group, girls in fifth or sixth grade begged their mothers for brassieres. When they got them, they were both humiliated and perversely proud to have the boys twang their bra straps when the teachers weren't looking. Irritating and obnoxious though the boys' behavior was, it was also a crude gesture of intimacy and interest. As they later would sometimes misinterpret sexual advances as expressions of love, young girls mistook much of this early teasing as a sign of personal affection.

Parents encouraged girls to think of sex as the ultimate intimacy. Girls were not taught, as boys were, that sex could be fun and pleasurable. To the contrary, the message was that it could be very dangerous and degrading unless it was combined with true love. Love would lift sex above the physical act, which most young girls thought frightening and repulsive, and make it almost ethereal. While they recognized that love should come first, some believed that if they "gave" sex, the boys would find it easier to love them. Instead of thinking of sex in terms of naked skin contact and penetration, many young girls twisted the facts into a romantic fantasy. When they had sex, they would be looking deeply into their lover's eyes. They would hear birds singing. The world would stop turning, and they would know they had found true love.

The onset of menstruation was a jolt for many young girls. Those who understood the facts of life knew they were now capable of becoming pregnant, a terrifying thought for any twelve- or thirteen-year-old, and this signal of sexual maturity made many self-conscious and fearful. For all the physical changes and added responsibility that came with puberty, there was little corresponding surge in sexual desire. Unless she masturbated, the average preteen girl had no idea what an orgasm felt like. While she may have been interested in boys and may have longed for the soulful kisses she'd seen in the movies, she was probably no more eager for intercourse than before, and her natural reluctance may have been strengthened by her parents' concerns that she not get "into trouble" and that she remain "a good girl." If she did have sex, chances are that she kept it secret from her parents and even from her closest girlfriends, lest they think her "cheap" or "loose."

Having treated girls as foreign creatures throughout the early grade school years, boys were fascinated by the sudden physical changes in their classmates. For the most part, the boys matured more slowly, so while the girls were turning into women before their eyes, the boys remained boys. And they responded accordingly, with teasing, snickering, more dirty jokes, and, for the more daring, an occasional "feel" or "goose" as a girl passed close by. Some girls took this badly, bursting into tears of embarrassment; some rather liked it. But for the boys, it was all simply playfulness. They were a little jealous of the girls' newfound maturity, and this was the only way they knew to express their own insecurities. They certainly couldn't *talk* to the girls — that would be mortifying at this age — so instead they acted out their curiosity and ignorance in ways that would make them look cool to their buddies. It was unfortunate if their behavior made some girls feel like sex objects, but it was understandable. After all, in their own way the boys were mimicking grown men who whistled at and ogled women on the streets. Since this was how adult men treated women, it was predictable that boys would treat girls the same way.

Boys realized that men view sexual performance as a sign of manhood and power. They also learned that it was a way to dominate the opposite sex. "Getting" or "having" a girl was a challenge to boast about, according to many fathers and older brothers — though the boasting should be done out of Mother's earshot. "Having" *many* women was the ultimate sign of masculine freedom and power, as proved by those rock-and-roll stars with their adoring fans and groupies. These messages produced both fascination and terror in many young boys. They were mesmerized by the notion of licentiousness, yet they struggled with the notion of having sex with girls who were just like their sisters or with women who were like their mothers. Who could make sense out of a system that taught them to respect and cherish the women of their family but to use and abandon other females? How could anyone tell where to draw the line? Was love based on treachery or on trust?

While boys were puzzling out these questions, their bodies began sending more urgent promptings, at first in the form of nocturnal emissions and later through sudden, often uncontrollable arousal. Unlike girls, they didn't have to masturbate or have sex to experience orgasm. While girls were still wondering about their sexuality, boys were suddenly grappling with strong physical urges. Given the tacit encouragement of their fathers, brothers, and male friends, it seemed only natural for them to try to satisfy these urges any way they could.

For the most part, boys' interest in sex was motivated almost entirely by physical desire and parental or peer pressure. Few girls felt equivalent urges at this age, but many felt an emotional longing for love that made them vulnerable to the boys' advances. This disparity in motivation only intensified the gap between the sexes left over from elementary school. The adversarial roles would take many years to become more balanced, if in fact they ever did. For some, the love-hate relationship with the opposite sex would get worse instead of better over time and eventually would disintegrate into outright hostility and rejection.

While society changed dramatically in some ways during the seventies and early eighties, tending toward more egalitarian thinking, these adjustments have done little to dispel youngsters' illusions about love and sex. In fact, in some ways, today's children are exposed to even more conflicting influences: While they are still fed fairy tales about romance, they watch their parents divorcing and perhaps dating multiple partners, and they see explicit yet impersonal sex around them on TV and in the movies. Today's pornography and films often show — or suggest — men and women in active intercourse. Rock-and-roll lyrics have grown more and more explicit and are now acted out in music videos. At the same time, sex is so glamorized that it seems irresistibly attractive and "cool" to many youngsters. There are rarely any consequences, such as pregnancy, disease, or heartbreak (love, not sex, causes heartbreak, the songs tell us), so there seems no reason not to "do it."

Up to a point, the increase in sexual imagery is in keeping with the increased openness of a culture in which sexual issues are publicly debated. But while open discussion can be healthy for both adults and children, the bombardment of sexual imagery effectively desensitizes youngsters to sex. Many young people view sex as a requirement instead of a privilege or choice of adulthood.

Even with the threat of AIDS, today's youngsters tend to be more influenced by the images of sex that they see in the movies, on television, and in "adult" publications than by concern over an illness that to them seems remote. Unless the disease claims someone they know, they often don't consider it a direct threat. The illusion of immunity and the pressure to act grown up, which are strong in all adolescents, particularly boys, encourage them to ignore the risks.

Evan was the kind of eleven-year-old all the girls despised. He talked constantly about "cruising for chicks" and "getting pussy," phrases his father and two older brothers had taught him. They had also introduced him to *Hustler* magazine, so he knew what the phrases meant — which gave him an important edge on most of his friends. While some of the boys were embarrassed by Evan's swaggering and boasting, all were impressed by his confidence and knowledge. When he bragged about his sixteen-year-old "girlfriend" who worked at the 7-Eleven, they went along to see him tease and taunt her until she finally told him to get out. "They all act that way when they want me," he said with a grin, echoing his father.

Evan's mother was distraught over her youngest son's behavior. He was the brightest of the family, and she'd dreamed that he would grow up different from the others. Unfortunately, he worshiped his brothers and his father. While his mother had quietly rejoiced in his good grades all through elementary school, the men in the family called him a "mama's boy" and joked that he would grow up to be a "fag" if he kept his nose in the books. His father, who owned the largest auto body shop in the county, was proud of the fact that he'd gotten rich without a high school education. He wanted his sons to join him in the business and to be just like him. Evan wanted to please his mother, but his father's influence was just too powerful.

When he entered junior high, Evan began to get into trouble. He had a young, attractive, female biology teacher, and one day he whispered to his buddy what a "nice ass" she had. She overheard him and grabbed him by the shoulder. He shoved her back. He was suspended for a week. His big brothers treated him like a hero. His father promised to "get that bitch." His mother went to church and begged for guidance.

Evan "got laid" for the first time at age thirteen, when one of his brothers persuaded a girlfriend to do it as a special favor. ("She's so hot for me she'll do anything," he told Evan.) Although Evan climaxed almost before they'd begun, afterward he told his buddies that they'd gone for hours and that "she couldn't get enough" of him.

After that, Evan became the terror of the eighth grade. He pulled up girls' skirts, maneuvered to look down their blouses, and clicked his tongue at them like his brothers had taught him. The girls responded by giving him the finger and calling him a moron, but he insisted to his friends, "They love it!"

The boys who had been his friends in grade school eventually turned away from him. Some were pressured by their parents to stop seeing him, and others decided on their own that he was too far out of control. But Evan found his way into another group, the guys who hung out and got into trouble. They smoked and stole beer from their fathers, and occasionally one of them would be taken in by the police for driving his parents' car without a license. Most important of all, they had a following among girls who were "easy."

These girls wouldn't even look at Evan before, but once he was a member of the BOD (Brothers of Doom), as they called themselves, the girls suddenly treated him with new respect and acceptance. They not only tolerated his come-ons but threw the jokes back to him. If he got serious and acted admiring, he found, they would let him get close, and a few even seemed to like it when he got rough. They said it was "exciting."

("Women like to get shaken up every now and then," explained his father. "They want to know who's the boss.")

When he was fifteen, one of Evan's girlfriends got pregnant. She had an abortion, but this development prompted Evan's mother at last to take action and bring him for counseling. Unfortunately, Evan's mother was too weak to provide an antidote to her husband's influence, and Evan was not particularly inclined to change his ways. He had been so heavily indoctrinated that he thought it normal to treat women badly. Therapy could work no miracles in this situation. Evan's attitude could possibly be reversed if, later in life, he began to be rejected by women he desired. But men with backgrounds like Evan's usually gravitate toward women who, because they come from abusive families, are accustomed to unhealthy relationships and, in fact, expect nothing better for themselves. So instead of directing the men toward mature love, they submit to their domination. The result is a sad dance of victimization that traps both the men and the women.

While young girls are frightened of sex, boys are frightened of love, which they've been trained to view as a trap. But many girls eventually convince themselves that sex can be used as bait for attention and approval from the opposite sex, and just as many boys learn (often from older boys) that if they say "I love you," girls will be more willing to have sex. Some begin to experiment with these "tricks" well before they are mature enough to handle the consequences.

Nicole had sex for the first time when she was thirteen. Gil was a college freshman home for summer vacation when he met Nicole. She told him she was sixteen and he believed her because she was tall and well developed for her age.

She was elated when he asked her out and she boasted about it to all her friends, who were duly awed. She was the only girl in the entire eighth grade who had even talked to a college boy who wasn't either a brother or a neighbor. This achievement won Nicole her friends' overwhelming respect and envy.

She didn't really need this extra incentive, however. Gil was movie-star gorgeous and drove an original 1964 Mustang painted "candied tangerine." He was also smart. A film buff, he could recite the key actors in every hit movie dating back to 1939. Appropriately, he took her to a screening of *Women in Love* for their first date. The sensuality on the screen made her already pounding heart break into double time. She could hardly believe he respected her enough to bring her to such a grown-up movie. But then, she reminded herself, he thinks I'm a lot more experienced than I am.

Gil did have his suspicions about Nicole. Her schoolgirlish mannerisms and the nervousness in her laughter tipped him off that she probably was not as old as she claimed. But she looked sexy and gave him a kind of respect — almost reverence — that he found very flattering. It was certainly not the kind of treatment he got from girls his age. Even if she was a kid, she might be fun for a short fling. He'd just go slowly in the beginning so he didn't scare her.

At eighteen, Gil was pretty skilled in the tactics of romance. He knew how to warm up a new girlfriend gradually so that he got what he wanted without having to fight for it. He met Nicole at the beach every evening when he finished work, and they went for an innocent walk. He took her to more romantic movies. He bought her little presents. He promised to invite her to visit him at college for a weekend in the fall. After about a week, he made his move, in the back seat of the Mustang at a drive-in theater.

Nicole had paid attention during the animated film about intercourse shown in her fifth grade sex education class, but she had never imagined that it would be so awkward and silly. Her parents had told her sex was an expression of love. To her it seemed more like an athletic competition. The wrestling into position, the struggle with the condom, Gil's strange jerky movements seemed almost laughable. The only thing that really impressed her were Gil's words as he climaxed. "I love you!" he panted and collapsed on top of her. Overwhelmed, Nicole began to cry and wrapped her arms around him.

Their affair lasted three weeks. At the end of his vacation,

Gil broke it off, saying they had to be free to date other people when they were apart. For about a month Nicole felt abandoned, but when new boyfriends began to appear, she cheered up. Some of the callers were friends of Gil's, others high school boys who had seen her with Gil around town. The word was out that Nicole was "experienced," and her popularity rating skyrocketed.

She never thought of herself as "fast" or "loose," though others called her these things behind her back. She figured that her affair with Gil had made her more mature than the other girls, and this was what appealed to the older boys. She never agreed to sex on the first few dates, and most of her relationships lasted a couple of months, much longer than those of her virginal girlfriends. Even though her affairs invariably ended with her in tears of desolation, she was comforted by the knowledge that her phone would ring again.

What Nicole knew, but never admitted to herself, was that none of the boys she dated really liked or respected her. And if she refused to have sex with them, they would stop calling. Then she would be forced to acknowledge her reputation, which by the time she reached high school had cost her most of her closest girlfriends. The same girls who had been so impressed by her "love affair" with an older boy had been disgusted when they learned that she was "giving away" sex. She told herself that they were just jealous, but she suspected the truth, and the spiral was pulling her self-esteem lower and lower. When Nicole first came to me, she was loaded with guilt, regret, and a severe loss of faith in love. It took many months before she began to believe that she could recover her self-respect and take control of her sexuality. Ultimately, she had to get out of high school before she was able to escape her reputation and have more balanced relationships in which sex was an expression of affection rather than of subjection.

Today's young people tend to have sex earlier in the belief that this will make them more experienced in love. But by rushing into physical intimacy when they're still emotionally immature, most are only adding to their own confusion. They barely know how to talk to each other when they start sleeping together. Aside from the risk of pregnancy and disease, this early sex has a tragic impact on their capacity for true love. There is no basis for trust, patience, or understanding in these premature liaisons. And with so much self-esteem riding on sexual performance, sex becomes tremendously threatening. The reality is never as good as it is in the movies, and the guilt and disappointment over this discovery can be crippling. At least if you viewed love purely as a popularity game, you had a chance to grow up a little before taking on the burden and confusion of sex.

However potentially dangerous *your* illusions may have been at age twelve or thirteen, you were essentially innocent. While you may have absorbed lots of conflicting images and conditioning from your early years, you still had not assimilated them into a personal approach to love. Even if you had started "dating," you would not yet dare say you were "in love." That would come in high school or perhaps college, when you began putting your illusions to the test and your heart on the line.

8

REHEARSAL GAMES

IT WAS A SWEET summer night in 1966, the kind of night created for a gently rocking porch swing or a stroll under a canopy of elms. At fourteen, Nina was particularly susceptible to the power of the stars and moon and the nearby rush of the harbor surf. Strains of "Sgt. Pepper" were still floating from the window as she left the party. Though eager to be one of the crowd, she had had enough of standing on the sidelines. It was clear that the boys were not interested in her, and at least in the darkness she could *imagine* how romantic it might be if one of them would pursue her.

New to the neighborhood and chronically insecure, Nina longed to be one of the poised, self-confident girls the boys went after. She knew she was pretty and bright, but she had no idea how to play up to the opposite sex, to lure and bait them. Instead, she was grateful for the slightest sign of interest, even if it was stupid teasing or a purely inconsequential conversation about the latest Rolling Stones album. She could kick herself for not acting more aloof and independent, but she simply was incapable of playing hard to get. In the full grip of puberty, she could not disguise her yearning for male attention and affection. Unfortunately, this only seemed to drive boys away.

So she turned her back on her girlfriends and their "steadies" and escaped to the comfort of the night. The rush of beach traffic had slowed. She listened to the gravel crunch beneath her feet as she started down the path leading to the dock. When she reached the waterfront she curled her body into a tight ball on the seat where in the daytime the lifeguard presided. Watching the dark silhouettes of the boats rising and falling, she didn't even hear the soft footsteps or notice as Jim mounted the dock behind her.

"Want company?" he asked, smiling.

She jumped, as much at the unexpectedness of his attention as at the suddenness of his presence. Until recently, he had been going with one of Nina's best friends. A couple of years older, he was very cocky and occasionally teased Nina in the condescending way an older brother might. But he had never sought her out alone, never invited private conversation.

"Company's always welcome here," she replied, hoping he couldn't hear her galloping heartbeat. She didn't know what to say next.

Jim skipped a couple of stones across the surface of the water. The ripples made circles of moonlight against the ocean's glittery blackness. Wordlessly, they watched the circles dissipate.

Jim had noticed Nina the first time she appeared on the fringes of the group, but he had been involved, so instead of coming at her directly, he had taken an oblique approach. He teased her to get her back up, to see if she had any fire inside. He watched her with the other girls and noticed that she was much looser and more confident with them than she was when boys were present. In male company she would stiffen and become painfully self-conscious. He wondered what would happen if he kissed her.

For him, that was the extent of the interest and the challenge — curiosity and little more. The product of a boarding school adolescence, he was accustomed to having his year split into fragments and had learned to grab his pleasure piecemeal, without heavy commitments. His previous relationship with Nina's friend had been perfect while it lasted. Lots of making out, casual conversation, no expectations. As soon as he was expected to invest more than that, he backed off. Now, with Nina, his guard was up because it was plain that she'd want more. The way she looked at him and all the other boys, she obviously was hungry for affection — not the physical kind he was prepared to offer, but the emotional kind that fed into girls' romantic fantasies. He knew he had to be very careful in satisfying his curiosity so that he didn't get pulled into these fantasies.

"So," said Nina uncertainly.

"So!" replied Jim. His teeth flashed in laughter. "Relax. I won't bite you."

"Oh no? What, then?"

"This," he answered, pulling her firmly toward him and guiding her face for a kiss . . . her first.

As her body moved toward his, Nina felt a moment of elation. At last, it was going to happen to her. And for those initial brief seconds, it was just as she'd imagined. The warmth of his body, the strength of his arms, the cool darkness enveloping them. That he was someone she'd admired but imagined unattainable made it even more exciting. As their relationship ripened, she thought, she'd learn what had prompted this sudden rush of desire on his part. But first, the magic of the kiss.

Then it was finished. They came together and it was nothing like she'd dreamed. Instead of velvety caresses and soaring ecstasy, there were wet, voracious lips and teeth grinding into her own. For the first time, she noticed his distastefully sour odor. And then, to her horror, he tried to thrust his tongue into her mouth. Hard and round, it parried with hers like a soccer ball looking for a way into the goal.

This was not a dance of unison, but a display of his power. The way he held her exuded his satisfaction in conquering her.

There was no affection or even emotion here. For him it was merely an exercise. Once she had more extensive sexual experiences, Nina would realize that Jim's game was really pretty tame, but at that moment she was devastated. It was not only the kiss but her own reaction that crushed her. If this was what love was all about (and she still believed that his desire to kiss her meant, on some level, that he felt love for her), her fantasies about it had been hopelessly naive. This was one of the great milestones in her life, yet it left her feeling cheap, dirty, and defensive. I don't like the way he kisses, but I know he'll make up for this in other ways, she consoled herself.

He didn't, of course. In fact, he was appalled at the way Nina behaved in the following days. At first, on the basis of a single kiss, she acted as though they were lovers. He thought he was letting her off lightly by shunning her rather than telling her outright that the kiss had meant nothing. But then she complained to all her friends that he was treating her cruelly. From Jim's point of view, it was sheer lunacy. He'd kissed her because she was pretty and he was curious — and that was *all*. If he'd had sex with her, she might have had grounds for complaint, but this was nothing!

A few years later, in my office, the memory of this first kiss returned to Nina in detail. At first, she concentrated on the pain of having her romantic visions so precipitously extinguished. She'd experienced similar disappointments in many later relationships, but until now she'd never traced them back to this particular moment. On reflection, she was able to put the incident into perspective and understand Jim's actions. She had not been the "wronged woman" at all, but a naively romantic little girl. They were merely acquaintances, barely even friends. She had no justification for expecting a "relationship" with Jim, any more than she had for being disappointed in his kiss. And yet her reactions were not unique; they were based on illusions of love that she'd garnered from romantic movies and the teenage romance novels she soaked up during sixth and seventh grades. Like so many bright, impressionable young girls, Nina expected a Prince Charming to sweep through her life and transform her into the belle of the ball. Had she recognized at the time the illogic of this notion, she might have pulled out from under its spell. As it was, she'd simply persisted in believing in variations of the same fairy tale. Maybe the first kiss was not the best test, she'd thought, but surely sexual attraction was the best way to measure love. Not until she finally let go of this reasoning and began to recognize the real requirements of love was she able to break the cycle of disappointment and pursue a mature love affair.

Learning the Moves

All the myths about love that you amassed during early childhood were put to the test during the high school years. It was at this time that you began viewing romance as a way to meet the emotional needs that were surfacing as you approached adulthood. Some of your early relationships no doubt were innocent experiments, but others set the course for your future love life.

Now, instead of imitating adult couples by playing house or worshiping teen idols, you began actively rehearsing for a deeper commitment. Suddenly, sexuality was a reality. Being intimate, having babies, and getting married were all frightfully possible, and as a result, love's illusions took on new and urgent implications. If you were like most young people, sorting out these illusions was the central preoccupation of these years.

The first relationships of adolescence, of course, bear little resemblance to adult romances. Most, like Nina's with Jim, are little more than encounters. Yet because they are the first such encounters, they take on all the importance of a devastating love affair. You probably can recall your first brushes with romance far more clearly than many later, more established relationships. Who can forget the strangeness of the first kiss, the nervousness of holding hands for the first time, or the palpita-

tions that accompanied that first trial run at sexual intercourse? The newness, the trepidation, the discovery of formerly
taboo sensations all conspire to make what will later become
commonplace seem like earth-shaking events. And in a sense
they are, for they set a precedent for many of the attitudes
about relationships that we carry into later life. If your first experiments in sex were positive, you probably developed a
healthy sense of your own sexuality, which may have eased
your passage into adult relationships. If you selected your first
romantic partners from among close and loyal friends, this too
set a good precedent for true love. However, because adolescence is a time of such deep emotional uncertainty and vulnerability, any feelings of rejection, disappointment, or pain
aroused by these first romantic forays might have left lasting
scars. Sometimes the only way to lift such scars is by reexamin-
ing the changes in behavior and attitude you experienced during this period.

The big social adjustment came when you shifted from
group activities to dating. While today's youths may experiment with sex at a much younger age, up to the late seventies
even those who went steady during junior high school rarely
spent much time alone with their partners. It was in high
school, particularly when boys turned old enough to drive, that
dating began in earnest, and boys and girls found themselves
alone together for the first time. Suddenly, you had to learn
how to talk and listen to your date, how to look at and, above
all, how to touch each other. This new intimacy raised the ego
stakes considerably because acceptance and rejection now involved sexuality as well as popularity.

If dating was so intimidating, why did everyone feel so compelled to do it? During this transition from childhood to young
adulthood, most teenagers are obsessed with two things —
being accepted and being grown up. It's therefore natural that
they also become obsessed with coupling. While many youths
are drawn to drinking, smoking, driving, using drugs, and
other restricted activities to express their quest for maturity,
nothing can compare with sex and love as expressions of adult-

hood. There are three reasons for this. First, being in a couple satisfies the yearning to be wanted and understood by another person at a time when one's parents can no longer fulfill that role. Second, among most teenagers, dating enhances social status and self-esteem because it seems such a grown-up and therefore courageous step to take. Those who don't date have difficulty relating to those who do and often worry that they may never catch up socially. And third, a romantic relationship offers an outlet for all the hormonal havoc created by adolescence. Even without "going all the way," having a partner to hold and kiss can help vent much of the physical frustration that comes with a body racing ahead of emotional and intellectual maturity.

Dating for all these reasons is natural and positive up to a point. Ideally, dating represents a healthy step toward maturity, an opportunity to experiment with affectionate relationships without putting deep emotions on the line. Adolescence is the perfect time for just this sort of exploration of oneself and others. Unfortunately, many youths instead get mired in false expectations, illusions, and misinformation. They are in a hurry for love even though they don't understand what love is. This makes them vulnerable to the lures of false love.

Fooling Around

If someone had asked you to define love when you were in high school, what would you have said? When I ask today's high school students to define love, they tend to squirm and shrug. Their answers are vague: "You can't define it." "It just happens." "It's a mutual attraction." "It's magic." "You know it when you feel it." The youths who give these responses are not sexually inexperienced, nor in other respects are they particularly naive. They simply never have been taught what to expect in relationships and have been exposed to too many myths about love. At their age, and perhaps even years later, you might have agreed with them.

Unfortunately, the floundering uncertainty that colors their responses underscores the romantic behavior of many adolescents who grow up to become adults troubled by false love. If love is based on magic, they reason, then it can happen to them at sixteen as well as at twenty-five. If it's a feeling, then the swoon of attraction they feel toward their current partner must be love. Though it's easy for adults to dismiss teenage romance as "puppy love" or "kid stuff," the assumptions that drive adolescents into exclusive relationships include many of the same assumptions that perpetuate the false love cycle for years in adulthood.

A teenager named Sandy heard me give a lecture on love at her school and called me the next day with an "emergency." When she appeared in my office, it was hard to imagine that she had any serious problems. At sixteen, she was bright, blond, bouncy, a touch overweight, but full of self-confidence. She had an extremely close, if slightly symbiotic, relationship with her mother, a widow in her late fifties. They were best friends, could read each other's mind, and loved each other tremendously but, as Sandy was realizing, had less and less in common as she grew up. Sandy's father had died when she was a toddler.

"So what's the emergency?" I asked.

"I met this guy at a party last night and fell for him right away. We went parking and fooled around — not all the way. I'm still a virgin! But far enough so I'm afraid he'll think I'm cheap. And what worries me is — I loved it."

Her sexual curiosity seemed healthy, if a little more aggressive than in most sixteen-year-old girls. She had a strong will to limit her activities to foreplay and seemed enough in control to enforce her will on her partner. We concluded that there was no immediate danger. She should see how the relationship proceeded.

Two days later she called to announce that it was all over. She'd gone to a movie with her young man and he'd had poor manners and had made no offer to pay. "He's an idiot," she said, dismissing him.

The next week she spotted a good-looking boy in a car stopped alongside hers at a traffic light. They drove side by side for several blocks, chatting and exchanging phone numbers. He called her that night. Her mother objected to her dating anyone she'd met in such a haphazard way, but they compromised and won her mother's approval for Sandy and the fellow to have lunch, chaperoned by her girlfriend. Before the meal was over, she'd made up her mind that he was "creepy" and came up with an excuse to leave.

A few days later, she was smitten by the twenty-two-year-old uncle of one of her girlfriends. Hours after meeting, they were locked in a passionate embrace, his pants off, hers barely on. Again she came in for therapy, chagrined but excited. The sex was exhilarating, the attention felt good, the romance was destined to last no more than a few days.

She went through six young men in less than two months, and she broke off the relationship each time. Yet on those rare days when one was not pursuing her, she was depressed.

Watching this pattern emerge, I could see that Sandy was struggling between both positive and unhealthy impulses. To her credit, she had a strong sense of her own limits. She would not have intercourse, nor would she become emotionally entangled until she was sure she was ready. Even though she said she "loved" each man who sparked her attraction, she never got to know him and was not deeply upset when the flirtation ended. To this extent, she was using her youth to meet and experiment with a wide variety of men. Her game of chase brought her a great deal of attention and boosted her ego tremendously. People who do not receive this kind of feedback as teenagers often move into adulthood feeling that they do not measure up, that they don't deserve attention from the opposite sex. Alternatively, they may become much more aggressive and fickle later as they try to compensate for being "ignored" when younger. This clearly would not be Sandy's problem.

The problem was Sandy's inability to see beyond the most superficial characteristics of the young men she dated. In her quest for an Adonis with table manners, she never gave herself a chance to discover her dates' interests, goals, strengths, or weaknesses. Part of the dilemma was that she didn't want a relationship that might compete with the one she had with her mother. She was afraid to make the separation that such a relationship would entail. Another difficulty was the absence of her father. Although she seemed on the surface to be at ease with the opposite sex, she had had no male role models while growing up and was a little afraid of what she might find if she got too close to her young men. Her sexual appetite and enthusiasm disguised this uncertainty quite neatly, but she came to therapy in the first place because she was not comfortable with this cover-up.

Before Sandy was able to have a deeper relationship she had to relinquish many of her expectations about romance and develop more meaningful standards for her dates. She had to trust that she could sustain a relationship past the first meeting without having sex right away and that she could feel genuine affection for a boyfriend without jeopardizing her love for her mother.

Because she was troubled by her conflicting sexual desires and her frustration that no man was ever "good enough" for her, Sandy was able to adjust her behavior and develop healthier, more realistic expectations of love while still a teenager. For others, the game of chase extends well into adulthood. If you're never taught to distinguish true love from false, playing hard to get can become habitual, and the excitement of being pursued can become addictive. No one denies the thrill of being lusted after by attractive strangers. Unfortunately, true love cannot begin to grow until this thrill subsides and your stranger becomes a familiar partner, flaws and all.

First "Love"

If you compare "serious" teen relationships with "serious" adult relationships, the key difference is the context, the time of life in which the affairs occur. It's the vulnerability, insecurity, and neediness of the age that often makes young love seem so poignant in retrospect. Your first affair may or may not have been consummated, but inevitably it was sexually turbulent. All the biological confusion of adolescence, the natural sense of being out of control, was filtered through the relationship and created something you might have sensed was magic. Without much experience to use for comparison and compelled by unrelenting physical urges, it was easy to mistake superficial attraction for love. The constraints against satisfying these urges — lack of privacy, parental prohibitions, fear of pregnancy — only made them that much more powerful. In the face of such obstacles, intimacy was dangerously seductive.

But physical desire was not the sole motivation — not for a serious affair. Teenagers often believe that love can resolve their emotional conflicts as well as their physical needs, including all the self-doubt that wells up as they confront their fast-approaching departure from childhood into the real world. They may become obsessed with the affair of the moment because they are afraid of the uncertainty that overshadows everything else in their lives. Even the most flawed, problematic relationship can serve as a kind of refuge from the outside.

Though their parents all tried in every way they knew, including sending them for therapy, no one could persuade Chris and Carol that they were making a mistake. They were in love, they'd say, defiantly stalking away. They were seventeen years old and "fully mature enough" to handle the feelings they had for each other. The fact that they spent every moment together, that they shunned all their other friends, and that they turned away from their families only confirmed to them the intensity of their desire. They were losing themselves in each other, and in the process, they believed, they were reaching for a higher spiritual plane.

Their parents thought that was hogwash. They were children playing make-believe.

But the harder the outside pressed in on them, the more

tightly Chris and Carol hung on to each other. They professed absolute, unwavering devotion, yet each fretted with jealousy when the other was out of sight. They told themselves that they understood each other totally, yet each worried how the other might react to increased pressure from parents, school, or friends. "Only you know what I feel, how I think," Carol told him, but she was not sure she believed that he did understand her completely. "You are the only important thing in my life," he told her, but he was never absolutely confident that he was the most important thing in hers. All their separate insecurities converged within the relationship.

Among the many impossible promises they made to each other, they pledged undying love. No matter what happens, they said, no matter what kind of a future we face, we will always have each other. Just as their best friends had provided a sense of safety and belonging when they were younger, this relationship gave them confidence against the void of objectives and prospects they now perceived in the rest of their lives. Both were bright, college-bound youngsters who, despite their romance, were maintaining good grades. But nothing was more important to them than being together. Their only emotional resource was each other, and that was draining them far more than either knew. Their union had no context; it was, in fact, nothing but magnified illusion. When the reality of the future at last began to press through their cocoon, the illusion splintered.

Against their parents' wishes, they had applied to the same university. Carol was accepted. Chris was not. She was devastated, guilty, but most of all fearful of going away without him for emotional support. He was angry and resentful of her for showing him up and suddenly began to feel suffocated by the web they'd bound around themselves.

The night after Chris's rejection arrived, Carol stole to his house at three in the morning, climbed the tree to his window, and slithered into bed beside him. They had slept together before, hidden in the sand dunes and once in a friend's vacant guesthouse, but never in one of their homes. That was not what Carol wanted now either. What she wanted was a reassurance of the magic she knew was fading. It was a desperate measure, an exaggeration out of a dated movie, but she was just obsessed enough to try it.

Chris was horrified. While they had been defiant in their relationship, they had always been cautious in their intimacy. Risk taking was not part of the attraction. Now Carol was pulling a stunt that was clearly intended to change the rules. A few weeks earlier, he might have found it titillating. Tonight he felt only alienated.

"You've got to be out of your mind," he blurted out. "Get the hell out of here."

"Love me," she whimpered.

"Not here, Carol!"

"I wanted to do something . . . crazy, to show how I feel about you."

"I know," he whispered, momentarily touched. He kissed her. "But you've got to go. I can't handle this."

"But you understand?"

"I understand." In that moment, his ego swelled with pride that she would go to such lengths to impress him.

Then his mother walked in.

Afraid that any harsh restrictions would drive them closer together, their parents expressed their outrage and penalized them with extra chores but did not forbid their seeing each other. It was a wise decision. Chris's ambivalence couldn't have withstood the added pressure of parental constraints. He would have relented and probably would have eloped with Carol. As it was, the relationship wavered for weeks after that, he becoming more determined to break it off, she becoming more desperate to hold him. What had been a pact against the universe turned into a tug of war between themselves. Sentiment and the comfort of her desire held Chris for a while, though he knew it was time to release himself from her claustrophobic grip. Insecurity drove Carol to encircle him, though she realized the romance was gone. The end was inevitable and painful for both of them. It represented not just the loss of a relationship, but the defeat of illusion.

Adolescent relationships like Chris and Carol's are burdened with impossible expectations that doom them from the start. Filled with conflicts between attachments to family and the emerging discovery of themselves as individuals, young couples find an escape in losing themselves to each other. Having a lover during the developmental transition of adolescence is like having an intravenous injection of validation. For a time, the relationship becomes a world unto itself, the ultimate source of courage for youths who are otherwise in a state of panic. Both fervently believe that they can meet each other's every need. Alas, no relationship can withstand such pressure. Despite their obstinate efforts to stamp out any hint of independence, the two souls do not merge. Their separate angsts do not cancel each other out. "Love conquers all," they've been taught, and they are desperate to prove this myth true, but they cannot.

Usually one of the partners recognizes that the relationship is really an elaborate stall, that the two of them, in fact, are not bravely facing the future together but are backing away from it. Once one partner gathers the strength to test life independently, the fantasy that they've been sharing explodes. The partner left behind often remains a candidate for false love, in varying versions, into adulthood. This is understandable: If you're unable to see that the fault lies in the obsessiveness of your desire, you're likely to blame your partner instead; and if you don't yet have the courage to move forward as an individual, your natural inclination is to find another partner with whom you can establish the same sort of irrationally intense relationship you had before.

Occasionally, the commitment to the fantasy is so strong that the young couple remain together, perhaps marrying. Sometimes they are simply afraid to face the world independently; sometimes the girl gets pregnant, and marriage seems the appropriate solution; and sometimes marriage is an act of defiance against the families. But even if they survive longer than a few years, such relationships rarely progress to true love. The burden of immaturity that marked their beginnings usually is just too great. Though teenagers struggle mightily under the yoke of parental supervision, most remain sheltered and relatively pampered until they leave home for college, careers, or marriage. Young people don't acquire truly realistic goals or a strong sense of purpose until they make this separation, and being in a tight relationship doesn't facilitate the process. To survive as a couple through this transition, both partners must come individually to the same objectives or else develop the sensitivity and skills to support each other's, and they must remain interested and committed to each other even as they change and mature as individuals. If you look at your high school yearbook picture and then turn to your college yearbook portrait, you'll realize that this means weathering a sea change. It's not surprising that couples who come together during adolescence are particularly susceptible to temptation outside the relationship later. A man who married at eighteen is bound to be curious about other women. *Am I attractive to them?* he asks himself at moments when his ego is drooping. *Would sex be better with another woman?* Because his realm of experience is so narrow, he may feel entitled to have affairs and perhaps to leave his wife when he finds a woman who excites him again. His wife, meanwhile, is feeling similar temptations.

Despite the very real limitations of young love, it strikes a dangerous chord of longing in all of us. Adolescent affairs are the stuff of tear-jerkers, those movies that make us long to relive the period when we experienced romance so intensely and pain so exquisitely. Unfortunately, in the process, teenage passions are often used misguidedly as a yardstick for true love. The woman who marries in her thirties may doubt her choice because her husband fails to evoke the passion she felt for her high school sweetheart. The adolescent whose girlfriend dumped him for a college man carries a torch for her for ten years in the hope that someday they'll live out those vows of undying love that they made in their sixteenth year. Such nostalgia proves not the validity of young love but the magnetism of youth and innocence. It's rarely the partner we mourn; it's the time and changes between then and now.

Losers in Love

Walter seemed to be a healthy, good-looking high school sophomore. He had an A average, enjoyed a solid relationship with his parents, and had never doubted himself until he entered his teens. But in junior high he had fallen under his older brother's shadow.

Billy had always been a ham and a socialite, even as a little boy. In high school he was president of his class and captain of the basketball team. His grades were never as good as Walter's, but he was popular. "Your big brother was a terror — and what a ladies' man!" the gym teacher would inform Walter, and there was no mistaking the approval in the man's voice or his tacit disappointment in Walter, who could barely make a basket, much less break hearts.

"Billy was going out on dates by the time he was Walter's age," their mother would say to her friends. Overhearing her, Walter could not mistake the tone of disappointment and concern in her voice.

Billy tried to help his baby brother, offering advice like "Come on tough" and "Let them know you're in control," but Billy could grin and say "Hey, baby" and have the girls eating out of his hand. If Walter tried it, they called him a creep.

In junior high, Walter wanted to be popular. Even though he failed at virtually every sport, he tried to make friends with the guys who were athletic because his brother told him that they would hold the social power in high school. Unfortunately, they ignored him, as did the girls who traveled in their group. And, of course, they were the only girls who interested him.

The girls who seemed interested in him were never good enough to suit him. One reason was that he was unable to accept the notion that they might be his friends without becoming his girlfriends.

When he entered high school, Walter became obsessed with fantasies of his own desirability and manliness. His academic accomplishments contributed nothing to his self-esteem. He no longer cared that he was unpopular with the "in" group; if just one beautiful woman would "want him," he thought, he'd know he was a man. This obsession took on such mammoth proportions that eventually his failure to win a girlfriend convinced him that something was seriously wrong with him. At his parents' urging, he began therapy, expecting to hear the worst.

Walter was astounded to discover that the problem lay not within himself but in his brother's image of social and sexual "success." This image had so dominated his perceptions that he never doubted it or even considered the possibility of relating to a girl as an equal. Nor had it ever occurred to him that he had many attractive strengths that the "jocks" in school lacked. The first steps in counseling, therefore, were to build his self-confidence so that he wasn't afraid to approach a girl and to help him redefine male-female relationships so that he wouldn't evaluate the opposite sex purely in terms of appearance and class popularity ratings. Then he had to give himself permission to become friends with some of the girls he'd snubbed in the past.

By the time Walter graduated, he'd achieved these milestones and had been out on a few dates. In college, free of his brother's shadow and his family's subtle pressure, he was able to have his first mature sexual relationships as well as many affectionate friendships with women.

Had Walter not managed to break out of the illusions his family unwittingly imposed on him, he would have carried them into his adult relationships, probably with the same miserable results as in high school, and the damage to his self-esteem would have intensified. Or he might have given up and retreated from love, believing himself to be inept and thus turning his failure into a self-fulfilling prophecy.

As Walter's story illustrates, you didn't need to experience romance in high school in order to be touched by its spell. You knew that "everyone else was doing it," and you knew that you were ready to test the myths yourself. If you had no opportunity to do this during adolescence, you became even more vulnerable to the myths when you began dating later. Moreover, you may have acquired the reputation (if not in the eyes of others, at least in your own) of being a "loser" in love. Because high school was a relatively closed society in which no one was a stranger, such labels could be socially crippling. Fortunately, there is life after high school. Once you left home, the assumptions that governed your early life, including many of your feelings of inferiority and your illusions of love, could be reexamined and questioned more freely.

9

TRANSITIONS IN LOVE

BY THE TIME you reached your twenties, the hormonal storm had finally subsided, and adulthood, that destination which for so long had been relegated to the future, was at last the present. The urgency of getting a date and being seen as "popular" had been replaced by the drive to complete your education, perhaps start your career, and, along the way, find a mate. Now it was time to begin the transition away from the family of your childhood and toward a family of your own.

This stage of development, when you acquired your finishing touches as an adult, was critical in determining whether you were ready to give and receive love in a mature relationship. If you emerged as a strong, purposeful individual at this juncture, then chances were you'd be able to sustain your identity in a loving partnership without feeling threatened or consumed by it. And if you also succeeded in making the transition in roles *within your family* from child to adult, then perhaps you would be able to make your own independent choices in love without being unduly pressured by your parents' expectations and illusions. In reality, however, not many young adults are able to achieve such direction and independence; the vast majority remain much more deeply influenced by their families than they would like to admit, even into their later adult years. In this way, the myths and illusions that contribute to the false love syndrome pass from one generation to the next.

The illusions about love that you absorbed in youth are reactivated as you prepare to transfer some of the emotional bonds from your original family to the family you will create when you marry. Even parents who are quite undemanding when their children are young sometimes become surprisingly intrusive in their grown offsprings' love lives. Whether you confront these pressures in early adulthood or sidestep them until later in life, when you finally succeed in separating your own priorities in love from your family's influences, you may find that your relationships reflect not only your parents' illusions about love but also unresolved conflicts from your childhood.

Parents and Lovers

Ever since he was a child, Alan had been hearing about the woman his parents wanted him to marry. She should be good-looking, but not too good-looking — you can't trust women who are *too* good-looking. She should have a college education and strong career goals but understand that when children come along, they take priority. She should be supportive but not submissive, clever but not smarter than Alan, and sensible but not boring. She should be an excellent cook and, above all else, she should come from an upstanding Jewish family.

Every time he dated a non-Jewish girl in high school his mother cried. He quickly learned to conceal his trysts from her by pretending to go to the movies with male friends. Occasionally he would bring home a female Jewish classmate for a study session, and this would appease his mother, but Alan never had any romantic feelings for these girls. He was snowed by the blond, blue-eyed Gentiles who surrounded him in most of his classes. The fact that his mother strongly disapproved only made them more tantalizing to him.

For about ten years he sowed his wild oats and never dated anyone Jewish. His mother occasionally took him to task. "If your father could see you he would disown you," she'd say. Alan remembered his father's tirades against *shikses*. He *might* have disowned him if he'd lived long enough, but instead he'd died when Alan was nine. For all her protests, Alan doubted that his mother personally felt as strongly as his father had about non-Jewish women, but he knew she'd be very upset if he ever married someone of a different faith.

By the time Alan reached his late twenties he found himself thinking more and more about marriage. He was getting tired of acting the playboy and wanted stability and permanence. He also wanted children. An only child himself, he found the prospect of family life extremely appealing. Besides, it would make his mother so happy to have grandchildren.

He had a girlfriend of nearly two years, Jenny, who was as close to him as any woman had ever been. They had been friends long before they started sleeping together, and as a result the relationship was extremely comfortable. She had been there for him when his best friend died. They shared many of the same interests and political beliefs. Their arguments were volatile but brief, their reconciliations passionate. Alan had considered asking her to live with him on several occasions, had daydreamed about marrying her, but never seriously entertained either possibility. He was afraid to get too serious with her because Jenny was Swedish. Her father was in jail in Europe for tax fraud. Although she was extremely bright and inquisitive, she had never been to college and couldn't cook anything more complicated than open-faced sandwiches. Alan didn't care about these things, but they clearly violated his parents' expectations for him.

Though he found these familial demands irritating and unreasonable, he couldn't help being haunted by them. After so many years of defiantly dating whomever he wished, he hated himself all the more for not having the nerve now to propose to Jenny. But somehow it seemed that the stakes were much higher in marriage. He didn't want to break his mother's heart by marrying without her approval. He was her only child, and she, now in her seventies, lived for him. She already was deeply saddened by his lack of religious commitment — it had been over ten years since he last attended temple, as she kept pointing out — and Alan thought that the prospect of having grandchildren who were not Jewish might just send her into despair. And in truth, he agreed on this particular issue. Although he didn't observe the rituals, he certainly considered himself a Jew, and he also felt that his children should appreciate their religious heritage. Grudgingly, he admitted that it would be easier if he took a Jewish wife.

So, while he still spent most of his time with Jenny, he kept his eyes open for someone else. As he looked around, most of the Jewish women he noticed only confirmed the stereotypes that had dominated his youth. He remembered how his friends had joked that all Jewish girls were pushy and spoiled. This brainwashing proved a formidable obstacle now as he tried to be more open-minded — until he met Natalie.

She fit his mother's description exactly. She was pretty and natural looking, obviously bright, and yet approachable. Alan met her while searching for some summer reading in the library. Natalie was checking out child development texts. "For my master's thesis," she explained. He quickly hid the covers of his thrillers and asked her to lunch. She suggested that he come home with her instead, since she'd invited several other friends over. Alan was struck by her self-confidence and focus. She told him that after she completed her studies she was going to Israel to develop child care programs in the kibbutzim.

Judging by the lunch she served, she was an excellent chef. Even the kosher food tasted good, Alan marveled afterward. Her friends were bright Jewish college graduates. Her home was clean and simple. She seemed earnest and guileless — the perfect woman to bring home to Mama. Why, then, did he leave her apartment and race back to Jenny?

It had seemed like a game as long as there were no possible candidates, but now he felt as if he'd met his destiny, and it was not a comfortable feeling. He could find no fault with Natalie, no excuses for *not* pursuing a relationship — except that he was intensely intimidated by her. She was so dedicated to the cause of Judaism that she made him feel more guilty, not less. He could never live up to the standards she set for herself and, presumably, would set for the man she married. Moreover, confronting someone who "should" become his wife was only making him ache for Jenny. Suddenly, Jenny represented safety, comfort, normalcy.

Arriving at her apartment, he charged through the door, swept her up in his arms and carried her laughing to the bedroom. After a night of intimacy and passion, Alan felt that he could never be this happy with anyone else.

Nevertheless, the next time he visited his mother and she began her inquisition about marriage prospects, Alan blurted out that he'd met someone who'd make her the ideal daughter-in-law. "Who is it?" his mother asked, her eyes lighting up in excitement. "Why don't you bring her to meet me?"

Alan hesitated and then took a deep breath. "Okay," he said with resignation, "I will."

"I'm going to take you to meet my mother," he announced that night. Jenny looked up, startled. He'd never made such a suggestion before. In fact, he had avoided talking about his family. She had tried on several occasions to get him to open up about his childhood, but he had resisted, except to talk about what an unyielding man his father had been. She could tell these discussions were painful for him and hadn't pressed for more. As their relationship deepened, she assumed, he would open up.

For her part, Jenny was willing to be patient. She had had dozens of boyfriends before, one more callous than the next. Alan was the first who was primarily a friend. He had nursed her when she was sick, helped her get her citizenship, and supported her financially and emotionally when she was out of work. While it pained her that he was so hesitant about committing his future to her, she suspected that his ambivalence about religion was a large part of the problem. It was primarily a matter of trust, she told herself. Once he trusted her enough to really open up and express his true feelings, they would be able to work out a solution. Surely, winning his mother's acceptance would help.

They made the visit the next weekend. Jenny was dressed modestly and carried a gift of cookies. Her gentle blue eyes warmed at the sight of the historic brownstone where Alan's mother had lived most of her life. She smiled at the musty smell of old carpets and drapes. "It reminds me of my grandmother's house in Stockholm," she whispered to Alan. He looked at her as if she were crazy.

Alan's mother's face fell the instant she laid eyes on Jenny, and her expression as she turned to Alan said, "This can be no daughter-in-law of *mine!*" But Jenny refused to be dismissed so easily. She had grown up with tough characters, and she could handle this one too.

"You expected someone else, didn't you?" she asked calmly and paused. Alan's mother said nothing. "Well, I'm not Jewish, it's true," she continued. "But I would like to get to know you. I hope you'll show me the same courtesy before you pass judgment on me."

Alan's mother was so taken aback by the young woman's directness and self-confidence that she forgot for a moment she wasn't supposed to like Jenny. In that moment, she glimpsed someone she admired and, indeed, was curious to know better.

Alan watched this split-second exchange in astonishment. He had expected his mother to terminate this relationship instantly, but instead he felt like a third wheel as Jenny settled herself in a large armchair and began talking comfortably about her memories of her grandparents and her childhood in Europe. It soon came out that she had relatives living in Germany, near where Alan's mother had grown up.

"Go get the tea, Alan," his mother instructed. "Your friend and I seem to have a great deal to talk about."

"I think it went well, don't you?" Jenny commented as they departed, three hours later. "Your mother was charming. What were you so afraid of?"

Alan was silent, fighting a cascade of conflicting emotions he couldn't begin to understand. Though he knew he should feel delighted, he resented Jenny's triumph and felt betrayed by his mother. What had she been talking about all these years? Had he so completely misunderstood what she was saying to him? Why did he care so much what she thought anyway?

"Are you going to stay tonight?" asked Jenny as they got back to her apartment.

"No," he said abruptly, then caught himself. "I mean — I have too much work. Maybe tomorrow." He kissed her quickly and turned to leave.

"I love you," she said, smiling. He turned back, a look of puzzlement darkening his face, then nodded and left.

He didn't see her the next day, or the day after. Nor did he speak to his mother. Instead, he buried himself in work and tried to shake off all the assumptions and second-guessing that had dominated his romantic life for years. Since boyhood, he had been rebelling against an illusion, and with the illusion finally revealed to him, he didn't know how to act or what to feel. Suddenly he was responsible for his own actions and choices. His mother's only certain condition was that he be happy. Yet now that that was clear, the building commitment he'd felt toward Jenny was suddenly in doubt. Had he chosen her purely out of defiance, as a kind of forbidden fruit, or was it love he felt? In therapy he tried to sort through his confusion.

"My heart is telling me to marry Jenny, but I don't know if I can trust the impulse," he said, trying to sum up his uncertainty.

"There's fear in your voice," I pointed out. "Perhaps you're still afraid of hurting your mother. Perhaps you're afraid of hurting Jenny. But it sounds like the only way you really might hurt either one would be to commit to something you don't believe in. You've never really allowed yourself to dismiss your parents' expectations and seriously consider what it would be like to be married to Jenny. I think now's the time to do it."

As Alan talked about their relationship, it became clear that, whatever initially had attracted him to Jenny, the bond that had evolved was substantial. They shared the same lifestyle, could talk to each other for hours, had the same basic goals. He had never felt as intimate with any other woman, and sex was always good.

But Alan still wasn't comfortable with the idea of marrying Jenny, in part because he had never dared ask her any of the "hard" questions. He wasn't absolutely sure she wanted children, and he certainly didn't know how she'd raise them. He didn't know what her true religious convictions were or what she wanted out of marriage. Not wanting to become too "serious," he had resisted finding out this deeply personal information.

It gradually dawned on Alan that his relationship with Jenny had been colored all along by his ambivalence toward his parents. Deep down he had always trusted and wanted to please his mother, yet he couldn't tolerate what he viewed as her narrow-mindedness about religion. Meanwhile, he was still raging against his father's rigidity and against the premature death that prevented them from developing the love that Alan always craved. He had conducted his love life like a confused and defiant adolescent, and Jenny was caught in the middle. She possessed the personality to please his mother, yet her heritage — that part over which she had no control whatsoever — would have been absolutely unacceptable to his father. In choosing her, Alan was still wrestling between the desire to be accepted and the desire to break away. This would have to stop, he realized, before he could make any decision about marriage.

Afraid as he was of losing Jenny, he had to objectively consider the differences in their backgrounds and personalities, differences that he previously had overlooked. He knew now that some of his parents' advice was wise and some was not, some for his benefit and some for theirs. They would have to sort it all out together if he was ever to trust his love. Too unsure of himself to undertake this process with her alone, he asked her to join him in therapy. She accepted, hoping that this would finally clear the way for marriage.

During their joint consultations, Alan and Jenny focused for the first time on the critical issues that would face them in marriage, beginning with children and religion. Jenny was surprised that Alan felt as strongly as he did about raising his family as Jews, but after some discussion, she agreed with him. Their children should have faith in God. Her own religious background was shaky, and she'd always admired the traditions and tenets of Judaism. In fact, maybe it wasn't enough that the children should be raised as Jews, she suggested. Maybe she should convert. Alan looked thunderstruck but pleased.

Next, they began to confront some of their other feelings about love and marriage. To Alan's surprise, Jenny had very definite expectations which she'd never before spelled out. She would not merely take fidelity and commitment for granted but would insist on them. She expected a great deal more time, trust, openness, and emotional intimacy than he had given her in their early years. She wanted the honesty and concern that marked these discussions to continue throughout their marriage. As he listened to her, Alan felt ashamed that he had been so guarded in their first years togther. She was far more sensitive and perceptive, but also stronger than he had ever realized. She had such high standards and yet had believed in him enough to wait for him to come around. This demonstrated a respect for him that he had never before acknowledged or returned. He might not deserve it, he promised, but he certainly was going to try to live up to it.

When at last they became engaged, there was no doubt in either of their minds that the decision was the right one or that it was theirs alone. If this was not exactly the daughter-in-law of her dreams, Alan's mother was satisfied that Jenny was converting and that the grandchildren would be raised within the faith. But most important, as his mother said on their wedding day, they loved each other.

There is love between parents and child. There is love between lovers. Ideally, the two should not compete, but unfortunately they often do. When this happens, both relationships may be compromised.

Parents naturally take a special interest in their children's love lives, for love generally leads to marriage, and marriage, in the traditional view, represents the end of the parents' official role in a child's life. Until you find a mate, your parents continue to have a certain authority over you, even after you've left home; but once you marry, they must abdicate much of that responsibility to your new spouse. Naturally, they hope for the best possible match, someone who ascribes to their own beliefs and will support the values and goals they have tried to instill in you. To this end, they may become directly involved in your romantic explorations, perhaps pressuring, perhaps hovering, perhaps merely monitoring from a distance — but probably passing judgment to some degree.

This involvement may represent nothing more than an unselfish desire for you to be happy and to build a truly loving relationship. More likely, it represents a mixture of unselfish and selfish desires. Not only do your parents want you to be happier through love, but they hope that your mate will also make *them* happier. The lines may be so blurred that even they don't realize the distinction. "Oh no," they may say if challenged. "We don't care for *ourselves,* but we know what's best for you." Sometimes what they wish on you is not in your best interests at all.

As you search for a partner in love, you can't help but be influenced by your parents' advice and desires — after all, you've been conditioned by them to agree with many of their preferences. Also, you realize that your mate will become part of the family, and you'll have to live with your parents' approval or disapproval as long as the relationship continues. But perhaps the most important reason you care what your parents think is that you yourself may be uncertain about what's best for you in love. Regardless of whether you follow your parents' advice, you inevitably take their opinions into account, even if only to reject them. Even if they've died, you may find yourself asking, "Would they have approved?"

It is appropriate to accept your parents' advice as long as you weigh their suggestions rationally and objectively and then use the good and throw out the bad. Unfortunately, the dynamics between parents and children are often so fraught with tension, mistrust, and confusion that you may never achieve such temperance. Instead, you might go to extremes, altering your romantic choices either to please or to thwart your family. Both approaches lead directly to false love.

True love requires a mature, responsible, and intensely personal commitment from both partners. Its purpose is to enhance and enrich your lives, not your parents'. Likewise, its ultimate success or failure will depend on you alone. Unfortunately, when parents are particularly meddlesome or you are particularly susceptible to their influence, romantic commitment is compromised. To secure it, you need to learn to pierce the emotional overlay that makes parental pressure so compelling. This means reading your family's motivations and then determining why they respond as they do. Only then can you be sure that your choices in love are truly your own and not just a reaction to family pressure.

Classic Pressure Plays

Every family develops a unique blend of dynamics and beliefs and thus has its own expectations regarding love and marriage for its youngest members. Religion, ethnic culture, race, and economic factors all play roles in determining a family's requirements for a prospective in-law. Despite individual differences, however, most of these expectations come together in a few classic pressure plays, some of which may be motivated by selfishness on the part of the family, some by selflessness, and many by a mixture of both. Once you understand how these pressure plays work and can identify the true motivations behind them, it will be much easier for you to manage familial interference in a mature fashion.

"Find someone who will fit in with the family."
This seemingly innocent plea encompasses a broad range of demands, some of which may be reasonable and some not. To the extent that it means "find someone with a similar background," the pressure is justified. For the most part, couples who share the same religion, race, and cultural background do tend to have more successful relationships than those who start out worlds apart. However, when this requirement conflicts with your own more liberal views, it becomes distinctly unreasonable. Then the only justification for the pressure is to satisfy parental ego or make your parents feel more secure. I remember a patient whose father wanted him to marry someone traditionally feminine, not too well educated, from a black lower-middle-class family like his own. He went so far as to set his son up with a friend's daughter when the young people were still in their teens — and violently objected when the boy eventually broke away and became engaged to a corporate manager. This father's motivation was not to make his son happy but to protect himself from having a daughter-in-law who might intimidate him.

In many other cultures, particularly in the Near and Far East, where a child's spouse routinely is selected by the parents and *the offspring accept this as a precondition,* the resulting marriage often evolves into a loving relationship, but in the West the results of parental matchmaking are often disastrous. Even if the chosen couple marry, the anger and resentment provoked by all the meddling can overshadow their personal commitment as husband and wife. Such marriages usually succeed only when the couple genuinely share their parents' values and beliefs or are willing to blindly accept their authority — when the couple trust that by following their parents' advice they will ultimately be happier themselves.

"Find someone who will take care of you."

This advice usually is motivated by parents' concern for both your needs and their own. Parents who are sick of their son bringing his dirty laundry home every weekend or of their daughter asking for money and borrowing the car are understandably eager to have someone else absorb these burdens. The son and daughter usually are just as eager to find someone other than parents to do the chores and foot the bills.

Unfortunately, this message misrepresents love as a kind of custodial arrangement. Instead of encouraging their children to look for life partners, these parents effectively are telling them to look for substitute guardians. The net effect is to emphasize their offspring's immaturity while predefining the spouse's role. It does not convey an image of love as a mutual and equal partnership.

What some parents really mean when they say this is "Find someone to take care of your emotional needs." As a general rule, this makes sense. Loving partners should be emotionally responsive and attentive to each other. When parents start defining these needs, however, they are out of line. It is not a mother's place to insist that her son be coddled by his wife, nor a father's to demand that his daughter's husband treat her like a princess. Often, parents who voice such demands are jealous of their child's lover. They are saying, in effect, he or she can't give you what I can. They know that the criticism strikes deep and may even divide the couple, but that may be precisely what they want. The truth is that the roles of parent and lover do not fulfill the same emotional needs and should not be expected to.

"Find someone who will make us happy."

Few parents have the nerve to say this outright to their children, but many hope and press for it in less obvious ways. Perhaps they never had a daughter or were never close to their own, so they urge their son to marry a woman who can be the daughter they always wanted. Perhaps they are getting older and are afraid they won't be able to take care of themselves much longer, so they urge their daughter to marry a man of means and conscience who can help support them. Or perhaps they always dreamed in vain of being successful and powerful and now hope to realize this fantasy by having their daughter marry someone wealthy and famous.

The message can be cloaked in advice that sounds as if it's for your benefit: "Find someone who has money . . . is young and strong . . . is well connected . . . has a college education." These suggestions may coincide with your own needs, but if they do not, your parents' motivation may be suspect.

Another warning signal is the tenor of your parents' concern. If they impose themselves on the selection process, proposing marital candidates, interrogating new prospects, demanding credentials and financial statements, their interest may be predatory rather than altruistic.

"Find someone who will marry you and have children with you."

The desire for grandchildren as a hedge against mortality is a strong motivation for many parents to press their children to marry. The trouble is that these parents sometimes discount love in their concern over reproduction. They may push for a prospective partner who cannot possibly meet the requirements of love but is capable of bearing or siring a child. By the same token, they may object to someone who is ideal in every other way but is unable or unwilling to produce successors. Families who take this stand often will resort to the most extreme means of pressure. Hal's father threatened to cut him off when he and his fiancée announced their engagement. Hal was twenty-four, Lynn thirty. She had two sons from a previous marriage and refused to have more children. Although Hal had some desire for children, he believed he could make this sacrifice for Lynn.

However, his father was determined that someone in the family provide an heir to carry on the line, and his sister had had a hysterectomy, so Hal was the only candidate. The sister and the father joined in a campaign to discredit Hal's fiancée. She would die before him, they said. Her sons were brats and would destroy the marriage. She was so much older than he. She'd been a failure in one marriage, why should she do better this time around? Even though Hal saw through their tactics, he was not unscathed. They played on his feelings of ambivalence about having children and created unwarranted doubts. He knew he could never forgive them if they coerced him into breaking up with Lynn, yet the pressure took its toll on the relationship. Finally, Hal realized he had to choose between them. He chose Lynn, and his father stopped talking to him. For Hal, the price of true love was his family's rejection.

Parental pressure on couples to marry before living together is often just as selfish. Most young adults who choose to live together feel no shame about doing so, but their old-school parents still may be shocked and embarrassed. Often, they want the young people to marry so they can hold their heads up high at the weekly bridge game and not have to think about sex out of wedlock. They may insist that they're just concerned about their child's "security" or mistrustful of the partner's "commitment," but the real concern usually is over form rather than substance in their offspring's relationship.

In today's world, your parents may urge you to marry because they feel this will cement a monogamous, heterosexual lifestyle, a hedge against the threat of AIDS and other sexually transmitted diseases. The motivation is certainly unselfish, but the reasoning is not altogether correct, unless they also insist that both you and your partner be virgins when you marry. More to the point, this thinking pits the threat of these diseases among heterosexuals against the importance of developing trust and personal commitment *before* the knot is tied. Even the desire for safety and security, if overemphasized, can lead to false love.

"Find someone who will make you happy."

Of all the pressure plays, this is the only purely unselfish demand. If parents stated it just this way, it would be difficult for
anyone to object. The confusion starts when your parents try
to administer your future happiness by suggesting more specific
criteria. Knowing that he is going to be a doctor, a mother
strongly discourages her son from dating women in professions
whose career priorities are likely to conflict with his. A father
whose daughter is a biochemist despairs when she professes
love for a struggling artist. These parents have no hidden agendas, and they are well within their rights to voice their feelings,
but in some families there's a fine line between expressing an
opinion and meddling. Genuine concern is easily mistaken for
jealousy, and well-meaning advice can be misinformed. It's
wise to remember that your parents sometimes, but by no
means always, know what's best for you, particularly when it
comes to affairs of the heart. Welcome your parents' desire for
your happiness and consider their comments and suggestions
with an open mind, but then let your own good judgment take
over.

The Selection Process

Your parents cannot influence your love life unless you let
them. Theoretically, you should be mature enough by adulthood to accept good advice graciously and disregard the bad.
Unfortunately, when the person giving the advice is your parent, your responses may get skewed. We all react to our parents' words and actions much more emotionally than to those
of others. While we may accept that a friend or business associate has differing attitudes about love, such disagreement with
our own parents is much more difficult to take in stride. Few
people are able to maintain equanimity in the face of parental
pressure. The emotional web of the family intervenes.

Some actively adjust their romantic choices to please their

families. Early in the search, this may indicate nothing more than uncertainty and indecision. Jan spent three of her college years with her first lover, a man whom her parents quietly opposed from the start. Ultimately, she realized that they were right all along. The man dealt drugs, was irresponsible and overdependent, and had no sense of personal direction. Jan had simply been too inexperienced to see him clearly. After breaking out of the relationship, she couldn't get over the fact that her parents seemed to be much better judges of character than she. No longer trusting her own instincts, she directed herself toward men she thought her parents would like. Her mother was fond of a man who was artistic, well spoken, well bred, and slightly balding, so Jan found a similar type and dated him for about three weeks. Her father was involved in international diplomacy, so she briefly dated a foreign service attaché. Her parents appreciated classical music, so she tried dating a cellist. The experiments continued for over a year.

None of these relationships worked out because Jan had no true personal interest in the men, but they did give her a useful range of experience. She learned some of the things she wanted to avoid in a partner as well as many qualities she desired. She also learned that it was pointless to try to match her partners to fantasy images of men who would please her mother and father. Not only was she unfairly typecasting her partners into absurdly narrow and superficial roles, but she was unfairly second-guessing her parents *and* giving them far more influence over her love life than they deserved or wanted. This realization made her much more confident and secure when she became engaged to a man without her parents' approval. This time she could sit down with them and explain why she loved him and why she was willing to risk their objections. They remained noncommittal even after she married him, but as they grew to know him they admitted they'd been wrong. On her own, Jan had made the right decision.

When the desire to please your parents extends beyond the experimentation phase, the results can be far less positive. Ideally, if you marry according to your family's specifications, you freely accept their guidelines. Perhaps you have questioned and tested your own attitudes and ultimately have come to agree with your family. Perhaps you have had such a positive, loving upbringing that you follow your parents' advice in an attempt to duplicate their success. The trouble starts when you allow the family to override your own needs and good sense. While you sincerely may want a partner who "fits in," you cannot expect this person to become as tightly enmeshed in the clan as you are. If you or your parents demand this level of involvement, the fallout will damage your relationship with your partner or with your parents or both. Love and marriage should represent a healthy separation from the family, but if your family is too closely involved in the choice of your partner, that separation cannot occur. If you allow your parents to persuade you to make choices you otherwise would not make, you may really be looking for acceptance and approval. Unfortunately, your own low self-esteem and self-doubts may be setting you up for trouble whether or not your family approves of your lover. If the family does approve, there may be a moment of gratification, but then the doubts will come creeping back because the source of the problems remains unchanged.

Rita thought she had found the answer to her deep-rooted family conflicts when she met Dwight. He had been a quarterback on the football team at Yale, her father's alma mater. He was going on to business school. He was tall, handsome, and sure to please her mother. He was also aggressive, outgoing, and effusively self-confident — all the qualities her parents had tried in vain to instill in Rita.

She had never lived up to their standards. She was intensely shy, had stuttered all through childhood, and, though she masked her insecurities by overachieving academically, felt like a complete failure in the eyes of her family. They wanted a cheerleader or a homecoming queen, and they got a bookworm. She wanted them to treat her like a woman, and they continued to call her Baby. Well, as soon as they met Dwight, she thought, they would start to take her seriously and show her the respect she'd always longed for. She could hardly wait to bring him home.

Dwight was attracted to Rita's gentleness and almost old-fashioned femininity. She looked up to him and made him feel just as successful as he hoped someday to become. To him, they seemed the perfect match. She never revealed the conflicts and insecurities within her, and he never suspected them. He was delighted and flattered when she asked him to come home.

At first, the homecoming was exactly as she'd hoped. Dwight was charming. Her parents were charmed. They marveled at her "good fortune" in finding this remarkable man. Her mother fawned over him. Her father engaged him in a long discussion of Yale's curriculum past and present. But as the weekend dragged on, Dwight attracted more and more of the spotlight and seemed to be enjoying it. He spent hours playing touch football on the lawn with her brothers and soon began teasing her with all the "little Rita" jokes she'd despised from youth. He sat talking with her family after dinner while she retreated to the kitchen to do the dishes. By Sunday morning they were all so preoccupied with each other that no one even noticed Rita's absence at breakfast. She had gone for a long walk to sort out her feelings of jealousy and resentment. By the time she returned, she recognized that she'd been trying to use Dwight to resolve problems that had nothing to do with him. She knew that his presence wouldn't make her any less of a misfit in her family. If this weekend was any indication, it probably would do just the opposite. Being with him didn't at all improve how the others treated her, and because he was so confident and outgoing, by contrast she felt even more shy and self-conscious than usual. To make matters worse, he was oblivious to her feelings.

After the weekend was finally over, Rita wanted to break up with Dwight but lacked the courage. She would have to face her parents' wrath if she did. She could just hear her mother saying, "You'll learn to love him," and her father, deprecatingly, "This is the best chance you're ever going to get, Little Sister. Don't blow it." They wouldn't care why Rita had made this decision, any more than they'd questioned why she was with Dwight in the first place.

She tried to express her feelings to Dwight, but the words stuck in her throat. He thought her family was marvelous. He thought it was cute how everyone treated her like a little girl. He would never understand how repressed and misunderstood she felt. And how could she blame him? He was with her because he assumed she was as happy, healthy, and well adjusted as she pretended to be. Instead of accepting and cherishing her for her true self, as she somehow had deluded herself that he would, he seemed to be demanding an extra layer of pretense to satisfy his standards on top of her family's. Rita had put up an extremely enticing front, and Dwight had fallen for it. Now, though, the pressure was too much for her, and she knew that, with all his other commitments, there was no room in his life for her imperfections.

So instead of leaving him directly she had an affair with her hairdresser, a man who knew nothing about her family, cared nothing about her past, and thought her every bit as worldly as her family wanted her to be. He actually looked up to her! This relationship was based just as much on illusion as her relationship with Dwight had been, except that the illusions were slightly different. She had hoped Dwight's self-esteem would rub off on her. Now she hoped this man could draw out what self-esteem she possessed herself. Neither effort succeeded. She quickly became uncomfortable with what she viewed as undeserved adulation in her affair. Then Dwight found out about the affair and refused to tolerate her infidelity. Her parents, when they heard, were outraged, mystified, and unforgiving. They suggested she get therapy to "fix whatever's wrong."

Recognizing that she did need outside help, Rita followed their advice. Her family wasn't thrilled with the results, but in time Rita learned to stand up to her parents and began to develop self-respect. She also stopped trying to use men to redress the pain and confusion of her childhood. She had to deal with her family separately and on her own terms. If, in the process, she chose a man who displeased them, she would survive.

Sometimes, of course, your family won't be at all impressed by the candidates you bring home. They may openly object or simply remain neutral. Either way, if you desperately want your parents' approval, this rejection can be devastating. It tells you that you've "failed" again, and it may intensify your self-doubt, making you even less sure of yourself with your next partner. You might keep trying to please your family until you hit the mark, although, like Rita, you must face the fact that this may buy you nothing. Alternatively, you can quit worrying about pleasing your family and concentrate on finding a partner you can truly love. This may be very difficult, however, if you have a deeply troubled family history. In this case, you might want to get professional help to resolve your family problems *before* you attempt true love.

Even in healthy families, parental rejection of a new partner can be confusing and hurtful. If you trust your parents, you may assume that they know more than you do. They know you better than anyone else, after all, and maybe they're in a better position than you to judge who's right or wrong for you. Yet if they are right in rejecting your latest romantic interest, that means you are wrong — a fact that is bound to bring your own uncertainties and ambivalences to the surface and may ruin what until this point seemed a promising relationship. If it doesn't, it may make you angry with your parents and may make them disappointed in you. These reactions might not fade until the relationship either disintegrates or proves itself over a number of years.

Not everyone is so eager to please, of course, and many, like Alan, use romance as a form of rebellion against family constraints. This is not necessarily a sign of weakness or low self-esteem, but of misplaced objectives. True love is no more a tool of defiance than it is bait for parental validation. You may love a person your parents can't accept, but when you choose a partner for the sole purpose of antagonizing your family, that's no basis for love. Even Romeo and Juliet are suspect. As teenagers from warring families, did they profess love for each other in spite of their families — or to spite their families? The fact that they died in each other's arms did not make their love true.

People often use the most superficial criteria when choosing a partner to spite their parents. His family is rich, so he marries a girl from the slums. Her family is white and bigoted, so she marries a black man. The chances of such marriages surviving are slim. Sometimes, the spirit of rebellion is so strong that the couple genuinely believe they love each other, but what they're mistaking for love is often the excitement of challenging the odds. This may last for several years, as long as the opposition is strong. But eventually families, friends, and neighbors lose interest, perhaps even accept their choice, and the couple must face how little substance there is between them. As the external resistance fades, so does their interest in staying together.

Defiant romance is a reaction to unresolved anger and frustration. Alan had never forgiven his father for dying too young and used his romantic escapades with non-Jewish women to try to get revenge. If his anger had run deeper, for example, if he'd been abused as a child, he might have taken up with women who were even more unacceptable to his family. Sometimes rage creates a desire to punish the family at any price, even if it means sacrificing one's own happiness, health, and even life. Therapy can interrupt this spiral and separate the processes of love and recovery, but true love alone cannot repair such rage.

Completing the Transition

Succeeding on your own at any age gives you the security of knowing that you can survive independently and that you need not fear solitude, even if you dislike it. If you have never allowed yourself the chance to try single living before getting heavily involved in a relationship, you may have difficulty accepting love as a choice and maintaining the degree of individuality needed to make it work. Instead, having a relationship may seem a necessity, a direct replacement for the protection and security your family provided you in childhood. If your relationship is based on this kind of underlying need, you may go to desperate lengths to preserve it, even if it causes you unresolvable pain and disappointment or dominates your identity. While the autonomy you gain through separating from your parents and living for a while as a single person by no means guarantees your romantic success, at least it can help you to see love as an asset to a much broader existence, rather than a key dependency.

Independence can change other attitudes about love as well. Away from your family, you can escape many of the roles that dogged you in youth. You can wipe the slate clean and start anew, but in a different, more mature context and on your own terms. As you look ahead to your future goals, you may adjust the qualifications you seek in a partner. Perhaps you'll stop asking what others will think of you if you date a certain person and begin asking what *you* think of that person. Perhaps the chase will seem less entertaining and the prospect of actually being in love more attractive. Perhaps you will see that love requires work as well as magic. If so, you're on the right track and may already have fended off many of false love's illusions quite successfully.

Now, as you read this, you may have a partner with whom you're attempting to build true love. Having disentangled the sources of your illusions and survived the search, the next challenge is loving.

PART III
REALITY AND ROMANCE

10

CHOOSING LOVE

"I THINK I WANT to settle down and get married, but I'm not making any progress." He stopped abruptly, and then, as if suddenly embarrassed to find himself with a psychologist, announced, "Everything else in my life is perfect. There's just this one problem, but it's really starting to bother me. I need to figure out what's going on."

I knew, without his telling me, that Jason's problem was *not* a lack of willing women. At thirty-eight, he had thick, dark hair that was carefully styled, a great tan, and a better physique than most twenty-year-olds. His clothes were well chosen, and his car, parked outside, was a triple black Mercedes convertible. If he was not one of the most successful and refined bachelors in town, he was putting on a very convincing act.

"I've always had my pick of women," he continued, as if reading my thoughts. "You might say I've been the quintessential playboy. But after twenty years of one-night stands, I feel like I need something more in a relationship. Trouble is, I don't know where to begin. Even choosing a woman seems impossible. I find something wrong with all of them."

Jason's romantic history was the classic male fantasy. He'd had a gift for sweet talk ever since he was a boy, and when adolescence had graced him with good looks as well, he discovered that women would fight for his attentions. He took full advantage of the situation, dating a different girl every weekend, but always kept the relationships casual and noncommittal. While he enjoyed women tremendously, he had little desire as a young man to spend more than a few days — a couple of weeks at the most — with any one partner. It was too exciting to be with a variety of women. In any case, his plans first to become a doctor and then a plastic surgeon ruled out a more serious commitment until he was established in practice. But once Jason had realized his professional ambitions, the level of temptation increased rather than decreased. His clientele were beautiful women, single and married, who became infatuated with Jason because he made them even more beautiful. He felt like a child in a candy shop, terrified that if he committed to one selection he'd be passing up something better. Instead, he felt compelled to try as many as possible.

Jason recalled that his dates often would tell him he was afraid of getting involved, that intimacy scared him. He never doubted the sincerity of these comments, only their accuracy. As far as he was concerned during his twenties and early thirties, dating was for fun. He never wanted for company, yet he had his freedom and never had to explain or apologize to anyone if he just wanted to go fishing with his male friends for a few days. Bewildered by his friends who chose to marry young and start families, Jason warned them that they'd be cheating on their wives before the first year was up. He really was telling them why *he* didn't feel ready to marry. There had been several women who seemed to "have it all," but Jason always seemed to lose interest in the relationship after one or two weeks. The women remained as attractive to him as ever, but he would feel confined by the situation. It was as if his freewheeling lifestyle and the constant ego gratification of having a new woman at all times were holding him hostage.

"If you've been this satisfied with your life as a bachelor," I asked him, "why are you thinking about settling down *now*? What's changed?"

"I guess part of it is that I'm just getting tired," he said, shrugging. "I don't need the constant stroking any more, at least not the kind of superficial stroking you get from someone you barely know. Although I have dated literally hundreds of women and slept with most of them, I've never been truly intimate with anyone. Every time my birthday comes around, I'm with a different woman. I never take a vacation with the same woman twice. I don't honestly *share* my life with anyone. When I receive a special honor for my work, for example, I get a lot of compliments, but no one really shares my pride or my pleasure the way I imagine a wife would. And, of course, I've never shared anyone else's accomplishments in that way either."

"You think part of it might be that you're getting older?" I suggested.

"Definitely. Although I've enjoyed being with lots of different women up to now, I don't want to become one of those middle-aged skirt chasers. I would much rather spend the rest of my years with one woman and maybe have a family."

"Even if it means adjusting your fishing plans?" I tested him.

"Well . . . any woman I married would have to be understanding about certain things!" he said with a laugh.

"You talk a good line, but you haven't convinced me that you *really* want to settle down. I don't think you've even convinced yourself. Tell me what's getting in your way."

"This is very hard for me to admit, but I don't really know how to function in a relationship."

It seemed that Jason was just coming out of a three-week relationship with a young woman he'd met on an airplane. Elizabeth had all the qualities he thought he admired. She was well educated and energetic — a vibrant redhead with great style and an independent career. Having recently decided to initiate his search for a wife, Jason wooed her aggressively. He persuaded her first to have lunch, then dinner, and, a few dinners later, a weekend in the mountains with him. Although he'd known women who were both more attractive and more intellectual, he tried not to compare her with anyone. As long as he succeeded in this effort, he felt that she'd captured his heart. Whenever he let those comparisons creep up on him, however, he couldn't help wondering if he might find someone "better" if he gave himself more time.

His doubts were exacerbated every time they disagreed. Jason had never bothered getting into meaningful arguments or working out compromise solutions to problems with his past girlfriends because it seemed so much easier just to back off when a relationship became tense. He now realized that this had become his automatic response to conflict of any kind. Though he wanted to work through the problems with Elizabeth, he didn't know how. Instead, he would either rage or sulk. If this were true love, he thought, there would be no disputes — but in his heart, he knew this was just an excuse for his own shortcomings. After each argument, he would apologize and promise to change.

At first Elizabeth was understanding, even quite touched by this image of the Don Juan who had never learned how to love. In her thirty-one years she'd known many men and had had several long-term, live-in relationships, but she'd rarely dated men as successful or handsome as Jason, and she'd *never* had a man profess such anxious, eager intentions for her. The thought that this prime bachelor was trying to remake himself out of love for her was extremely seductive and gave her ego precisely the same boost all those willing women had given Jason's. However, Elizabeth's ego was already quite secure, and his promises went only so far with her. She quickly saw beyond what Jason was saying and began to concentrate on what he was doing within the relationship. She was patient up to a point, but when his apologies kept repeating themselves without leading to any substantive change, she had had enough. While Jason claimed to share all her major life goals —

marriage, a family, an active athletic lifestyle, and a successful career — and her basic attitudes about religion, politics, culture, and the like, he clearly lacked the skills to hold up his end within a loving, intimate relationship. From where she sat, it was impossible to tell whether he was even capable of developing these skills, and she'd been disappointed by too many immature men before to risk another heartbreak with Jason.

When Elizabeth broke up with him, Jason realized for the first time that just wanting to be in love was not enough to bring him love. The shock of losing her was more than just a jolt to his ego. It made him reevaluate what this relationship meant to him. In her absence, he forced himself to face and accept the fact that she was not perfect and that no one could ever meet his standards for perfection. He also realized that perhaps *he* was the most flawed of all. He desperately wanted Elizabeth back, but he knew he had to inspect his own behavior and make some serious changes before he stood a chance. This became his major goal in therapy.

Comparing the way Jason managed his surgical practice and his behavior within his romantic relationships, I could see that he had difficulty relinquishing control. Subconsciously, he expected his dates to look up to him and follow his orders just as the nurses and assistants in his office did. When the women in his relationships challenged him, he felt that his authority was being questioned and he couldn't stand that. This impulse extended even to minor disputes over what wine to order at dinner or what movie he and his date would see. When a woman refused to accept his decisions in the past, he would stop dating her. In love, he came to realize, he would have to learn how to surrender control in exchange for compromise.

To his employees' and partners' astonishment, he began testing this new approach at work. To *his* astonishment, the result was a dramatic increase in efficiency and productivity. The people around him had many extremely valuable insights that they were eager to contribute if only he was willing to listen. When he approached them as a fellow member of the team rather than as a benevolent dictator, he discovered, they were far more forthcoming and honest. For the first time, they seemed to genuinely enjoy working with him, and as they came to trust that the change in him was real, he could feel the defensiveness melting on both sides. He learned to accept that he was sometimes wrong, and he discovered that compromising could be relatively painless. It was not easy to change such a deep, lifelong pattern, but Jason soon realized that the rewards were well worth the effort.

His plan was to work through these changes in therapy and in his professional life before returning to Elizabeth and requesting another chance. While Jason couldn't stop thinking about her, he was afraid of "failing" again if he tried before he was fully prepared. It took time to persuade him that this was not a pass-fail proposition, but a mutual effort that he and Elizabeth would have to share. Learning to surrender some of his passion for control was important, but it was only the beginning. The trust, compassion, devotion, and intimacy that make love so rewarding would come only if he and Elizabeth worked together to forge a lasting relationship.

Elizabeth was suspicious at first. She doubted that Jason could possibly have achieved such a critical change in attitude. But her affection for him and her own desire for true love pushed her to see him again. She was impressed by the obvious effort he had made *and* by the increased gentleness and openness it had produced in him. He was more relaxed and much more accessible than before. They still had the inevitable collisions of opinion from time to time, but it was clear now that he respected her right to a vote as well as his own.

Jason and Elizabeth were married eighteen months after they began dating again. It was not the ideal marriage he had imagined as a bachelor. He found many faults in Elizabeth, and she pointed out many in him. She was not always obliging when he wanted to go fishing. And sex was not always as thrilling as it had been when he had a new woman to explore each night. But on a deeper level, they made each other feel happier and more fulfilled than either one had ever felt while single. They had a future together. They were creating true love.

This couple's marriage succeeded — and is still thriving after seven years — not simply because of Jason's actions or because of the striking attraction between them. It succeeded because *both* were prepared to choose love, and *together* they had the foundation for a secure, rewarding marriage.

Establishing the Foundation for Love

How can you tell if you and your partner are ready to choose true love? It involves much more than simply wanting a fulfilling relationship; it requires *mutual* commitment. But there are two kinds of commitment. You both may be committed to having a relationship. You both may be committed to your affection for each other. Alone, neither of these commitments is enough to sustain true love. Each of you needs to be ready and willing to take on the responsibility of a mature relationship in general and of this one in particular.

If your partner is perfect for you in all other ways but refuses to enter a permanent relationship, there's no foundation for love. Loving someone is a voluntary but requited act — you cannot love someone who refuses to love you. You may feel an attraction or need for that person, but that's not the same as love. Only when the commitment flows both ways can a relationship survive and grow. Love without sharing and unity is false love.

To be sure that you and your partner are ready for *mature* love and will not get sidetracked by the illusions of false love, ask the following questions of each other.

• Are you old enough, and is your life stable enough? You need strength to handle the responsibilities of a relationship without withdrawing every time difficulties arise. One of the reasons that couples who marry during high school or college so often pull apart is that their personalities and egos are still developing and are constantly changing during these times. They do not have the secure foundation they need as individuals to understand and meet the demands of marriage.

For the same reason, it's a mistake to begin a serious relationship when you are not feeling and behaving normally, even though you may *want* a relationship most when your life is off balance. Under these circumstances your new partner sees only the unhealthy side of you, which sets you up for an essentially unhealthy relationship, with one person as the "rescuer" and the other as the "victim." And when you're feeling rejected or needy, even if you're not normally a dependent person, it's easy to misread a new partner. If the replacement relationship lifts your spirits, you may mistake your gratitude for love.

While the drama of personal struggle may be compelling for a while, almost no one can stand the pressure cooker of continual turmoil. We all need the relief that joyousness, relaxation, and a sense of humor bring, and we look to love to provide this kind of pleasure during the good times as well as spiritual support during the hard times. Without a healthy balance in your life, you can hardly expect to achieve a healthy balance in love.

• Have you dated a broad enough mix of individuals to satisfy your sexual curiosity and ego? True love is monogamous and permanent. Therefore, the time to experiment with a variety of different romantic partners is while you are unattached. The more assured you are that members of the opposite sex find you attractive while you are single, the less tempted you'll be by their advances after you commit to your partner. Also, there's nothing like experience to teach you what you're *not* looking for in a partner as well as what qualities you value. The more you have dated, the more confident you'll be when you finally select a permanent mate.

• Are you able to present yourself as you are, not as you wish your partner to see you? Creating a false image of yourself almost inevitably will damage your relationship in the long run. Even if your intentions are good — because you want to hide character traits that you dislike in yourself or because you want to avoid conflict — you can't keep up the act indefinitely, and when the truth comes out your partner may feel hurt and resentful at having been deceived. The revelation will also unleash understandable questions about your self-esteem, honesty, and sincerity. You cannot expect your partner to love you without knowing who you are.

- Are you ready to be an equal partner in a relationship? This was the area where Jason needed to mature. Being a partner means being able to surrender control at times. It means being able to be flexible in your own needs and desires for the sake of the other person or the relationship. It means being able to compromise and sometimes even admit that you're wrong. Being an equal partner requires that you give as freely and with as much pleasure as you take.

- Are you prepared to fight for the relationship? True love is not perfectly serene. No matter how devoted you and your partner may be to each other, you sometimes will disagree, you will face problems and difficult decisions about your life together, and you will have to fend off the illusions of false love that inevitably will beckon from time to time. You must be willing to defend what you believe is best for your relationship, even if it sometimes means compromising your own individual interests or impulses.

- Are you willing and able to keep sexuality in perspective so that you can take the relationship past infatuation? The sexual lust that fuels infatuation is extremely compelling, and when it recedes, as it inevitably does from time to time in every long-term relationship, the letdown can be confusing and disappointing. As long as you need the perpetual sexual excitement of infatuation, you will remain vulnerable to false love. Only when you accept sexual intimacy as a fulfilling part, rather than the sole focus, of the relationship can you be comfortable with the ups and downs of sexual desire in true love.

Once you've determined that you and your partner both are prepared to accept the general conditions of true love, you need to make sure the underlying bonds are there to hold the two of you personally together as a couple. These strengths will form the foundation for your love, sustaining and supporting your relationship through the challenges to come. They fall into the following eight general categories:

1. Physical attraction and sexual compatibility. The attraction need not be instantaneous or electric. With many loving couples, it builds gradually and gently, sometimes taking years to fully ripen. All that's really required in the beginning is some attraction, mutual openness, affection, and desire for intimacy.

2. Shared goals, interests, and belief systems. Primary among these must be the goal of developing a truly loving relationship *with each other*. You also need absolute agreement about the choice to have or not have children, attitudes about raising children, lifestyle preferences, and career priorities. Couples with similar religious, ethnic, and political beliefs tend to be more united than those with disparate backgrounds, but differences can be overcome if the mesh of goals and other interests is strong. More superficial interests, such as a mutual passion for jazz, tennis, Hemingway, or ballet, can make a relationship more entertaining but are not necessarily vital.

3. Mutual respect, acceptance, and the desire to please each other. In relationships based on false love, these attitudes often flow from one partner only. The wife may honor and obey her husband, for example, while he treats her with scorn. In true love, there must be balance, and both partners must accept the responsibility of living up to each other's expectations.

4. Mutual honesty and trust. Deceit has no place in true love. It breeds mistrust and division. At the outset, you and your partner must be truthful, both with yourselves and with each other.

5. Realistic expectations for each other and the relationship. Your expectations should be based both on the requirements for true love and on your individual personalities and needs. Discuss them openly, recognizing that some are non-negotiable while others need to remain flexible. The basic rules of love — fidelity, honesty, commitment, and intimacy — cannot be compromised; if either of you is unable to meet these conditions, you are not ready for true love. Expectations regarding patience, humor, habit, sociability, and other specific personality traits must be tailored to the individual. If your partner is quiet and shy, don't expect to change him into a gregarious socialite. On the other hand, don't expect him to always remain precisely the same. There must be room in your relationship for both of you to grow, and growth inevitably means change. If your expectations of each other are too rigid, you will stifle each other and jeopardize your love.

6. A balance of dependence and independence. True love requires the connection, but not the submersion, of two individuals. Mature lovers do not merge completely, as obsessive couples do, nor do they remain essentially disconnected. Rather, they interlock, so that a portion of their lives and identities become shared. In diagram form, the three possibilities look like this:

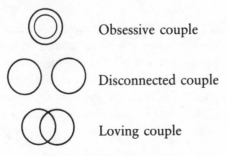

Obsessive couple

Disconnected couple

Loving couple

To succeed in love, you and your partner must be able to rely on each other for comfort and support without expecting *all* your needs to be met within the relationship. Part of your life must remain separate. You need some friends, activities, and interests that your partner does not share. In addition to the personal benefits you derive from these outside sources, they provide ideas, energy, and information that you bring back to keep the relationship opening up and developing.

7. A cooperative approach to problems. Conflict and struggle are intrinsic to life and therefore also to love. You and your partner must accept this fact from the outset and figure out how you will deal with problems when they arise. Ideally, the process of working through difficulties should help you understand each other better and, ultimately, bring you closer together.

8. A shared life. True love does not occur spontaneously, and it does not develop overnight. For most of us, it takes years to reach fruition, and the simple experience of *being* together as a couple becomes a major source of cohesion. Facades fade away as the layers of defenses diminish. Through the routine of daily life, you and your partner come to know each other's secret yearnings and subtle talents, discover and meld to each other's inner rhythms, and realize the kind of joy that comes not from laughter or pride but from the lasting unity of love.

The 90:10 Rule

Theoretically, if you and your partner meet these eight criteria, you should feel no hesitation about committing to each other. In reality, though, even if all the essentials are there, one or both of you still may suffer from precommitment jitters. Usually, it's because you focus on the qualities that your partner lacks. The most insignificant blemishes become magnified under your scrutiny, shaking your desire and your confidence in the relationship. When this happens, remember the 90:10 rule: If your partner meets 90 percent of your requirements for love — and that must include *all* the key characteristics described in the last section — don't let the missing 10 percent sabotage your relationship.

The 90:10 rule prevented Felicia from throwing away an opportunity for love that ultimately ended in a very successful marriage. At twenty-eight, she was a rather plain but noble-looking young woman with a strong commitment to her career as a social worker and an infectious enthusiasm for life. She could make another person feel comfortable almost immediately and never seemed to have difficulty starting or sustaining a lively conversation. Men were magnetized by her unpretentious self-confidence.

It was Felicia's choices in men that had thwarted her in the past. Because she was blinded by the illusions they projected, she generally had selected men who were very charismatic but selfish and either emotionally insensitive or too needy. She already had spent several years in therapy working through the mistakes that had plagued her past affairs. Now she made a conscious effort to look past the veneer in potential partners to find the personality and temperament within. She no longer mistook infatuation for love; she wasn't seduced by wealth or glamour; she understood that it requires more reciprocal effort than magic to make a relationship work. Her vision was clear, her motivation strong. She was ready, she thought, for a mature and lasting love.

Her efforts paid off when she met Bart. There was no immediate physical attraction, but the emotional rapport was instantaneous. He had an easy laugh and a ready smile, and as he talked he used his entire body, moving fluidly, to draw Felicia in and hold her, riveted. She was amazed by the candor with which he confided his personal losses and disappointments as well as his successes, which included the creation of a nonprofit foundation for environmental protection. The eagerness with which he described his plans for the future made Felicia feel that she'd found a kindred spirit. They spent their first few dates talking until dawn, sharing their dreams, hopes, fears, and uncertainties.

Bart had a similar response to Felicia. At first glance, he'd dismissed her because she had too much bosom, too little waist, and was a little too dark for his liking. There was something about her that drew him back, however. He had rarely seen a woman with such natural vibrancy, and when they struck up their first conversation, he felt that they were in stride with each other.

Before they even shared their first kiss, they'd discussed each other's religious practices, political beliefs, family history, literary and film preferences, career goals, and lifestyle choices. They differed enough to have a few spritely arguments on their early dates, but on the core issues they were together. As this realization dawned on them, their physical attraction ignited. What had started as a comfortable friendship suddenly opened up into a rich romance. By the fifth date, as they sat in an open-air amphitheater listening to the city philharmonic play Vivaldi, both were privately contemplating marriage.

And then it happened. They were dining one evening not long afterward, and Felicia became tangled in what seemed an unending web of Bart's "failings." First, there was his left profile. From where she was seated, she could see how thin his hair was on this side. Soon he would start to grow bald — and in a rather lopsided fashion. That would accentuate his ears, which were unusually large and rather strangely shaped. Then she noticed how his Adam's apple bobbed each time he swallowed, like a golf ball rising and falling in his throat. And he had the irritating habit of replacing his used fork on his placemat instead of resting it on his plate. These were the kinds of things that would send her screaming out of the room after they'd been married awhile, she imagined. These were the kinds of things that would make living together unbearable. Long after Bart, unsuspecting, had left her apartment that night, Felicia still was dwelling on these "failings."

The next day, in therapy, she confessed her misgivings, and we discussed the 90:10 rule. We started by listing the qualities that were essential for true love. Bart seemed to have all the necessary individual traits, and their relationship, until last night, had seemed primed for true love. Even now, the only missing element was Felicia's commitment.

Next we ran through the incidental characteristics Felicia found desirable in Bart. Her list included all the idiosyncrasies that endeared him to her, such as the way he told a story, his love of gardening, his rather old-fashioned style of dress, and the cornflower blue of his eyes.

Finally, we turned to the qualities that had trapped her the night before and struggled to see if she could come up with other complaints. She was able to add a few, but when she compared these shortcomings with all his virtues, she quickly saw the madness of her struggle. Imagine what she would find if she subjected *herself* to this kind of analysis! The only possible outcome of such intensive scrutiny would be a life devoid of love.

While Bart, on the other hand, was aware of Felicia's frailties, he didn't go through the same kind of agonizing. He understood the wisdom of the 90:10 rule intuitively and felt confident that the ratio was strong enough to support his ardor. Although they were not officially engaged until they'd been dating for nearly a year, his desire to have her as his wife never wavered after that evening under the stars. On her wedding day, and on many another day in the following years, Felicia silently thanked the 90:10 rule for saving her from one of the biggest mistakes of her life.

Going Home

"You do understand that my parents are a little different?" Scott asked, nervously clutching the steering wheel. "They're not like me."

"I know, I know," Dale retorted. "Your father was a fighter pilot and your mother was a nightclub dancer. Beyond the history, how different can they be? They're your parents. That's all I need to know. The real question is, what if they hate me?"

"They're not going to hate you," Scott replied. "They may think you're too good for me, but they're not going to hate you!" Already the anxiety level was creeping up, and they hadn't even arrived.

"If we'd met each other's parents a year ago it wouldn't have been so frightening," she continued. "Now I feel as if my entire future is in their hands."

"Look," he said, stopping the car before pulling into the driveway. "I love you, no matter what they say. Think of this as a courtesy call. A necessary formality. If you all like each other, fine. If not, it won't make any difference in our relationship."

Dale nodded, but she knew that was rubbish. If she and his parents didn't like each other it could eventually become a serious obstacle to the relationship. Scott might be able to persuade himself that he didn't care, but he couldn't fool her.

The house was pretty much what she'd expected — a typical midwestern tract home with a postage stamp yard and a two-car garage, in front of which two elderly American cars were parked. Scott's parents, however, were nothing like she'd imagined them.

His mother, who rushed out before they were parked, was wearing white, tasseled cowboy boots, tight white stretch pants, and a snug pink sweatshirt. She engulfed Scott as he stepped from the car and, for several long seconds, bemoaned how thin he looked and how long it had been since he'd been home.

Scott made the introductions as they entered the house. "Gil, Gil!" Maureen interrupted, calling for Scott's father. "Come see Scott and meet his *girlfriend!*" In the living room, Gil looked up from his newspaper. Dale made a mental note of the plastic sheeting on the sofa.

"How are you, son?" Gil called, ambling toward them. "Good to meet you, young lady." He grinned and then fixed her with an eagle eye. "You going to marry my boy?" Dale glanced at Scott, speechless.

"Oh, Gil!" Maureen exclaimed breathlessly. "You're embarrassing both of them! Hush now!"

"It's nice to meet you both," Dale said stupidly, unable to think of anything more appropriate. After a beat, she extended her hand to Scott's father. He grabbed it enthusiastically.

"Come sit down and tell me about yourself," he said. Dale sent Scott a look that said, "Please don't leave me here alone!" but Maureen was already whisking him off to the kitchen.

Scott had warned her that his father was a character and his mother was a little clutchy, but she had never guessed they could be this different from their son. Scott was a college-educated stockbroker who went to the ballet and art museums. He collected Oriental antiques and had traveled throughout Europe and Asia. His parents were from another world entirely.

Gil spent the next half hour telling Dale war stories about Korea, leading up to the revelation that he had met Maureen at the USO there. She'd been a dancer. They were married the week he got home and Scott was born nine months later. It was the best decision he'd ever made, he informed her, and he hoped Dale would be as good for Scott as Maureen was for him.

While Gil was talking, Dale wondered what kind of a childhood could have allowed Scott — or pushed him — to make such drastic changes in lifestyle after leaving home. Then again, what if he was *not* as discriminating as he appeared? What if it was all an act, and his idea of a cozy home was just like this — furniture draped in splash guards, shelves overflowing with souvenirs from Disneyland. . . . Her throat locked at the thought.

Maureen called everyone in to lunch. In the center of the table was a large casserole filled with macaroni and cheese. The glasses contained milk. "Scott's favorite menu!" Maureen chirped. Funny, thought Dale, he never told me.

She swallowed a bite or two. Fortunately, Maureen kept her busy answering questions about her own family. No, she wasn't an only child. She had a brother and a sister. No, she didn't come from near here. She'd grown up in Seattle. Yes, she had a job as a law clerk, and yes, she had finished law school and passed the bar.

"I think it's just wonderful for young girls to have a job when they're starting out," said Maureen, her singsong voice rising and falling. "It's such a help to a husband. I worked when we were young. Of course, I quit the minute I knew Scott was on the way." She threw Dale a challenging glance.

"We've talked about that, and Scott and I both agree that I'd keep on working whether or not we had children." Dale hadn't meant to play into Maureen's hands this way, but she just couldn't restrain herself. She wasn't about to let this woman dictate her life on the very first meeting.

Maureen pounced immediately. "So you *are* engaged! And this is how we find out!" she cried.

"Mother," cried Scott, clearly exasperated. "It was only speculation. We're considering the possibility. We're not *planning* anything yet!" He was trying not to look at Dale, but she could tell he was furious with her.

"Well, I think it's a great idea," cut in Gil. "You'd better see what Scotty was like as a little guy before you decide to tie the knot."

Pushing back from the table, he led Dale back into the living room and presented her with several family albums. While Scott tried to reassure his mother that they weren't planning to elope, Gil provided Dale with a running commentary on the most intimate moments of her lover's early life. She saw the requisite bearskin rug photos, pictures of him sucking his thumb and dragging a blanket. She heard how he wet his bed for three years and how they had to call the fire department to get him down from a tree in the school yard when he was eight. Humiliated as she was for Scott, Dale was more than a little amused to see this side of his past. She was in love with a thumbsucker, a tree climber, and a macaroni fanatic!

By the time they finished with the albums, Scott had persuaded his mother to apologize to Dale. "I didn't mean to offend you," she said. "It's just that Scott's my only baby, and it's hard for me to turn him over to another woman."

"I can imagine," said Dale. In fact, she wasn't sure she would handle it much better if she were in Maureen's shoes. Differently, no doubt, but not necessarily better.

"I hope we'll have a chance to get to know each other better before you young folks do decide to set a date," Maureen said graciously.

"I'm sure we will," Dale assured her, taking her hands.

On the ride back to the city, Dale prodded, "Why didn't you ever tell me your parents were like that?"

"I warned you they weren't like me."

"To put it mildly! I'd never guess in a million years that they were your parents."

"Well," he said, grinning, "I can hardly wait to meet *your* family!"

There comes a time in almost every long-term romance when you and your partner will meet each other's families. This can be an important milestone in the relationship. It may happen early on, or you may postpone the encounter as long as possible — perhaps even for years — but generally the sooner the meeting takes place, the easier it is for all involved. When the relationship is just beginning, both your parents and your lover are curious about each other, but not especially nervous. If they don't like each other, they can reassure themselves that the relationship is uncertain. There's plenty of time yet for re-evaluation. The longer you've been dating, however, the more "serious" it is considered, and the graver the consequences if the two sides don't like each other. For a father, meeting his daughter's boyfriend of two weeks is a minor event, but meeting the man she's been living with for four years is like being introduced to his son-in-law after the wedding.

Though you may feign nonchalance, you probably care very much what your family thinks of your lover and vice versa. No matter how independent, self-confident, and well adjusted you may be, the day you bring a new partner home to "meet the folks" is almost always fraught with tension — and because you're caught in the middle, you'll probably feel it far more than your partner or the family. Your beloved is passing judgment on them, and they are passing judgment in return — but both judgments reflect on you.

However much you may wish for mutual admiration, it's extremely unlikely that the two will hit it off perfectly. Usually, either the lover thinks the family is odd or distasteful, or the family thinks the lover is inappropriate. Or they both simply dislike each other. Your reaction may be to grin and bear it at first, but if the friction continues, you'll become defensive. You may resent your partner's criticism of your family just as much as you do your family's objections to your relationship. And even if they all do like each other, you may feel left out and become defensive about that!

Meeting the other family can be just as anxiety-provoking, but it's usually a great deal more interesting. For one thing, your partner's tribe is an unknown commodity. No matter how much you may have heard about them, they are unlikely to conform to your expectations. Even if you never want to see them again, you probably will be glad to have satisfied your curiosity.

Another benefit to meeting the other family is that it provides new insights into your partner. As Dale discovered, family members are often very forthcoming about a son's or daughter's early years. Even more important, the family dynamics and personalities of parents and siblings will often reflect behaviors and attitudes you may have overlooked in your partner. The adages "Like father, like son" and "Like mother, like daughter" are truer than most of us would like to believe.

The danger is in placing too much importance on the family. Some people are more interested in the family than in the partner. For example, an only child from a strait-laced aristocratic family may long to be part of a large family that expresses love openly and warmly. Someone from a poor background may be attracted to a partner whose father is rich and powerful. Someone whose parents are illiterate may be impressed by highly intellectual families. But the idea that you can make up for all you missed in your own childhood by being "adopted" into this family fold is an illusion — and it's not fair to use your partner this way. Even if you marry into the family of your desire, you will remain somewhat of an outsider. You won't be able to remake your childhood or substitute this family for your own.

To judge a partner too harshly on the basis of family appearances is also a mistake. Many people escape appalling childhoods to become fine, honorable individuals. While it's useful to understand a partner's past, it is not fair to use his or her family as a strict yardstick of character. Nor is it wise to seriously criticize your partner's family based on a superficial meeting. No matter how unacceptable they may seem or how different your partner may seem from his or her kin, within the fold are certain loyalties that no outsider can possibly penetrate. If you try to mess with those allegiances, you're likely to receive a stinging rebuke. Love does not give you license to attack the other family unless there is cause for serious concern. If there *are* severe problems — for example, if one parent is truly dangerous or disturbed — you must consider how the situation will affect your future relationship and decide whether you are willing to accept this added burden.

While it's true that you and your partner are, in a sense, interviewing members of your future families on these first meetings, it's important to remember that you do not have to adopt their way of life or yield to their opinions. Ideally, as your relationship matures, you will create your own standards and lifestyle. It will be more pleasant if you are able to establish a warm connection with both sides of the family, but your success as a couple does not depend on it.

To Marry or Not to Marry

Once you and your partner have made the commitment to love each other, the next natural question is whether to marry. Prior to the 1960s, very few unmarried couples openly lived together. If you were in love and wanted to spend your life together, it was assumed that you'd marry. By the mid-1970s, however, it was common even for couples who made no pretense of true love to live together. To share a home — and presumably unrestricted sex — was considered by many the only sensible way to test the viability of a relationship. Today, the pendulum seems to be swinging back to the center. Marriage is back, and some of the pitfalls as well as the benefits of living together have been exposed. In the current climate, you have the opportunity to consider all sides pragmatically, with relatively little societal pressure, before deciding what's best for your relationship.

While there is no significant difference between divorce rates for couples who marry before living together and for those who live together first, the data are somewhat deceptive. There are not many statistics for the couples who live together and then break up without marrying or for those who remain together without ever marrying. In fact, logic strongly suggests that the trend toward living together has prevented far more divorces than it's created.

The most obvious benefit of living together is that you have more time to spend with your lover and on a more natural basis than you ever have when dating. You discover the full spectrum of each other's habits and moods as you test your compatibility on a purely practical level. Creating this "fit" in the context of daily life is essential to your success as lovers, and it makes sense to start before you become husband and wife.

The most common complaint about living together is that it detracts from the mystery and romance of new love and makes marriage less meaningful. Once you've lived together, the honeymoon is more of a vacation than a new beginning. This is a valid argument only if you and your partner are absolutely certain that you share true love and are realistic about the changes that will occur as you adjust to daily life together. However, until you *have* lived together you may not really know each other well enough to make an informed commitment. While the ethereal considerations that dominate early romance are important, most of the energy you'll expend in a long-term live-in relationship, whether married or unmarried, will focus on the mundane.

The most compelling argument against living together is that it is a very convenient stalling maneuver for someone who is feigning true love. Ideally, once you understand and accept the concept of true versus false love, you will be immune to partners who themselves are susceptible to illusions and who may profess commitment to you without realistically understanding the dynamics of true love. The reality, unfortunately, is that there are no guarantees for any relationship. To an extent, love is always a gamble in the beginning. Even in the most secure relationships, it sometimes takes years before both partners are absolutely sure of each other's devotion. Should you happen to fall for someone whose intentions are not what they appear, living together may set you up to be used and disappointed. If you have had a lengthy courtship and you are prepared for true love but your partner is wavering, it may make sense to press for marriage. For all its advantages, living together involves no binding commitment. The arrangement can be dissolved overnight, and despite a few highly publicized "palimony" settlements, there are neither financial nor legal penalties in most such breakups. If you are uncomfortable with this lack of structure, you will do better to view living together as a step *toward* marriage rather than a substitute for it. Establish a clear understanding that the purpose of living together is to lay the foundation for commitment, and set a time when you'll decide whether to take this step or break up.

If, however, you are very secure in your love and do not want children or need the financial protection afforded by marriage, you may choose to live together indefinitely without legalizing the union. For some, the relationship is more dynamic simply because of the fact of not being married and the awareness that the only thing holding them together is their love. Such couples claim to work even harder to retain each other's interest because the threat of temptation is that much greater. There is nothing wrong with this approach as long as both partners are equally comfortable with the arrangement. Usually, though, there comes a time in the relationship when at least one of the partners becomes disenchanted with this unstructured approach and wants to get married.

For most couples, marriage represents not a test but a celebration of love that brings to the union a sense of pride and accomplishment. However committed you and your partner may have been before, marriage will crystallize this commitment in a way you probably cannot anticipate beforehand. Publicly announcing and legalizing your relationship is bound to make you feel more secure and less isolated. You are no longer simply two individuals; you now share an additional identity as a couple. This engenders a powerful psychological feeling of being desired and taken care of, and because there is less fear of rejection, it also promotes increased openness and honesty.

A more concrete argument in favor of marriage is that it provides a legal and ethical foundation for bringing children into the world. The legal constraints of marriage encourage partners to stay and work together through times of stress when they might otherwise falter. Few experiences in life are more stressful — or rewarding — than having children. At times, the stress outweighs the rewards and can strain the parents' relationship. Marriage helps to keep the couple unified, which is beneficial for them and vital for the family. In the event that this or other stresses are too great and divorce ensues, both parents will be legally compelled to continue living up to their parental responsibilities. Any child coming into today's uncertain world deserves at least this degree of protection.

If and when you do decide to marry, you may want to consider a prenuptial agreement. This contract specifies what pre-existing property is to be kept by each of you, in case you should ever divorce. If you and your partner are both young and have no major assets when you marry, an agreement is unnecessary, but if one or both of you have a substantial amount of wealth, the precaution of a prenuptial agreement makes sense. While this discussion may seem ·out of place when you've just established that you are truly in love, it's wise to remember that your relationship will always be subjected to pressures and temptations from outside, and sometimes these forces can invade even very strong and loving marriages. A prenuptial agreement is merely a form of insurance that if these stresses should prove stronger than your love, you will end up no worse financially than when you started. Many couples convince themselves that they'll never need a prenuptial agreement, the illusion being that if they don't prepare for disaster it will never happen. But in itself, this contract is no threat to love, and there is no conflict between having one and being in love. The real issue is how you and your partner handle the negotiation.

Confronting such a potentially inflammatory issue at a time when you're convinced your love will last forever is hardly easy and may put considerable strain on the relationship if it is not approached sensitively and justly. The key point is to introduce the notion early in your engagement or even before. Waiting until the last minute before the wedding is bound to create distrust, resentment, and anger. If, instead, you deal with this decision in the beginning, in the same way you confront the question of having children or balancing your careers, it will fall into perspective as a purely pragmatic safeguard rather than appearing as a divisive maneuver.

When it comes to drawing up the document, fairness should

predominate. You probably are not eager to view your marriage as a business arrangement, and it's never easy to see your love affair reduced to twenty-five pages of legal text focused on dissolution. The only way you can come through this process unscathed is if both you and your partner are satisfied that the terms are reasonable. The agreement should focus primarily on assets that exist prior to your marriage, and it should specify that different terms are to go into effect following divorce and following death. Separate provisions may be made to safeguard the interests of your children.

If your partner desires a prenuptial contract and you don't, you need to make a special effort to keep the issue in perspective. Otherwise it may threaten your relationship unnecessarily. This began happening to Marissa two weeks after she'd become engaged.

Her fiancé, Jeffrey, had considerable assets, including cash, bonds, real estate, and a trust fund his grandfather had established for him. Marissa, a moderately successful interior designer, was not financially naive, and she was well aware of Jeffrey's inheritance and investments, but she had absolute confidence in their relationship. Besides, she believed that they would always remain friends even if they broke up, and she had no intention of "going after his money."

He broached the subject as they were leafing through catalogues of silver patterns. Trying to be tactful, he asked, "What do you know about prenuptial agreements?" Marissa flinched involuntarily. In fact, she knew almost nothing about them except that they premeditated divorce. It was as though Jeffrey had taken their shining moment and dashed it with cold water.

He tried to draw her into a rational discussion, explaining his parents' concerns about keeping the wealth in the family and describing the pressure they were exerting on him to protect his inheritance in the event of divorce. All Marissa saw was accusation. She felt he was calling her a money grabber and stripping their relationship of the mutual trust and protectiveness they had so carefully nurtured over their two-year courtship.

When she arrived in my office, she was seriously considering canceling the engagement. Jeffrey's gentle appeals for reason and understanding had had no effect. She needed an objective observer to help her understand that this was not a frontal assault or a one-way proposition. She had to pull out of her romantic cloud long enough to see her marriage in the context of their lives as individuals. Both of them had been very independent before meeting and would retain a certain amount of independence even when married. They had agreed that this was as it should be. All Jeffrey was asking was that they return to the original level of independence in the unlikely event that the marriage didn't work out. He was trying to invite her participation in the agreement and wanted to make sure she was treated fairly. Her stonewalling was far less reasonable than his request.

Once Marissa accepted Jeffrey's right to a prenuptial agreement, the next challenge was to work with him on the terms. It was a far cry from selecting items for the gift registry. Just as she was starting to view herself as Jeffrey's wife and soul mate, she had to imagine he was divorcing her. To ease the process, Jeffrey insisted on the simplest possible document, written in plain English rather than legalese and consisting primarily of a specific list of the holdings that Jeffrey would retain following divorce. If he died, it stated, these assets would be held in trust for any children they might have. To provide for Marissa in the event of his death, the contract required Jeffrey to obtain an insurance policy equal to the value of the holdings listed. All assets acquired after their marriage would be considered joint property.

Once they started drawing up this document, Marissa's objections quickly began to fade. Jeffrey showed her such respect and was so determined that she be treated fairly that it was impossible to view this as anything but a kind of partnership agreement. She actually found that she enjoyed dealing with him on this level; it made her feel more mature, more his equal. It also made her realize how childish her reservations had been. As difficult as it might be to face these decisions now, it would be so much more traumatic to do it in the midst of divorce proceedings.

A prenuptial agreement represents a positive intrusion of reality over illusion. While it certainly is not a mandatory requirement for marriage, neither does it have to be divisive or depressing. If you and your partner genuinely love each other and care for each other's well-being, you should be able to cooperate in this process just as you will cooperate later in acquiring a home, arranging for your children's schooling, writing your wills, and making the many other business decisions that will confront you as husband and wife. This may not be your idea of high romance, but it can pull you together even as it guards against your pulling apart. It is as valid a preparation for marriage as buying a ring or taking a blood test.

Surviving the Honeymoon

When you're in the midst of celebrating your engagement, planning a wedding party for two hundred guests, packing for your honeymoon, and opening wedding presents, it's easy to let ritual overtake reality. One illusion that runs the deepest, particularly with women, is the notion that a magnificent wedding and an idyllic honeymoon are the perfect way to inaugurate a marriage. While weddings and honeymoons are customary and certainly are often joyful and rewarding events, they have almost nothing to do with the reality of *being married*. A fairy tale marriage ceremony is no guarantee of a fairy tale life. After all, many divorced couples had sensational weddings, which they remember with great longing and nostalgia. "Our wedding day and honeymoon were the only truly happy times in our entire marriage," more than one couple has told me. These are often couples for whom the illusions of romance are stronger than the desire for true love.

Even when you are truly in love and want your wedding to symbolize your commitment to each other, it's easy to let the event overtake you. One way to avoid this is to make sure that the ceremony you choose is something the two of you want for yourselves and not something that is imposed on you. This is your special day and should belong to you in every sense of the word. Too often, it is held not for the benefit of the bride and groom as much as for their family and friends. Weddings are often used as a status statement for the newlyweds' families. The more opulent the event and the more powerful the guests, the more satisfied the parents are — regardless of how the young couple feel about it. One of the reasons this happens is that the families help finance the event and therefore feel entitled to take control of it. Traditionally, the bill for the wedding went to the father of the bride, the idea being that he was "giving away" his daughter to her new groom. While there aren't many in America today who would embrace this antiquated notion, it still is customary for one or both of the families to pay for the celebration. Given that a medium-sized wedding typically costs thousands of dollars, few young couples are able to pay for their own, and so most accept their parents' generosity — but at what price? Generally, they end up with a very different affair than they would like: more guests invited by their parents and fewer of their own friends; more arguments with each other and with their parents; and overall, more headaches than they would have with a ceremony that fit their own budget. Furthermore, couples whose parents pay for their weddings often feel permanently indebted, and the parents may feel entitled to encroach on the marriage in other ways later. If the marriage doesn't work out, the couple's guilt over this "wasted" investment exacerbates the disappointment and anxiety surrounding the breakup. Even if it means disappointing your parents and stretching your pocketbook somewhat, your marriage probably will get off to a smoother start if you control your own wedding.

This is not always easy to do, of course. Parents usually have a tremendous emotional investment in "getting their children married," and they often insist on being involved in the planning of the event. If excluded from the decision making, they may feel slighted, and some even threaten retaliation, such as disinheriting the couple or refusing to attend the ceremony. Others are well meaning but get so caught up in their own image of the "perfect" wedding that they can't understand the couple's desire to do it differently. If your parents resist your wedding plans, try to figure out what's motivating them. Look for areas where you might compromise, and offer concessions. As important as it is to have a wedding that suits you and your partner, it's also important that your families be allowed to share in the celebration without feeling hurt or embittered by it. The less personal conflict that surrounds this day, the more joyous it will be for all of you.

One way to reduce the stress and conflict over your wedding is to keep it scaled down. It doesn't *have* to be large and extravagant to be meaningful. If you and your partner agree that having a grand wedding is important to you and you won't have to bankrupt yourselves paying for it, then that is what you should have, but be sure you both are prepared for the work it will entail. The larger the ceremony, the more nervous you are likely to be; the less contact you will have with your guests individually; the more you will be involved in ritual procedure; and the more rest you'll need afterward.

Whatever type of ceremony you choose, try to keep in mind that this is just one day in your life as a couple. Even while the primary focus is on the details of the big event, don't forget that the purpose of this event lies in the days, months, and years to follow. You make a big mistake if you strive so hard for a picture-perfect wedding that you are barely speaking to each other by the time you exchange your vows. Relaxing your expectations for this one day may help you see your way more clearly to the days to come.

The same rule applies to your honeymoon. If you can accept this as a time simply to be alone together free of distractions and worries, it's a wonderful way to unwind after the wedding is over. The danger is that you'll feel obligated to make your honeymoon the "happiest time of your life." Particularly if you haven't lived together before, your expectations may be enormous. You naturally will expect superb sex, brilliant conversation, romantic adventures, and sublime intimacy. If the honeymoon — or your partner — disappoints you, is the marriage a failure? And even if you do live up to each other's most unrealistic visions during this week or two, you are bound to return to your normal selves once you're back home, and how will you handle the anticlimax then? Viewing your honeymoon simply as a relaxing vacation will help to limit your expectations and your disappointments. Remember that this is just the beginning of your marriage, not its culmination. As passionately as you may feel for your partner the day after your wedding and as romantic as your honeymoon may be, you probably won't realize the full depth of your love for years to come.

11

LIVING LOVE

ROSALIND HAD a disconcerted look on her face as she settled into her chair.

"How was the honeymoon?" I asked.

"Wonderful!" she answered, her voice cracking just slightly.

"The Bahamas, right?"

She nodded.

"And the wedding went well?"

"It was perfect!" Again her voice was poised on the edge. Having seen Rosalind in therapy on and off for more than three years, I was familiar with this tentative tremble. In the past, it once had meant she was about to get passed up for a promotion, once that her father was terminally ill, and once that she was considering quitting her career as an investment banker. It had never been a signal of joy or satisfaction.

"Then what's *not* perfect?" I inquired.

Her eyes began to well up. "I feel as though everything is over," she blurted out. "I worked so hard for so long to find the right man, to work out our relationship, to plan our dream wedding and honeymoon . . . and now I'm looking at him and thinking I'll never be independent again. I'll never be intimate or have sex with another man again. And I'm sitting here facing all the same old problems at work. You know, I'm not sure I can handle the added strain of holding up my end of the marriage on top of my career. How do I get on with my life now and keep all the balls in the air?"

Rosalind's concerns were more than just post-honeymoon blues. She was confronting for the first time some of the basic truths about love that she'd previously overlooked in her eagerness to get to the altar. At thirty-five, Rosalind had wanted desperately to be married and yet was also quite set in her ways. She was intensely ambitious at work and very exacting with herself and others around her. Her husband more than lived up to her standards and respected her independence, but her doubts were not whether she had chosen the right man. She didn't know if she was capable of reorienting her life to make room for marriage. She was struggling with the notion of permanence and the realization that even though she loved her husband, this love would not automatically resolve her other problems — and it might make her life even more complicated.

What Rosalind was overlooking, and what we tried to put back into perspective during her next few sessions, were the positive changes her marriage would bring to her life from now on. The most obvious, and perhaps most superficial, was the relief from loneliness. Rosalind had long ago stopped enjoying life as a single woman. Until she'd met her husband, she'd been extremely lonely and bitter about men. During their thirteen-month courtship, he'd dissolved her loneliness and restored her faith in the opposite sex. In her current moment of doubt she might deny that he'd worked miracles, but she couldn't deny how unhappy she'd been before they chose to love each other.

An even more compelling benefit of their marriage was the solace and support they could give to each other from now on. Once she got past these newlywed jitters, Rosalind could ask her husband's help in resolving many of the worries and uncertainties she formerly brought into therapy. True, her husband was a CPA, not a pyschologist, but Rosalind was not mentally or emotionally ill. Most of her problems were the minor stuff of everyday life and seemed overwhelming to her only because she kept them bottled up. Before, she'd had no one else close enough or trustworthy enough to accept her confidences, but now in her husband she had a partner and confidant. Not only was he willing to listen, but he had a vested interest in helping her work out healthy solutions.

As we delved deeper, it became clear that what worried Rosalind most was what she viewed as a conflict between her work and her marriage. "I've been feeling so distracted for the past months," she explained. "Before, I was very driven. I knew absolutely everything that was going on in the office. I have this five-year plan for myself, and I never used to have any doubt that I could make it to senior vice president on schedule if I just stayed in there and fought hard enough."

"And now?"

"Now I'm not sure. I feel as if I've softened up. Not that I don't work hard, but the fight has gone out of me. That executive position still looks good, but I just don't know if I've got the energy to battle my way up the corporate ladder *and* keep my marriage alive. And if I had to choose one over the other . . . well, it's a tough call."

Rosalind was saying that she might be willing to toss away a vital, satisfying marriage in order to pursue a self-created theory that if she devoted every moment and every ounce of energy, she would get into the boardroom. Even if her theory proved correct, then what?

"My career has always been so important to me," she mused. "Since I was a little girl, when my grandfather used to tell me I'd be the first woman president, I've imagined myself at the top of something — a government, a company, an industry. Long before I ever imagined myself as a wife I saw myself as a success. But it's true, I've never come up with a really satisfying explanation for *why* I want to be rich and famous. I realize there's no guarantee it would make me happy. It's just sort of ingrained in me."

There was nothing wrong with Rosalind's desire to be married and have a successful career. In all likelihood, she needed both to be happy. The flaw in her reasoning was the notion that the two goals were incompatible. What she gradually came to realize was that by relaxing her expectations and her behavior in general, she would actually become more successful in both arenas.

To help her accept this, we explored the changes in her job performance since she'd met her husband. At first she insisted that she'd been more aggressive and more in control while on her own. But when she considered the work she'd actually produced, the deals she'd made, and the comments of her superiors, she conceded that things actually had gone better for her since her love life had ignited. Even though she felt that she'd gotten "soft," what her colleagues and superiors at work perceived was that she'd stopped being hostile and snoopy. Instead of trying to do everyone else's work and worrying about who was getting the credit, she performed her own work at the top of her ability and pulled out of office politics and gossip. Perhaps most important of all, she was much more pleasant and convivial with her coworkers. Love made her feel less jealous of them and less threatened by their successes. The change was slow and subtle and therefore easy to miss, but it nevertheless was strong evidence that true love had helped rather than hindered her career.

Rosalind eventually came to learn that love is an overlay that meshes with a life filled with other commitments, interests, people, and goals. It neither replaces nor competes with that life, but it *can* enrich it and sometimes can ease it. She was correct in assuming that love also would add a new layer of complications, but she was wrong in concluding that these would conflict with her other priorities. If her groom's kiss could not transport her to a world of enchantment, it did promise respite, distraction, support, and renewal that would make the real world that much easier to navigate.

Once Rosalind had put her marriage in perspective and granted herself permission to sustain the balance of life "outside" and "inside" the relationship, her doubts began to subside. The peace she found at home did take some of the edge off her ambition at work, and she realized that her five-year plan was slipping away from her. It became clear that she would not become a vice president with her firm before she turned forty. In retrospect she doubted that she realistically could ever have achieved this goal, though she was promoted several times and ultimately directed an entire department.

Then her husband was offered a major promotion that required a move to Chicago. Before getting married they had agreed that they would never make such a move unless both wholeheartedly wanted to do it. Privately, she had vowed never to compromise her own career aspirations for her husband's. But when faced with the decision, she felt her resolve melting. Her ambitions were not in competition with his, she now realized. They had to decide what was best for them as a couple, and *as a couple,* they stood to gain far more than they would lose by moving. Ultimately, they arrived at a modest compromise: he would not accept his new job until she'd determined whether she could find a position in Chicago that was comparable to or better than her present one. Coincidentally, one of the colleagues with whom Rosalind had been in stiff competition early in her career had moved to Chicago just recently to join a mutual fund management team. Despite their initial antagonism, they had become good friends after Rosalind underwent her "post-marriage transformation," as he jokingly called it. Now he considered her a strong team player. When he heard she might move to Chicago, he recommended her for a position at nearly double her present salary.

In her final session, Rosalind's voice was clear and confident. "I certainly was a foolish bride," she reflected, thinking back to her newlywed doubts. "Just think what I'd have lost if I'd opted for ambition over love!"

Bridging the Gap between Love and Life

Rosalind's concerns about the role of love within the broader context of her life were not unusual or invalid. Many couples are astonished to discover, once they're married or have lived together for an extended period, that the permanence of true love is not always easy to accept. While it may be natural in the glow of infatuation to yearn for your lover's everlasting devotion, this prospect can seem quite chilling once you have made your pact and begin realistically anticipating the rest of your life together. It's almost inevitable that your more exhilarating adventures as a single person will haunt you from time to time and that you'll have to tailor some of your more fanciful dreams so that they're compatible with your partner's. You may find yourselves competing with each other in subtle, unspoken, and perhaps unrecognized ways, perhaps resenting each other's social or professional achievements. All of these are signals that you have not yet fully relinquished that part of yourselves that will form the core of your union as a couple. This doesn't mean that you're not committed or that you don't love each other. It simply means that you're still testing the limits to find what's "inside" and what's "outside" your relationship.

Establishing this balance is one of the most difficult parts of building love during the first few years, and for some couples it remains forever problematic. Certain decisions must be made as a couple, while others should be made independently by each partner. You need to share some activities and occasions and to experience others separately. Some problems you have to resolve on your own, others together. How do you decide which aspects of your life are yours alone and which are yours as a couple? While every couple is different, in almost every long-term relationship there seem to be four basic sources of conflict that center on this issue:

- Competitiveness
- Personal crisis
- External relationships
- Personal change

Examining these in detail can help you develop the necessary guidelines for establishing balance in your own relationship.

Competitiveness

Competitiveness exists to a certain extent in virtually every relationship. In small doses, it can be healthy and may help sustain vitality. But the couple who occasionally battle each other furiously on the tennis court or in intellectual debates over dinner are different from the couple who constantly argue about who's working harder, who's earning more money, or who's "better" with the children. While the first couple uses competition to stimulate each other, the second may allow it to ruin the relationship.

It is almost impossible to moderate the level of competitiveness in your marriage until you both recognize the need for balance between your lives as a couple and your lives as individuals. Within the relationship you are equal partners, and you have to learn to operate as such, with both investing the same general amount of energy, attention, and effort to keeping the household and the relationship afloat. As individuals, however, it's neither reasonable nor desirable to expect equality. You each have unique talents and operate within different sets of circumstances. Personal specifics aside, society dictates that men and women will achieve different levels of recognition in most cases. But ironically, it's precisely this societal inequality that leads to much of the competition on the home front. The woman who is fighting for equal rights in the workplace has a hard time swallowing the fact that her own husband earns nearly twice as much as she and is promoted at work more frequently. The man whose wife's part-time wages barely cover the cost of day care for the kids can't understand why she insists on working and why she can't find time to iron his shirts. Accepting that you each must have an outside life — and that *the rewards from your separate activities flow directly back into the relationship* — is the first crucial step toward eliminating this corrosive brand of competitiveness from a marriage. Once you've established this premise, you can examine the specific issues that trigger competitiveness in your relationship.

For most newly married couples, the primary source of trouble is money. To an extent, this is inevitable in a culture that links personal worth so strongly with one's earning power and in which women as a rule are paid less than men. The problem often is most severe when the man is the family's sole breadwinner and excludes his wife from financial decision making. But even in a two-career couple in which husband and wife work the same number of hours a day, chances are that the husband will bring home more money. And if he brings home more money, he may feel entitled to control how that money is spent. The flip side of this is the wife who is so determined *not* to become classically dependent that she keeps her earnings apart from her husband's and insists that they contribute equally to the running of the household. This means that he ends up with more money in the bank, and they accept a lower standard of living in order to stay within her budget.

One problem in all these cases is that the couples are not looking at the *proportion* of earnings each person contributes to the relationship. While the controlling husband may be investing more actual dollars in the household, the working wife may well be contributing a larger aggregate percentage of her salary and therefore making a larger financial sacrifice than he. Meanwhile, the woman who's so determined to split the household costs evenly is guaranteeing that her sacrifice is greater than her husband's. And the housewife generally is making the greatest sacrifice of all — running the household, raising the children, and supporting her husband's career without any monetary compensation. But equalizing the percentage of earnings each person contributes does not adequately solve the problem of financial *competition* between the couple. Until both partners consider their money as "ours" rather than "mine" and "yours," the basic inequality will remain, and a certain amount of resentment, jealousy, and power playing will be difficult to avoid. This cannot help but undermine the relationship.

Ideally, you and your partner will have discussed the management of money before marrying. Possibly you agreed that it was best not to share control of the family finances. There may have been a host of reasons for this. Many women, early in a relationship, honestly believe that they want to be "rescued" from their own financial insecurity and so consent to letting their partners "take care of them" rather than demanding access to their husbands' bank accounts. Many men feel threatened by the idea of a wife who has her own income and so choose women who agree to be fiscally submissive in this way. Other couples are persuaded by the rising divorce rate that they must squirrel away separate funds as "protection" in case their marriage fails. While there is nothing wrong with having separate bank accounts, the effects can be pernicious when money is used by one partner to subtly dominate or threaten the other. One may be contributing the lion's share of the budget, and the funds may reside in different accounts, but unless the family finances are jointly managed — unless both partners feel that they are working *together* to support their common goals — it is almost impossible to prevent money from becoming a competitive and divisive issue in the relationship. Moreover, it can be very difficult to reverse the situation later; the partner who controls the money may resist, arguing that this was the "deal" going into the relationship. Therefore, it's important to review the financial terms of your marriage as early as possible to make sure they protect you rather than expose you to the threat of competitiveness.

Merely agreeing to be jointly responsible for the family's finances does not rule out competitiveness, of course. You each will have your own personal desires and priorities for spending money. One may think it's essential to have a new car, for example, while the other is determined to buy a new bedroom set. It would be wonderful if you both could have exactly what you want whenever you want it, but this is rarely possible. Whenever there is a limit to your spending, you will need to negotiate compromises so that neither partner feels neglected or exploited. While many of your expenditures justifiably will be for the household, you each deserve to have certain discretionary personal expenses as well. The trick is to jointly moderate your desires so that you are able to meet your own needs and your mutual needs as a couple. If you don't learn to do this, even seemingly trivial stand-offs can escalate into major disputes.

Competition can also arise over time and energy: who's working harder in the relationship and deserves the most credit. This often is much less obvious than competition over money and occurs much more spontaneously. For example, you have a hard day at work and struggle through an hour of traffic to come home and find your spouse calmly reading the newspaper and waiting for you to start dinner. You explode because you feel you're doing far more than your share — and you want some time to relax and read the paper yourself. But the blame may be misplaced. Your partner had nothing to do with the traffic or the hassles you experienced at the office and may not even want to have dinner right away. Rather than expending competitive energy bickering, your attention would be better focused on calming down and paving the way for a pleasant evening for both of you. If you don't want to make dinner, say so, and try to negotiate a mutually satisfactory alternative. Going out, ordering food in, eating cold cuts, or even skipping the meal would be far more constructive than arguing or grudgingly preparing dinner and glaring accusations at your partner for the rest of the night. Again, while this example may seem petty, over time these kinds of competitive collisions can erode the foundation of true love.

Time competitiveness can get much more serious when one partner is a workaholic and the other is trying singlehandedly to keep both the household and the relationship intact. In many cases this dilemma is caused by financial need; if you have children and very little money, one or both of you may have to work days, nights, and weekends to make ends meet. But as stressful as this situation may be, it generally is not as threatening to true love as the *compulsion* to work regardless of economic need. Ideally, your work should be both personally gratifying and beneficial to your home life. If the time and energy you devote to your career consistently detracts from the quality of your home life — by making your family unhappy or estranging you from your partner — then the balance of "internal" (mutual) and "external" (selfish) interests is upset, and work takes priority at the expense of love. In this situation it's essential to find out what is really motivating the workaholic partner.

If they're honest, many men who keep long hours will admit that they do so to avoid getting caught in what they view as the tedium of child care. They love their wives and families, but at the end of a long business day they just don't want to deal with the hassles over dinner, baths, and bedtimes. As justified as the men may feel in this attitude, however, most wives would argue that they too have full, tiring days (many in fact work professionally in jobs as demanding as those of the men) and deserve the extra help of a supportive husband and father. When this is the case, it needs to be discussed openly and some sort of trade-off arranged so that neither partner becomes overburdened and resentful. Dividing up responsibilities or alternating days of child care duty not only will spare you warfare but probably will allow both of you to become closer to your children.

When the motivation for working overtime is to avoid one's *partner,* of course, the situation is more ominous. In this case, the long hours are not born out of selfishness as much as they are manufactured in reaction to something that is happening within the relationship. They are not the threat to true love, in other words, but a symptom that the relationship is already in danger. Juggling schedules or demanding more time together won't resolve this situation. You'll need to examine what is going on — or not going on — in the time you currently spend together and try to make the partnership whole again. We discuss this process in more detail in the next few sections.

While it's true that some people genuinely are driven to overperform, overwork, and overachieve, in successful love relationships this need can be satisfied without distancing the other partner. Concessions can be made, such as including the spouse in business-related trips and social engagements; setting aside a portion of each day and specific weekends and vacations to spend exclusively with the family; and doing a certain amount of business from the home. The bottom line, however, must be an attitude that your partner and family come first, and business interests are secondary. If these priorities reverse, then work almost inevitably will become a threat to true love.

The competition that arises over the practical running of the household is tangible and immediate, but career competition can be much more destructive. While a couple who squabble relentlessly over who's spending more money may be otherwise content to live together for the rest of their days, the strain is much harder for the overcompetitive husband whose loving wife has suddenly been promoted to company president, leaving him "behind" as a middle manager. For many individuals, career status is a matter of core identity, and they simply cannot tolerate becoming subordinate to their mates in this regard.

Ironically, these same people often choose partners who seem equally destined for stardom — though perhaps in a safely different field — because this feeds into their own self-image. They believe that marrying a person who seems to be going nowhere can only bring them down, while marrying someone who's more successful will make them look and feel inferior. The illusion is that both partners in the marriage will rise to the top at the same pace, but of course this almost never happens. A competitive individual who certainly wouldn't hold back his own career in order to let his partner "catch up" may become outraged when his partner passes *him* by, even when the newfound success is in the form of an unexpected promotion or prestigious award.

This kind of competition works away at the very heart of a marriage. The drive to get ahead takes precedence over all other commitments, including love, and the competing partner can see the relationship only in terms of "me versus you" as opposed to "me *and* you." What's missing in this concern over separate identities is any sense of the shared identity created through marriage. Remember, the rewards from your separate activities flow directly back into your relationship, benefiting both of you. The more successful your partner is, the more successful you appear to the outside world, including your own friends and coworkers. More important, however, your respective accomplishments should be a source of mutual pride, because you both contributed to them by supporting and nurturing each other's talents and ambitions. Ideally, you will be rooting for each other to advance as far as your abilities allow, and you will recognize the important role you play in each other's achievements.

Parenting is potentially an even more dangerous area of competition. It should be obvious that children thrive when their parents are unified. The trouble is that, as a parent, you tend to become so emotionally involved with your children that it's easy to become jealous of anyone else who gets close to them — even if that person is your spouse. Up to a point, this is natural and even beneficial for the children; the subtle competition for their attention is one of the ways they learn that both their parents love them. But sometimes the competition gets out of hand, and the children become the focus of an unwitting power play between the parents. You may honestly believe that you understand your children better and that their welfare is too important to compromise your decisions, but if this means that you exclude your partner from major parenting decisions, then not only is it *not* in the children's best interests but it may threaten your marriage as well.

Of all the pursuits you and your partner share, the raising of your children should be the most important and the most cooperative. Your children *need* you both to agree on the key decisions affecting their lives. You each have too great an emotional investment and too great a responsibility to your children to allow their upbringing to become a sparring match between you. If you plan to have a family, it's critical that you discuss your attitudes about parenting early in your relationship. Recognize that you sometimes will have to compromise your desires, both as individuals and as a couple, for the sake of your children but that if you share equally in their care, the extra love and delight they generate will make your marriage much, much closer and more satisfying. Be sure you both are prepared to accept this higher goal before becoming parents.

In the daily routine of life as a couple, you probably will find many little spats erupting for no apparent reason. What's really happening is not so much competition between the two of you as it is competition between the *reality* of married life and your *illusions* of what it should be. If you're still clinging to the notion that you and your beloved will never disagree or be grumpy with each other, you're feeding right back into the false love syndrome, which whispers that every little fight is a sign that you've made a mistake, that you've chosen the wrong mate.

If you accept this fear, your natural inclination is to give up, pack your bags, and renew your search for your one true love; there's no incentive to *solve* the problems. If you are willing to resist the false love syndrome, however, you must recognize that even minor spats can become a constant and dangerous irritation. While it's true that all couples have disagreements, those who have *successful* long-term relationships are able to resolve their conflicts so they do not become chronic.

To solve problems within your relationship, you must first decide that you want to do so. This may mean pushing away some of your illusions about your partner and your relationship; it may mean swallowing some of your pride and competitiveness. It also means facing the issue — and your partner — squarely, without complaining to your parents or friends. Be prepared to work together to find a solution that will not punish either person. You need to be able to compromise when necessary. If you can't, you will be constantly at odds, and even if you have a truly loving relationship, it may not survive.

Personal Crisis

Personal tragedy can tear the fabric of true love even more severely than competitiveness can. It's very difficult to prepare for catastrophes such as illness, unemployment, or death in the family. If you've never lost anyone close to you, you may not understand how you or your partner will feel when grieving for a parent or a child. If you've never experienced serious injury or illness, you may not know how to respond if your partner develops major health problems. And if you've never had financial or career problems, you may be ill equipped to handle such disasters in your marriage. Lack of experience is not the real obstacle, however. What allows personal crisis to destroy a marriage is the illusion that tragedy will never strike and the unwillingness to accept it when it does.

It's easy to succumb to this illusion if you and your partner are healthy, happy, and reasonably successful when you begin your relationship. You naturally avoid thinking about all the awful "what-ifs" that could darken your contentment. If you don't think about disaster, maybe it will never happen to you. The real danger in such blind reasoning is that you will start applying an unnatural standard to your life and your partner. "In sickness and in health" read the standard wedding vows, but if your idea of sickness is nothing more than the common cold, what will you do if your partner develops cancer or is crippled in a car accident? The tendency to fall apart — or flee — is much greater if you've never contemplated such events than if you've made a conscious decision to remain strong and firmly committed in times of crisis.

Many people are self-confessed cowards who faint at the sight of blood or run at the first scent of trouble. There is nothing wrong with such behavior, but it's no excuse for backing away from crisis that affects loved ones. When a disaster or tragedy befalls your partner or your children, you are obligated to conquer your own weaknesses so that, within reason, you can offer maximum support. If there is any doubt, either in your mind or in your partner's, that you will be there for each other, that doubt will take its toll on the relationship not only when crises occur but even when things are running smoothly. This uncertainty will undermine your basic trust in each other.

Once you have discovered that your partner is unwilling to come through for you in times of crisis, the ensuing resentment can be even more devastating than the crisis itself. This was what Jane discovered in the aftermath of her brother's drug overdose, when her husband, George, refused to take a day off from work to fly with her to the funeral. Like so many others, he was patronizing. He offered superficial condolences, bought her a scarf "to cheer her up," and called her parents to say he was sorry. But for all that, George might as well have been one of her friends at work. As her husband, he acted as though her brother's death was a nasty inconvenience. Never once did he ask if there was anything he could do to soothe her grief or even to help with the funeral or estate transactions. That George had barely known Jane's brother was immaterial; he was embarrassed by the ugliness of the death and what he viewed as the cowardice of anyone who would take his own life. Furthermore, he was intimidated by the depths of his wife's grief. For him, it was far easier to tell himself how strong and capable Jane was than to involve himself in a process that might pull him in over his head. He didn't want to share her suffering, so he chose to downplay it. Under the circumstances, Jane didn't have the energy to fight him. She did what she had to do for her family and let George go about his life as if nothing had happened. And on the surface she appeared just as efficient as he painted her, but it was only because she had no choice. Once her grief let up, anger poured in to take its place, and it eroded her commitment to George. Were it not for marital therapy, which forced George to confront the damage that his involuntary selfishness had done to the relationship, they might never have fully recovered as a loving couple.

When you face difficulties solidly together, resolution will come much more swiftly, and you are likely to emerge more united than ever. This is not to say that you can defeat every obstacle or that merely being unified will safeguard you from stress, sadness, or frustration, but it may well prevent you from being devastated by circumstances that are otherwise beyond your control.

The time to start discussing these kinds of eventualities is early in your relationship. Talk about how you each react individually to severe stress and how you might help each other through it. In particular, focus on the situations that are most likely to confront your marriage, such as the death of your parents, serious illness or injury, problems involving your children, or perhaps legal troubles.

Consider not only what you would ask of each other in such situations but also what you would *not* ask. In other words, at what point would you be willing to set each other free? Having emphasized the importance of facing most personal crises together as a couple, it's also important to realize that some situations can be insurmountable. Romantic illusions of eternal devotion aside, there are limits to the strength of love, and situations such as terminal or incurable, degenerative illness clearly test these limits. If the terms of the relationship demand that the couple remain locked in devotion "unto death," the healthy partner may feel irrationally guilty for not being able to give one hundred percent at all times. In some cases, the demands of supporting and comforting a dying partner are so great that the survivor has neither energy nor interest in continuing life afterward. Such a penalty is well beyond the scope of true love, and it's up to both partners to recognize this.

When Harold was diagnosed as having cancer, his doctors told him that there was a sixty percent chance he would die within the next two years. In the meantime, he would spend most of his time in and out of the hospital for surgery and chemotherapy. Harold was forty-five at the time and had been married for nearly fifteen years to Maggie. She was thirty-five and was devoted to him, but every time Harold looked at her during the weeks following his diagnosis, he was overcome with guilt. They had no children, and she was extremely beautiful and youthful. Harold knew that Maggie would probably remarry after his death and have a full, happy life. This didn't mean that she loved him any less; it was just reality. Recognizing this, Harold was torn between his desire to hold on to her as long as possible and his feeling that he should spare her the pain and what would probably be a hopeless struggle in his final months. Had the odds been different or the treatment less devastating, he never could have imagined letting her go, but under the circumstances her presence filled him not with determination to recover but with despair that he was causing her such agony. One month after he learned he had cancer, Harold told Maggie he wanted a divorce. She wept that she could never leave him, but he was resolute. He could not go through what was ahead of him knowing that she was being victimized as much as he.

After the divorce and at Harold's insistence, Maggie forced herself to go out with friends and resume the independent life she'd had before marrying. She could not develop any interest in other men, and she visited Harold frequently, but she did feel somewhat liberated from the sense of obligation she had felt during that month following his diagnosis. The doctors no longer conferred with her about every detail; she no longer felt compelled to be at the hospital for hours on end; and she didn't feel guilty about focusing on her career instead of on Harold's condition. Rather than reconstructing her life in the midst of deep grief, Maggie was able to do it with the comforting knowledge that Harold was still there. While she persisted in hoping that he would recover, her existence did not hinge on this unlikely eventuality.

As for Harold, the divorce had a strangely energizing effect on him. When Maggie visited, he felt that she was coming of her own free will, not out of wifely duty. He did not feel that he was tying her down, and he could see that her life was moving ahead. Instead of depressing him, that knowledge excited him and made him intensely proud of her. It also encouraged him to conquer his own illness because, unconsciously, he was determined to "win her back." In setting her free he had created a challenge that was more compelling than anything Maggie could have done for him as his wife. Yet if he failed — if his illness defeated him — he'd have the comfort of knowing that he'd helped her recover.

Incredibly, Harold beat the odds. It took nearly four years of treatment, including several rounds of surgery, but there came a day when he was proclaimed cancer-free. Maggie was out of the country on business, unaware of the steady improvement in Harold's condition. He waited for her to return and then he called her to request a "date." Now that he'd been granted his reprieve from death, he was terrified that his plan would backfire, that Maggie would have chosen another man already, but his fears were unfounded. His announcement of health and his subsequent proposal seemed the answer to her dreams. In some ways, this episode had changed them both dramatically, but their love had never faltered.

Personal crisis and the choices it necessitates can destroy the balance between your needs as individuals and as partners in love. Not all couples could survive the kind of breakup Harold imposed on his marriage, but neither does true love always survive when the couple "stick it out" indefinitely. Only you and your partner can tell where the limits of your love lie and how much you can or should expect each other to endure in order to stay together. For the sake of your relationship, however, confront this issue *before* it becomes a reality.

External Relationships

Comedians use mother-in-law jokes as a standard stock in trade, but for couples who are divided over allegiance to family members and personal friends, the issue is not funny. Particularly when the conflict involves parents, the layers of guilt and loyalty that tie you to your first great loves can prove a formidable opponent to the newly formed bonds of true love. When all the people you love most in the world can't stand each other, you naturally feel torn apart.

Such rivalries occur in varying degrees in most relationships. After all, committing to true love does not mean that you're also willing to embrace your partner's parents, relatives, squash partners, and best friends from high school. Nor should you be expected to be closely involved with all your partner's external relationships. Maintaining individual ties with people outside the couple is essential to the balance of love. The danger occurs when these outside relationships threaten to dominate or conflict with your life as a couple. *True love must take precedence over all other relationships*, or the trust it demands cannot be sustained.

Much to some parents' dismay, this rule holds even with regard to previous family ties. A relationship is an intensely private matter between two people; all others, including family, are outsiders. They can neither share nor dictate the terms of your love. They can, however, interfere if allowed too close. As a couple, you need to be vigilant against inappropriate intrusion. This may mean limiting visits or even prohibiting certain topics of discussion, such as marital roles, childrearing, personal finances, or any issue you consider personal and privileged. Occasionally, it may mean withholding information, particularly if one or both of you are making an important personal decision (to have a child, to move, or to make a major career change, for example) or are working through specific problems in your marriage. Even if parents try to maintain a proper distance from their children's marital affairs, the suggestion of change or crisis often overwhelms their good intentions and they may become more intimately involved in the situation than they should be.

Your parents, perhaps unconsciously but nevertheless compellingly, may try to persuade you to stay within their fold. But when you marry or commit yourself to a partner, you transfer your primary family responsibilities from your parents and siblings to your partner and future children. This does not mean that you shouldn't try to compromise when rivalries develop, but when compromise fails, your duties to your spouse should come ahead of your duties to your parents. Confusion about this is one of the most common sources of marital conflict among couples in therapy. In Steve and Patricia's case, it was also one of the most agonizing.

Patricia and her mother-in-law had never gotten along. Steve's mother had opposed the wedding and had urged him to find a more "respectable" (meaning socially elite) wife; she was ashamed that her son wanted to marry the daughter of a shoe salesman. When Steve refused to acquiesce to his mother's demands, she boycotted the wedding. That was fifteen years earlier, when his mother was in her fifties and his father was still alive. But the animosity continued and intensified when Steve and Patricia had children. By then his mother was a widow, and with Steve her only child, the grandchildren became the focus of her life. She lived nearly fifty miles away, but she visited frequently and often differed with Patricia about childrearing practices. Sometimes the air was so thick with tension during her visits that Steve retreated to his hammock outside, and afterward Patricia would make him vow not to let his mother return for at least a month. The rivalry escalated severely, however, when his mother, now in her seventies, broke her hip. The injury and age toned her down and made her more accepting of Patricia, but Patricia had neither sympathy nor empathy left for her. *She* had made the effort in the beginning, she felt, and Steve's mother had simply waited too long to come around.

Steve was caught squarely in the middle, and for months he squirmed helplessly. On the one hand he felt horribly guilty about letting his mother live by herself, visiting only every few weeks. His wife was younger and stronger, he thought, and should be better able to handle the situation. The right thing to do would be to have his mother live with them. On the other hand, he knew the pain his mother had inflicted on Patricia over the years. Even more, he knew how unpleasant the household would be with the two of them under one roof. His mother was more moderate now, but she was still the same woman.

When they came for therapy as a couple, the first task was to help Patricia gain more insight into Steve's conflict, but without making her feel cornered. This meant establishing that their marriage had top priority. When she was reassured that Steve's mother posed no threat to his love for her, Patricia allowed herself to open her sights a little. One of the reasons she loved him, after all, was his strong morality and sense of responsibility. She didn't begrudge him his guilt or his love for his mother; she just couldn't stand the woman. Even the children were lukewarm toward their grandmother, Patricia pointed out. They enjoyed the gifts she brought but hated the way she was constantly correcting their grammar and trying to improve their manners.

Steve understood Patricia's and the children's feelings and readily admitted that his mother was a difficult woman, but that didn't change the fact that she was his mother. If Patricia's parents were still alive, he pointed out, she would feel just as responsible for their welfare. The fact that they weren't, however, was contributing to her resentment of the existing situation.

Another part of the problem was the dynamic that occurred every time Steve's mother visited. Because she traveled what for her was a considerable distance, she felt that she was entitled to special attention when she arrived. In her mind, she was a guest in Steve's house, and should be treated like one. Patricia, however, was not about to put the entire household on hold every time her mother-in-law appeared. If the kids had a soccer game or a birthday party that conflicted with their grandmother's visit, the children's activities came first. If the family was busy with a project, like cleaning out the garage or raking leaves, they went about their business, often leaving the elderly lady to sit alone watching. This made Steve's mother furious, but Patricia argued that she was always welcome to pitch in and help if she felt left out; she was, after all, a member of the family. But that rarely happened because Steve's mother never felt relaxed or comfortable enough to join the others. For her, these visits were special occasions, and she was an outsider.

It was clear that the situation was not beneficial for anyone. They would all need to make some compromises to come up with an alternative. Having the mother live with the family would never work, Patricia insisted, and Steve agreed. But, he suggested, what if she lived close enough that he could keep his eye on her and she could visit on a more relaxed basis? Patricia was skeptical, fearing daily, miserable encounters with the old woman. Steve persisted, warming to the idea. There were numerous elderly people in the neighborhood, far more than where his mother was currently living. If she was nearby, it would be easier for Steve to find the time to visit her without having to include Patricia or the children. Once she felt comfortable with the area and less like an outsider with the family, his mother might even be able to babysit for them. Ultimately, Patricia capitulated, on the condition that if her mother-in-law in any way infringed on their relationship or the children's well-being, they would have to find a different solution.

Ironically, it took more time for Steve to persuade his mother of the plan. In her old age, she was intimidated by Patricia and was afraid of stepping on her daughter-in-law's toes any more than she already had. Further, it was difficult for her to give up the apartment where she'd lived for the past ten years. But the same arguments that had worked on Patricia ultimately worked on Steve's mother, and she moved into a small apartment just a couple of blocks from the family.

She and Patricia never did become true friends, but the proximity gave them a chance to reverse much of the hostility between them. Steve's mother was careful not to abuse her welcome, but as she adjusted to more frequent, casual, and briefer visits, she gradually shifted from being an outsider to being a member of the family who felt enough at ease to help out when she could. Her relationship with the children also improved as they got to know each other. When she died about three years later, no one in the family had any regrets about having brought her to the neighborhood.

In Steve and Patricia's case, a certain amount of sacrifice was necessary, not just for his mother's sake but also for the sake of their marriage. Had they not been able to reach some compromise, the emotional toll on Steve inevitably would have strained their relationship and made him even more resentful of Patricia than she was of his mother. By being honest with each other and arriving at a solution together, they averted what might have been a disaster for the entire family.

While it is incumbent on most couples to try to find such compromises where parents are concerned, the picture changes slightly when conflict arises over personal friends. In a healthy relationship, each partner should have some separate friends. If you have only mutual friends, this may be a sign that your relationship is unhealthily tight, that you've lost the balance between "outside" and "inside." This predicament is rare, but its opposite is not. Often, one partner will have so many or such strong outside friendships that the other partner is forced to compete with them. The real trouble arises when this partner feels threatened by the other's friendships.

This may happen in a variety of ways:

- Once a year, the husband goes mountain climbing with a group of his buddies, one of whom is a well-known womanizer. Even though she has no desire to climb mountains, the wife resents his taking a week off and leaving her at home. Furthermore, she is obsessed by the notion that his bachelor friend (whom she despises) will lead her husband into an affair while away.
- She has a girlfriend whom she's known since grade school. When the two of them are together, they giggle like children at secret jokes only they can understand. Even when her husband is in the same room with them, he feels excluded.

Moreover, he personally dislikes her friend. He considers her loud, pretentious, and boring. He can never understand what his wife sees in her, and that makes him worry that his wife and her friend, on some subtle level, are alike. These concerns occasionally are validated when his wife becomes unappealingly boisterous in her friend's company. Were the friend a stranger or someone who worked in his office, he'd probably find her innocuous, but because she suggests and brings out qualities in his wife that he can't abide, he finds her threatening.

- Both partners have active careers and social lives and have never challenged each other's personal or business relationships. When she becomes friendly with one of her male clients who happens to be unusually attractive, wealthy, and single, however, her husband gets worried. He doesn't have any doubt of her commitment or love for him, but he has no basis for trusting the client to respect their marriage. Given an alluring enough proposition, his wife could hardly be blamed for having an affair.

- As long as the husband's male friendships didn't involve her, they never bothered his wife. Most of his acquaintances dated back to college and were based on past history. Her misgivings arose when the other guys started getting married and when men's nights out turned into social events for two, three, or four couples. She felt obligated to participate, making small talk with the other wives and pretending to enjoy herself. But she was not naturally gregarious. She had little in common with the other women and even less with the men. For her, these gatherings were torture, but her husband was so caught up with his friends that he just assumed that she too was enjoying herself. She was afraid that if she told him the truth he would simply go out with them, leaving her behind. That had been acceptable when it was only the men, but now the idea made her intensely uncomfortable. What would they all think of her? Wouldn't her husband resent her? Might he or the others feel compelled to get him a "date" to fill the table? Somehow, what had once been a comfortable part of his separate "outside" life was now encroaching on their life as a couple.

These are just a few illustrations of the potential for trouble that lies in external relationships. But as with conflicts over family relationships, most problems can be prevented if both partners agree to put their own relationship ahead of all others and are willing to compromise to avoid resentment. The solution depends on the specific situation and the personalities involved. The husband who disliked his wife's childhood girlfriend might be satisfied if they would simply cut back on their time together or meet away from the house. Alternatively, his wife might explain the situation and ask her friend to be a little less boisterous when the husband was around. The mountain climber might have to reduce the time away from home, find a way to include his wife, or persuade her that she can trust him. She might offer to go along, arrange to take a vacation with her own friends while he's away, or trust her husband's promises of fidelity. In some situations, however, like that of the career women with the jealous husband, the only realistic solution may be to forfeit the friendship. In a case like this, the wife could maintain the required business association without allowing it to progress into something more familiar and dangerous. If she truly loves her husband, she owes him this degree of self-restraint.

All of these solutions assume that both partners are able and willing to discuss their feelings frankly, without fear of derision or backlash. This is particularly difficult in a situation like that involving the shy wife and her husband's college buddies. She can't afford to let herself be intimidated by the fact that those relationships predate her own or by any presuppositions about the men's influence on her husband. He may be sensitive enough to pick up on her feelings without her having to confront him, but if she says nothing, he can't be faulted for missing the problem. Nor can he fault her, however, for not wanting to participate in these reunions. Neither his friends nor their wives were of her choosing. The logical solution is for him to arrange to meet his friends either individually or, as they used to, without women. His wife has no right to demand that he give up the friendships, but she can expect him to make some concessions out of respect for her and their relationship.

These kinds of conflicts are inevitable in most long-term relationships. You and your partner are not clones of each other, and you naturally will have some differing opinions about the people in your life. But unless you each consciously moderate your independent friendships, both in terms of the time and emotional involvement you invest in them, they can pose a serious challenge even to an otherwise strong, enduring love relationship.

Personal Change

Perhaps the most frightening prospect for couples newly in love is that they may change so much as individuals that someday they no longer will be compatible. While it's true that everyone is growing and changing all the time, the kinds of radical developments that can destroy a relationship are unusual, at least among those over age twenty-five or so. By the time most people approach thirty, they have a fairly secure idea of who they are and what they want out of life. Those who don't are more likely to find themselves in false love relationships than in true love. Even among young adults who are still developing, when two people are mature enough to choose true love, they often are committed enough to adapt the relationship so that they both can grow without sacrificing their love.

Most of the changes that ripple the surface of true love, then, are relatively minor. Often they turn out to be nothing more than passing whims, "crazy ideas." Your partner comes home one day and tells you he wants to quit his job, pack up the apartment, and move to a farm in the country. If you're smart, you'll indulge him rather than challenge the idea head-on. Maybe you'll take a weekend trip to the country to price some farms and find out how much pigs and chickens cost to buy and raise. Perhaps you'll spend an hour calculating how much it would cost to get the operation running and how much you'd have to earn back to make a profit. Before you complete your investigation, your partner's urge most likely will have passed, but he'll appreciate you all the more for going along with him. If, on the other hand, you tell him his notion is stupid or ask what's wrong with him, he may become defiant and press the issue past the point of reason. You'll have turned an innocent daydream into a source of anger and contention.

There will be times, of course, when the changes in your partner are real, and directly affect your life together. The hardest to deal with are changes that require joint participation, the most critical of these being a change in attitude about having children. If you start your relationship mutually determined not to have children and then one of you decides otherwise, it doesn't mean you've stopped loving each other, but it could ultimately result in the end of the relationship. Having children is one of the few decisions that permits neither compromise nor concession. For most people, it is such a profound desire and such a major life goal that it requires two strongly committed partners; anything less may compromise the well-being of the children and the marriage. If you very much want children but your partner refuses, your resulting sadness and disappointment are likely to turn into deep resentment as time passes.

Therefore, beginning early in your relationship you should openly and intensively discuss your feelings about having children. One conversation is not sufficient. You need to understand the feelings and motivations behind each other's positions. This will help you gauge how deep your convictions are and whether they are likely to change in the future. How you would deal with such changes, of course, is the key question, and it may be impossible to predict this ahead of time. The issue may not be closed until you either have children or are past the childbearing years, but keeping the issue open for discussion at least will help you anticipate any changes of heart and give you the perspective to rationally assess your own position.

Much of the strain that occurs during pregnancy and early parenthood results from the changes the father and mother separately experience during this time. Aside from the obvious differences in their physical experiences during pregnancy and childbirth, men and women also go through different emotional responses. Most women accept the changes their bodies undergo during pregnancy as the necessary price of having a baby. They cope with morning sickness, varicose veins, heartburn, sleeplessness, and loss of sex drive, trusting that they'll return to normal once the baby arrives. In the meantime, they want to be reassured and, perhaps, indulged — but they understandably are preoccupied by the changes going on within them. It's a rare woman who is as attentive to her partner during pregnancy as she was before. This preoccupation with the baby intensifies after delivery and usually does not subside for several months. In part, the preoccupation is a matter of time and energy, both of which a young baby drains quite efficiently. Nothing undermines love like exhaustion! But the overwhelming emotional distraction of maternity is also the result of hormonal changes that take place during this time. New mothers feel a surge of affection, joy, amazement, and devotion to their infants that is often even stronger than the swoons of romantic passion. This emotional bombardment may temporarily make it difficult for a woman to be as intimate in love as her husband desires.

Not surprisingly, the father-to-be may feel a little left out and consequently be less enthusiastic and supportive than his wife would like. While she receives all the attention, the baby showers, and the concern from others, he's often rewarded with nothing more than a few congratulations and a fistful of obstetrical bills. The physical changes pregnancy causes in his wife may also make him uncomfortable. Despite the popular notion that women become more beautiful when pregnant, many men feel just the opposite and become less and less interested in having sex with their wives as pregnancy progresses. Even if they remain interested, the desire has to be mutual, and many women simply don't feel very sexy during pregnancy. The medical prohibition of sex for several weeks after, and sometimes before, childbirth imposes an additional barrier to intimacy between a couple.

When you and your partner understand and respect these differences and work to maintain physical and emotional intimacy throughout this period, you will find that certain compromises are essential. You may have to adjust your accustomed sexual positions and practices. Time alone together, which you used to take for granted, must now be scheduled between the demands of baby care. Both of you may have to make an effort to give each other attention that used to require no effort at all. Your willingness to make this effort is a mark of your love for each other.

When such compromises are not made, real damage may follow. Some men have sexual affairs during and immediately following their wives' pregnancies. They may be sending a signal that they want out of the relationship, but most just need some attention and excitement. As they see it, their wives are preoccupied and uncooperative, and they're justified in going elsewhere. When a husband is unfaithful, he usually is feeling considerable anger and resentment over what he views as his wife's self-absorption and lack of understanding of his needs. The real problem often is not lack of love, but lack of communication and effort. When both partners are willing to confront the sources of this infidelity, serious damage can be averted. Infidelity during pregnancy is not necessarily a sign that the marriage is falling apart, but it does indicate a critical period of transition.

Such transitions, though painful, can bring you and your partner closer together in the long run. Emerging secure in your love, you will be more understanding and responsive in the future and less likely to neglect or blame each other. You may also have a clearer understanding of your responsibilities and expectations within the family.

A different type of personal change that commonly, and often unnecessarily, tears couples apart is the "midlife crisis," which usually strikes around age forty. The crisis, of course, is caused by the simultaneous realization and rejection of the fact that one's life is half over. The standard reaction is to grasp for youthfulness in any available form while fleeing from all reminders of one's true age. For some, the totems of youthfulness are possessions, such as a new convertible or sports car, a chic wardrobe, a home gym, or a back yard pool. For others, material comforts are not enough; they demand a complete change in lifestyle. This may include an abrupt shift in career, location, exercise regimen, diet, social life, or — the ultimate — in romantic partner.

The main reason people grasp at these changes is that they view everything in their existing life as a reflection of the past. And nothing reflects the past more vividly than the spouse who has shared it with them. The same man who took his wife into his loving arms at age twenty-five may turn on her at forty, not because of anything she's done but because she serves as a constant reminder of his own mortality.

Those who choose the most drastic overhauls may argue that they have been "wasting time" up to this point, that they are going to "grab their last chance" to start a new life before it's too late and they're *really* old. In reality, they're simply trying to run away from time. The idea that we can rejuvenate ourselves by changing our surroundings or habits is, of course, illusion. And the most dangerous part of this illusion is the idea that swapping true love for a younger partner will bring happiness. Not only does this devastate the spouse left behind, but the relationship that follows is almost always based on false love. The new lifestyle and companion that are supposed to be so uplifting often end up making midlifers feel even older and more miserable.

Fortunately, not everyone goes through a major midlife crisis, and some don't have any at all. Unfortunately, it's almost impossible to predict who will coast through to the golden years and who will experience turbulence. One preventive measure is to start making long-range plans early in your relationship. Imagine yourselves growing old together, and decide together how you want to spend your later years. You may even plan a joint midlife change, something that you both dream of doing but that career and family obligations currently prevent. The important thing is to face the reality of aging. Midlife crises generally hit hardest those who have always considered themselves immune to time. They're the ones who jokingly say their clock stopped at thirty. Because they've never been willing to imagine themselves as forty-year-olds, they're shell-shocked when their fortieth birthday inevitably arrives. Taking your partner's hand and looking squarely into the future may spare you this crisis.

Personal change in almost any form challenges your unity as a couple because by definition it is something that occurs within one individual. Therefore, unless you maintain strong, ongoing communication and sensitivity as a couple, such changes are likely to lead you further and further apart. By continually reaffirming and strengthening your identity as a couple, you will reduce the temptation to follow your impulses at your partner's expense, but you also will acquire the mutual flexibility you need to bend the relationship for positive change.

The following six-step strategy, a kind of ongoing needs assessment, can help you achieve these goals when you feel yourselves drifting apart.

1. Identify the change. Ignoring a problem — any problem — within your relationship only makes it worse. You must face it before you can resolve it, and the earlier you do this, the better. Couples who break up because of personal change usually find, in retrospect, that the changes were ob-

vious for a long time, but they chose to ignore them for fear
of upsetting the marital balance. Ultimately, the partners
grew so far apart that they lost the core of their love. Had
they acknowledged the changes *as they began to develop*
the partners might have been able to affect the course of
subsequent developments so that the relationship could
grow with the individuals.

Claude began to recognize his own unhappiness long before his wife, Phyllis, did. He had just turned fifty, and on
the surface he had it all: a top position in a major advertising firm; a bright, witty, committed wife; two healthy,
happy teenage sons; a large, comfortable home in a fashionable district. But he was exhausted and dissatisfied much of
the time and turned to therapy to find out how he could
turn himself around. His therapist asked him to describe his
vision of an ideal life. The answer, to his surprise, tumbled
out spontaneously. He wanted to sell the house, move to a
smaller community, and become an artist. Overjoyed that
he had found a solution so easily, Claude raced home to tell
Phyllis. In response, she looked at him as if he'd lost his
mind. "You're crazy!" she said and marched him into my
office. She wanted me to "fix him."

2. Objectively assess why the changes are taking place. Had
Phyllis been able to take this step on her own, she and
Claude might have resolved the issue by themselves. Instead, we looked together for the sources of Claude's sudden announcement. They emerged quite quickly once we
began to explore *why* he was so dissatisfied. As remunera-
tive as his job was, he no longer felt that it was rewarding.
He had studied painting in college and originally intended
to become an artist but had gotten sucked into advertising
out of a need to support himself and, later, his family. For
years he had been so determined to succeed as a father and
a businessman that he hadn't given much thought to his
lapsed aspirations. Now his old dreams returned to him,
largely because he felt neglected at home. Phyllis's daily

schedule overflowed with volunteer work that frequently kept her out late at meetings. The kids had their own active lives. Claude felt as if he were slipping through the cracks in his own family, and his job simply couldn't compensate.

Personal change is almost always a reaction to other events or conditions in one's life. These may lie within the relationship. They may be outside influences, such as family, friends, career concerns, or economics. They may be natural occurrences, such as aging or illness. Most often, as in Claude's case, a combination of circumstances provokes the change. Both you and your partner need to understand what is behind any "crazy" behavior before you can determine whether it's a passing fancy or a serious development. The secret is to forget momentarily that you're intimate partners and view the situation as an outside investigator would: weighing all the evidence and using logic, rather than emotion, as your guide.

3. Identify and voice your own needs. How are the personal changes affecting you and your relationship now, and where will they lead in the future? If the changes are in your partner, what adjustments would you need to make to keep step, and are you willing to make them? What do you need from your partner that you are no longer receiving? These were the questions Phyllis had to answer in order for Claude to understand her point of view.

Initially she resisted, arguing that her life was perfect as it was, that she couldn't imagine why Claude was "doing this to" her. This, of course, just made Claude feel more neglected and defensive. Only when he threatened to leave her to carry out his plan did she realize how serious the situation might become. She calmed down and tried to explain her own expectations in a more rational way.

Phyllis loved Claude and was committed to him and their life together. In her mind, this had never been in doubt. Her life had become very busy, it was true, but Claude had never objected before. In fact, he had encouraged her to keep herself busy because, he said, it made him feel less guilty about the long hours he had to spend at work. Phyllis simply had become so preoccupied with her volunteer responsibilities that she never even noticed that she was spending more time away from home now than he was. That certainly didn't mean her activities were more important to her than her marriage, but she did take great pride in them, and she could not bear to give them up, which she felt she would have to do if she capitulated to his "whim."

Phyllis was also concerned about the financial ramifications of Claude's plan. She loved their home and was not willing to sell it. She liked their lifestyle and felt that they both would be miserable if they had to rely on his artistic talents (about which she was skeptical) to support them. Even if they could give up the second car and the pool, she argued, how would they pay for the children's college education? The uncertainty that was built into the plan might excite Claude, but it made her very nervous.

4. Reaffirm that your relationship and family deserve priority. It's easy to forget priorities when you're preoccupied by goals evolving from work or other outside interests, but as soon as you lose this common thread, your relationship may be in danger. This was what had happened to Phyllis and Claude. They had not stopped loving each other, but they had drifted so long without actively tending to their relationship that their other interests had started to take precedence. It took therapy to make them recognize this shift and recover their commitment to each other.

One of the dangers of waiting too long to deal with change in your relationship is that you or your partner may lose sight of your previous order of priorities. Suddenly your work or your private dreams seem more important, and the fabric of your life together begins to unravel. Once you've reached this point, it is very difficult to reestablish the three-way balance — individual/couple/individual — that is the essence of true love. If you address problems early, however, you can rely on your mutual commitment to help you stay on course together.

5. Compromise. Taking into account the needs of the family and each other's needs as individuals, you next must decide together what adjustments you each have to make to keep moving forward. For Phyllis and Claude, the key areas of disagreement centered on relocating and sacrificing their basic lifestyle. Although Phyllis wasn't entirely convinced that Claude had enough talent or artistic drive to survive as an artist, she agreed that he should have a chance to try. She even agreed to make certain economic sacrifices to enable him to do this. She just was not willing to give up her home or security. So Claude traded his executive office for a consulting position that provided a reliable, if lower, income and permitted him time to paint on mornings and weekends. Phyllis cut back her volunteer schedule so that they could spend two or three evenings together, and gradually they recovered the strength that had been draining from their relationship. If Claude never did become a successful artist, neither did he sacrifice his marriage to find this out.

   It's important to recognize that your concessions won't always be evenly distributed. Usually, one of you will feel you're giving more than the other, and sometimes this will be true. But that's beside the point as long as the net result is satisfactory to you both. The ultimate goal is to remain supportive of each other and not allow your personal differences to turn into competitions for power.

6. Get outside help when necessary. One of the most important traits of a healthy couple is the ability to recognize when they can't solve their problems alone. As simple as step-by-step strategies may appear in books, applying them to real life is much more difficult. This was why Phyllis and Claude could not get back on track by themselves. For you and your partner, it may help to practice on the minor issues that arise early in your relationship. This will prepare you for dealing with more serious problems later. But what

if your partner is fired and responds by becoming deeply depressed or drinking heavily? What if you develop an overwhelming desire to have children and your partner adamantly refuses? What if you can't shake your partner's midlife crisis? Professional therapy can help you put the pieces back together.

Many people are afraid of professional counseling. In some cases, they know they've been dishonest or hurtful and don't want to be found out. In others, they suspect the situation is even worse than it appears, and they don't want to confront this. And in still others, they just don't want to be bothered with the conflict and pain that therapy stirs up in the process of healing the wounds. But avoiding therapy does not spare you from pain; it simply postpones and usually intensifies it. Don't be so proud or embarrassed that you don't seek the help you need when you need it.

The Basic Rules of Love

As comforting and enriching as true love is, it must be able to bend with both the major and the minor stresses of daily life. The issues we've discussed are just a few of the challenges you are likely to face as your love develops. There probably will be many others that are unforeseeable. The following basic rules of love can help you overcome such conflicts, whether large or small.

Give and demand equality at all times.

This does not mean that you both must do an equal number of chores around the house or that you must have exactly the same duties in the family. It does mean that you each have the right to an equal vote in how the household and family are run, that you make all major decisions together, and that you respect each other's viewpoint. In short, equality in love means that, regardless of who makes more money or has more power in the eyes of the outside world, neither partner is more important than the other within the relationship.

Talk and listen openly and honestly.

Communication is like the nervous system of love. If the system is healthy, information and feelings are constantly being transmitted from one person to the other. There are neither secrets nor lies, and both of you are equally willing to send and receive the messages that keep you tied into each other's life because you understand that, no matter how intimate you are, you cannot read each other's mind. You value your own body of experience enough to share it with your partner, and you value your partner's experience enough to listen and ask questions without being judgmental. If your individual lives become very disparate, you may need to make an extra effort to read or otherwise educate yourselves to maintain open dialogue. Developing your shared interests will also prevent you from drifting too far apart. Unfortunately, communication often becomes most difficult just when it's most necessary — when you are in conflict or under stress. The best way to make sure the system functions during these difficult times is to use it fully at *all* times. The two of you need to spend some time every day talking *alone together* about the issues and events in each other's life. As natural as this may seem in the beginning, it requires much more planning and commitment once you have children and develop other obligations outside your marriage. If you allow this ongoing exchange to lapse or become one-sided, the precious balance between your inner world as a twosome and your outer worlds as individuals may falter.

Recognize and confront problems directly.

Accept the fact that you sometimes will face difficult problems and that you won't always agree on how to resolve them. The more you disagree, the more important it is to address the situation head-on, exchanging and listening to each other's opinions. Many couples subconsciously sidestep the major problems in their life by focusing on symptomatic details or by creating additional confusion as a distraction from the central issues. Rather than working together to reach a decision, for example, a couple divided on whether to have a second child might argue endlessly over the first child's day care arrangements or evade the conflict by immersing themselves in plans to remodel their home. The longer a problem is allowed to languish and the more threatening it is to your underlying stability as a couple, the more of a smoke shield you are likely to construct to avoid facing the facts. This is why you need to be honest with yourselves and each other and to act immediately to resolve disputes as they arise.

Share responsibility for problems and solutions.
If either or both of you are too proud to shoulder the blame when you've erred, then chances are that you're too proud to maintain true love. You cannot survive as a loving couple unless both of you are able to admit your mistakes and say you're sorry. Apology is often the best way to defuse an argument and open the door to compromise. By the same token, if you work together to reach a successful solution to your problems, the pride you feel *as a couple* will deepen your love for each other and enrich your life together.

These are simple rules, but if you both adopt them, you will find that they can guide you through almost any difficulty. It may help to review them together periodically and to make a conscious effort to apply them on a daily basis. They can't help you if you follow them only during times of crisis or if only one of you accepts them. Living love, like choosing love, is a mutual proposition that must continually be reaffirmed. In the next chapter, we examine what happens when that mutuality falters.

12

DOUBTING LOVE

"WE HAVEN'T HAD good sex for months," said Michael, clenching his knees with both hands and rocking slightly from side to side. "When we have intercourse, which isn't often, she either fakes orgasm or lies there as if she's waiting for me to get it over with. At first I thought she was just preoccupied, or maybe it was a shift in hormones, like after she had the babies, but this is different. It's getting worse, not better."

"This sounds as if there's more wrong than just sex. What else is going on?"

"We hardly ever see each other. When I get home, she's in the middle of fixing dinner and refereeing the kids. Then there's the grind of dinner, bathing and putting the kids to bed. By the time there's a minute to talk to each other, she's either watching TV, reading, or going to bed. On weekends, she usually dumps the kids with me and goes to the gym or has some project or other at school."

"It's difficult to deal with problems when you're both so busy. What happens when you do talk?"

"Most of the time, we're so angry we end up insulting each other. But we never argue about the big issues. It's the little things that seem to take most of our attention. She yells at me for leaving the cap off the toothpaste. I get angry because she leaves her shoes all over the house. She complains about the way I wash the dishes. I bark at her for washing the lights and darks together. She says I don't spend enough time with the kids. The bickering is endless . . . and exhausting. I know I should be able to stop it, but she seems determined to provoke these fights, and I get sucked in. Do you think she wants out?"

Michael seemed genuinely distraught. He and his wife, Miriam, had been married for seven years. It was his third marriage, her first, and he'd always suspected he was the more committed one. So he had come to therapy alone at first to sort out his own feelings and suspicions. But no matter how much he wanted to resolve his marriage, he couldn't do it by himself. To produce any real results, both of them would have to come together for counseling. He said he thought he could persuade Miriam to come.

When they arrived for their first joint session, the frost between them was evident. Miriam fiddled ceaselessly with her wedding band and directed her eyes anywhere but on her husband. Michael fidgeted, watching her as if for a signal either to start fighting or to reconcile.

"Why don't you tell me how your relationship started?" I suggested.

Miriam rolled her eyes. She obviously didn't have much faith in this process.

"We met in the park," volunteered Michael. "She was walking her dog and I was jogging. I tripped over the leash."

"You always were a klutz," remarked Miriam, as if it proved that he'd been wrong for her from the start.

"Then what did you see in him?" I asked her.

She glanced at Michael, her expression softening just slightly. "Well . . . he's often very funny. He's very, very smart. He's nice looking." She took a deep breath. "And he was willing to spend more than two days with me, which is more than I could say about any of the other men I was dating." She shrugged, as if that was the end of it.

"Michael?" I asked. "What attracted you to Miriam?"

"It was a physical attraction at first, I guess," he said, eyeing her for feedback. "I liked her looks, her body, her feistiness. She's bright and energetic. And the timing was right. As Miriam said, she was ripe for a real relationship, and so was I." He wore a puzzled, nostalgic expression as he stopped talking.

"How long were you together before you married?"

"Two years," answered Michael. "We started living together after two months."

"When did you have your first child?"

"Almost exactly a year after we got married," answered Miriam. "And the second came along three years later."

"Did the relationship change after you had children, Miriam?"

"Actually, Michael was terrific about my being pregnant. He went through both births with me and was very supportive. Those first years were the good times. Too bad they couldn't last." She sighed and chewed on her thumbnail, fighting back tears.

"When did things start going wrong?"

"I told you," said Michael. "I first noticed about three months ago, when sex began to slide —"

"It started a long time before that!" broke in Miriam angrily. "We stopped talking months before the problems showed up in bed."

"Did you try to tell Michael you were dissatisfied?" I asked Miriam.

"I did everything but leave notes for him! I told him he was working too much, that I felt he was neglecting me and the children. I asked him if we could go out more often, just the two of us. I told him I was bored, that it didn't seem like we had anything in common anymore."

Michael looked astounded at this revelation. Where had he been?

"What did he say?" I asked.

"His eyes would glaze over. He'd start talking about how overburdened he was at work, as if I should feel sorry for him.

He completely missed the point — until I got so annoyed I stopped wanting to have sex with him."

"You're having an affair, aren't you?" Michael yelled. "That's what's causing all this!"

"That's bullshit and you know it," she erupted. "Just where would I get the time? Stick it in between Johnny's scout meetings and Katie's swimming lessons? Come on! If anybody's having an affair it's you, with that new office temp who keeps calling you at home."

"I only wish it were true!" he snarled. "Obviously, I've been faithful to *you* for too long!"

"Hold it, hold it," I interrupted. "Before you get carried away, let's try to get one thing straight. It's clear there's a lot of anger and resentment here, and that's making it very difficult for you to deal with each other on any other level. You're going to have to get past this emotional barricade if we're to make any progress." For the next twenty minutes we tried to back away from their accusations and focus instead on what they hoped to accomplish through therapy. When at last they calmed down, I zeroed in. "Saving a marriage that's troubled, as yours is, requires a tremendous effort from both of you. If we're going to proceed, you each need to make the commitment. Are you sure you *want* to come out of this together and are you willing to put in the necessary work to make that happen, Michael?"

He paused to collect himself. "I don't want to give up. We wouldn't be here if I did."

"Miriam?"

"I have to admit there are times when I wish I were single again. But then I think about the kids. And I'm not twenty anymore. Besides, I quit working when our first was born, and God knows how I'd support myself." She glanced at Michael. "I look back on the good times with Michael, and I think I'd give anything to get them back, but we seem to have drifted so far apart that I've nearly lost hope. If there is hope, then yes, I'm willing to try to save the marriage."

"Not exactly a ringing endorsement," muttered Michael.

"From listening to you, I'd say there's a lot of miscommunication going on," I said. "You're both going to have to stop being so defensive and make a serious effort to hear what the other is saying. This is going to require spending more time — *making* more time — to explore the issues that are really bothering you, not just the minor irritations. We'll start this process in counseling, but you need to carry it through at home so that it becomes an ongoing part of your relationship. You've gotten lazy about your marriage and preoccupied with your own individual lives. You can start to turn things around if you start treating each other with respect. If you keep acting the way you have been, you're probably just going to drift further apart."

Both looked skeptical.

"If you're going to go through with this process," I continued, "you'll need to follow some basic rules. If either of you is seeing somebody else, you won't be able to deal effectively with the problems in your marriage. You can't possibly give each other the attention and commitment that's necessary if part of your energy is going to someone on the side." Miriam's flinch was barely perceptible. "Also, even if there are times when it seems you may not be able to work through this, try not to threaten each other with divorce. If you truly want to save your marriage, then that goal needs to be foremost in your minds. Stop blaming and start listening. Don't be afraid to face the parts of your relationship that need fixing. This is going to cause a storm, and you'll probably feel a lot worse before you start feeling better. But this is the *only* way to make your relationship whole again!"

Michael and Miriam accepted the terms without enthusiasm. They were not optimistic, but neither had they given up hope entirely. Both recognized that their relationship had a durable foundation. They had simply neglected the structure of intimacy.

It took nearly three months for Miriam and Michael to begin reversing the damage. During this time they opened a great many wounds and did a lot of talking, a lot of crying. They had to confront and deal with problems that had long been festering below the surface, particularly Miriam's conflicting feelings about being a housewife. Initially, she'd volunteered to quit her job as a dental hygienist when her first child was born. She and Michael had planned to have two children, and Miriam felt strongly that she should be home full-time during the early years. But after a year or two, she started to feel twinges of jealousy and resentment toward Michael. He was a fairly high-paid engineer when they met, and over the course of their marriage he leapfrogged several times to different companies, doubling his salary with each move. While she was delighted to have the additional income, she envied the excitement and ego gratification that were Michael's personal rewards at work. She felt that she was sliding into his shadow and that even he was starting to take her for granted. Though she adored her children, she was feeling bored and trapped at home. Much of her day was spent watching soap operas and ferrying the children around town, and she yearned for a change of pace. When she mentioned going back to work, Michael protested that they had plenty of money and the kids needed her. Besides, she didn't want to go back to being a hygienist, and she had no other skills.

She tried to vent her energy by throwing herself into parent associations and signing the kids up for countless activities, but her greatest release came at the gym, where she spent most of her time when the kids were at school and on weekends when Michael was home. There she found herself eyeing — and being eyed by — attractive younger men.

Not knowing how to assimilate her frustration in any other way, she began considering divorce. What she really was missing, however, was Michael's reassurance and support. He had always felt she was at least his intellectual equal, but for a long while he'd neglected to express this attitude. He thought she understood how he felt. He didn't think she still needed to hear that he loved and valued her. This assumption was one of the main reasons they found themselves in crisis. What he learned as they worked their way back together was not only that she needed this reassurance from him but that he badly needed it from her as well.

As Michael and Miriam reunited, they put to rest many of the petty grievances that had been simmering below the surface ever since their courtship. They negotiated a household policy covering the laundry, toothpaste caps, shoes, dishes, and all the other minutiae that had sparked past feuds. Michael stopped belittling Miriam's need to work and suggested that they hire a part-time housekeeper so she could either get a job or go back to school. And they agreed to spend at least one half hour a day and one evening a week alone by themselves, without the children, television, or other distractions. As they recovered the intimacy of talking and simply spending time together, their sex life gradually returned to normal.

Neither Michael nor Miriam would ever go through this crisis again voluntarily, but there's no doubt their relationship benefited from it in the end. It forced them to recognize that their love would not cruise indefinitely without fuel or direction. Even though their foundation was solid, had they languished much longer they probably would have split up, becoming yet another statistic in a divorce rate that has hovered around fifty percent of all American marriages since the mid-1970s.

The Rise and Impending Fall of Divorce

For the past two decades, this alarming divorce rate has documented the power of false love in our society. It no longer is considered a disgrace or an automatic mistake to leave your partner. In fact, you may win more approval for leaving a troubled marriage than for committing yourself to make it work. Practically speaking, it is much easier to get a divorce today than it is to heal an ailing marriage. It is also easier to blame your partner for life's difficulties and disappointments than it is to deal with them directly.

A large part of the problem is the glorification of false love through the media, which hold out insubstantial but glamorous relationships as a never-ending lure. Like a powerful career, fashionable clothes, prestigious cars, exotic vacations, and a lavish home, the relationships portrayed by the media are a symbol of status rather than of emotional health or personal well-being. Such a relationship is not a goal but a possession, and as such it can be traded in when it wears out. The fact that this model of soap opera romance is so popular demonstrates the strength of false love's seductive powers, not only in novels and on the screen but also in real life. True love may be deeper and richer, but it doesn't glitter, and it requires hard work.

Several factors are beginning to subtly undermine the power of illusion over marriage, however. One is the simple reality of divorce. Reports from the field have come in now from several generations: Divorce is not a short-term crisis that you endure and then put behind you; the trauma of a failed marriage has long-term consequences. Regardless of how socially acceptable divorce may be, losing an intimate partner is painful and disorienting. Divorce represents a major change of life, a loss of companionship and, in many cases, of personal focus. Most devastating of all, it represents the loss of the hope and faith embodied in marriage.

Being single also has lost much of its allure in the last few years. The epidemic of AIDS and other sexually transmitted diseases has transformed dating from a recreational activity into a potentially life-threatening exercise. For those who have never been married, there is no choice but to accept this fact and get on, carefully, with the business of finding a partner. For those who are divorced, however, it's more difficult to be philosophical. The physical risk of being single may seem an additional punishment for "failing" at marriage. Among women in their thirties and forties, the fear is exacerbated by the ratio of eligible men to women, which stacks the odds against divorced women marrying again.

The upshot is that many couples who might once have split up at the first murmur of trouble are now either sticking it out or, like Michael and Miriam, working to undo the damage. The temptation to bail out remains strong — illusion has a tendency to override even life-threatening realities — but despite false love's continuing temptations, the pressure is mounting to make marriage work. This is why so many of today's troubled couples are turning to counseling rather than immediately filing for divorce. It is also why this chapter is a necessary part of our discussion about reality and romance.

The Myth of "Falling Out of Love"

Couples often worry that they are "falling out of love," but the truth is that you can't fall *out* any more than you can fall *in* love. Loving someone is a choice that, once made, must be renewed continuously throughout your relationship. Ceasing to love also is a choice, if not always a conscious one, and usually is prompted by false love's seductions. And unfortunately, even true love does not provide absolute protection against illusion.

The most secure relationships experience cycles of passion and doubt. As devoted as you may be to your marriage, there are bound to be days when you feel a little bored and entertain fantasies of a different partner. When you're overwhelmed by a major change, such as moving, changing jobs, becoming pregnant, or being a new parent, you probably will be less interested in your partner and in sex. The same may be true of periods when the two of you are preoccupied with outside work or activities or when you're in conflict. These lapses of "love's magic" are both normal and inevitable. They are *not* valid reasons to doubt your love, but if you don't make the effort to restore intimacy between these lulls, then they may evolve into a legitimate threat. This is what happened to Miriam and Michael; they had the necessary base for a lasting relationship, but they became lazy and complacent, stopped reconfirming their love, and let the walls collapse around them. By the time they entered therapy, the spiral was spinning so far out of control that they'd nearly forgotten whether they had ever had true love in the first place.

The complacency in their relationship, which alone is destructive enough, was compounded by Miriam's individual unhappiness, which she was unwilling to resolve on her own and so blamed on Michael. This is a very common pattern. One partner becomes disenchanted with "life," a term that might mean work, family, self-esteem, age, and/or health, and looks around for a scapegoat. The neglected relationship stares back, the perfect candidate. If only you could get out of your marriage, the fantasy whispers, you'd be free to start over and do things *your* way for a change. The illusion adapts readily to the specific source of malcontent. For example: If only you could be single again, you'd feel younger; if only you could get away from your partner's nagging, you'd stop feeling like a failure. The truth is that the relationship is rarely the source of such problems.

Why, then, do people so often take out their unhappiness on those they love the most? Number one, because the lover is convenient and less likely to strike back than someone outside the family; and number two, because people who do this tend to have such low self-esteem that they often can't solve their problems in a more constructive manner. The man who hates his job but lacks the confidence to quit or confront his boss often feels safe in blaming his wife. She is available and accessible, and he is not afraid of her. Moreover, she knows him so well that she serves as a constant reminder of his own inadequacies, for which he resents her. By accusing her, he manages to sidestep his responsibilty to solve his own problems. And because he believes she won't retaliate, he feels free to level his complaints at her. Little of this is conscious, of course. Even though he's staying out late, ignoring her, and finding fault with almost everything she does, the husband may not even realize how hard he's being on his wife. Having convinced himself that he's sacrificing his happiness and success for *her* sake, he's genuinely astounded when she accuses him of not being supportive or of being too self-absorbed. Defiantly, he responds that she's impossible to please and has never really understood him. And so the situation spirals, with both partners engaging in a potentially terminal dance of destruction.

This scapegoating syndrome often becomes a kind of buffer against reality. Even if she tries to be understanding and help him resolve his problems, the disgruntled husband may keep his wife at arm's length in order to maintain his fantasy of a magical solution. Accepting his wife's help in resolving his problems would mean accepting his own share of responsibility as well as committing himself to practical action. Sometimes it can seem less painful to let a marriage disintegrate than to face the facts.

Such individual crises attack even the strongest marriages at their core: mutuality. When one partner stops communicating and trusting the other, the relationship stops being mutual, and without mutuality true love cannot survive. Marital counseling usually won't help until the errant partner undergoes individual therapy, starts to accept and deal with his or her personal problems, and renews a commitment to the relationship. Only at that point is there a realistic basis for turning the situation around.

Preventing such crises requires, first of all, accepting that true love does not guarantee that you'll live happily ever after. True love certainly can *contribute* to your happiness, but it cannot be expected to compensate if your life beyond the relationship is in a shambles. Nor can you reasonably blame your partner if you fail to take responsibility for dealing with your own external problems. True love entitles you to expect support, not salvation, from your partner.

The second key precaution is to make a conscious effort to keep the lines of communication open at all times. The more you and your partner confide in each other, the better equipped you will be to support each other as troubles evolve, and the less likely you'll be to blame each other. This mutual support can provide extra ammunition to combat your individual problems while at the same time strengthening your relationship.

Ultimately, the prognosis for your relationship in the face of adversity depends largely on the inner strength that each of you possesses as an individual. If you are resourceful at solving your own problems, you can apply the same skills to problems affecting both of you. If you take responsibility for your own lives, you are better prepared to share responsibility for your relationship. If you are emotionally secure as individuals, then you'll be less motivated to blame each other when external problems get out of control. In short, the happier and more confident you and your partner are individually, the more successful your love is likely to be.

Coping with Temptation

Former President Jimmy Carter made headlines when he acknowledged that he sometimes had "lust in his heart." Some people were righteously indignant that the president should make such a confession. Some mocked him for stating his fantasies so benignly. But the reason his remark made history had more to do with America's pretensions than with Carter's personal predilections. This passing comment struck at a basic truth affecting all couples. Almost *everyone*, including those whose marriages are sublimely happy, has fantasies about different sexual partners. The point Carter was making was that these fantasies can coexist with true love as long as they are recognized as illusion. Danger arises only when we allow temptation to overpower commitment.

While everyone has fantasies, of course, not everyone has an equal opportunity to act on them. Obviously, if you are rich, beautiful, or powerful, you're more likely to receive attractive sexual offers than if you're merely "average." You're also more likely to meet potential partners if you travel a great deal or work with a wide variety of individuals. The fast-paced executive life is more conducive to philandering than is the life of a housewife — one reason why some men don't want their wives to have independent careers.

If you're often on the receiving end of appealing propositions, you need to exert far greater self-restraint to remain monogamous than if you have to do the propositioning yourself. And by the same token, a fleeting sexual encounter — a failure of will, in effect — is far less likely to be meaningful than a premeditated, ongoing affair. The brief encounter constitutes a challenge to true love, while the affair constitutes a threat. Neither can be condoned, but the affair is vastly more serious.

Because sexual temptation is such a strong undercurrent in our society, with some studies indicating that as many as seventy percent of married men and women have had extramarital sex, it's important to understand the difference between a sexual fling and a sexual affair. Many men and some women feel a genuine desire for impersonal, supplemental sex without any pretense of love. For some, it's simply a matter of "not getting enough at home," which usually can be remedied by more communication and sexual honesty within the marriage. For others, the lure is the ego gratification of attracting someone new and different, a hunger that ultimately must be controlled by sheer self-restraint. These kinds of encounters all amount to a form of masturbation, however. They require no emotional investment, and when the sex is over, they're over. This is not to say that they're healthy. Extramarital flings often are symptomatic of sexual problems that need to be worked out within the marriage, and if discovered they can unleash a tremendous amount of pain, guilt, and resentment between the partners. The added risk of contracting a sexually related disease and passing it on to one's spouse and children now makes any kind of adultery physically as well as emotionally dangerous. While many philanderers argue that the boost to their self-esteem and sexual confidence actually *benefits* marriage, in reality extramarital sex is almost never truly "safe" or "innocuous," and it certainly is not good for a truly loving relationship.

An affair is much more menacing, however. Even though the primary attraction may be purely physical, the intention in an affair is to keep it going, to turn it into something more than a one-time fling. Usually, having an affair serves as an escape from marital difficulties. Instead of confronting the problems and undertaking the hard work of resolving them, the disenchanted partner finds a much more pleasant (at least temporarily) distraction in taking a lover. Of course, it doesn't always occur in such a premeditated fashion. Most people who have affairs would argue that "it just happens." Consider the following examples:

- The frustrated wife confides in her friend at work and is so overwhelmed by his ability to comfort her that she convinces herself she's falling in love with him. Most likely, she's confusing sympathy and sexual attraction with love. With the excitement gone from her marriage, she may feel she has nothing to lose, but if she allows the affair to continue, it probably will precipitate a real crisis at home. She will then have to choose between what's likely to be a superficial relationship and the grueling and uncertain process of salvaging a marriage that has been ripped by infidelity. Even if her affair could be built into a truly loving relationship, she and her new partner first would have to overcome the guilt and trauma the affair has created.
- The bored husband finds himself alone with his neighbor's beautiful wife and discovers that she's as attracted to him as he is to her. The attraction feeds their egos, and their familiarity makes it easy for them to have an affair. Because both couples are such good friends, the adulterers may feel that they'll never be suspected, but they could well be found out, and when this happens the hurt, outrage, and humiliation will be all the worse because the affair is "between friends."
- Worried that the divorce statistics inevitably are going to catch up with her, the neglected wife starts an affair as a "protective" measure. She sees her boyfriend only occasion-

ally, and her husband never finds out about it, but the fact that she's dividing her body and emotions between two men quickly takes its toll on her marriage. She's less willing to tolerate her husband's distractedness, but also less inclined to confront him. It's so much easier to take what she needs from the affair. Ultimately, her fear of divorce becomes a self-fulfilling prophecy because she can't love two people at once. No one can.

The fact that almost everyone is tempted at least occasionally to have a sexual fling and that many are tempted to have a more substantial illicit affair doesn't mean that you should succumb to these temptations. Whatever short-term selfish gratification infidelity may bring, it produces far more long-term harm and usually expands whatever confusion or pain already exists within a marriage. While most internal marital problems will involve only you and your partner, the moment you start having an affair you expose a much larger circle to potential pain. Should word of the liaison leak out — and it inevitably does if the affair continues for any length of time — it will hurt not only your partner but your children, your family, and your extramarital partner's family. If divorce is widely accepted today, sexual infidelity still is not.

The solution to marital disenchantment is not to escape into someone else's arms but to find and resolve the sources of disenchantment. If the problems cannot be resolved, then perhaps the marriage will dissolve, but you need to make your own decisions without someone on the sidelines influencing your judgment. Wait until one relationship has ended before starting another.

Once you've been unfaithful and have realized that it was a terrible mistake, you're faced with the issue of confession. If your partner suspects nothing and you feel driven to "come clean," examine your motivation first. People who spontaneously confess to infidelity are usually trying either to assuage their own guilt or to punish their partners. Assuming you truly love your partner and are determined never to stray again, there is no valid reason to inflict the kind of hurt and doubt that this news inevitably would provoke. Such a confession would needlessly punish your partner and might spark a crisis where none previously existed. It would stir up resentment and mistrust, even if the infidelity took place years before. There is no statute of limitations on the pain of betrayal, and the process of slicing open the relationship and trying to work together to resolve other sources of conflict becomes much more difficult once you've exposed past dalliances, however much you may regret having had them.

Some people do report that the night after they confessed to having an affair, they had great sex with their spouse. In part this is because there's a certain titillation to imagining your partner with someone else. The idea of a partner's affair also arouses sexual competitiveness. Many look to sex as a quick fix for the problems that led to the affair in the first place. It never works this way, however. Usually in a matter of days — or hours — the recriminations intensify and the sexual passion becomes submerged in anger.

But what if your partner accuses you? In this case, you have nothing to gain by covering up. Explain the facts as gently as possible, stressing that you've made your mistakes and are committed to never repeat them. Try to use this discussion to explore some of the ways you can strengthen your relationship to protect you both against future temptations. If the revelation causes a great deal of pain and guilt that you cannot handle by yourselves, get professional help.

Getting Help

What if, despite all your precautions and hard work, temptation or doubt overcomes you? Even couples who have a strong foundation of true love occasionally find themselves in this position. If your relationship is relatively new or its base is not too secure, you may be especially susceptible to panic. Whatever the sources of the crisis, however, when it strikes, you and your partner have only three options:

1. Accept the situation and live with it as is. Some people would rather have a troubled relationship than none at all. Others are willing to accept false love for the sake of money, power, excitement, or other trade-offs. There is nothing wrong with this decision as long as it is a considered one, and no one else is hurt by it.

2. Get out. This is a last resort. Tempting as it may be to bail out whenever the relationship gets rocky, this impulse is antithetical to true love. If you believe you have true love, or at least a strong base for true love, you can only harm the relationship by running every time there's a conflict. And if you keep running from one relationship to the next, you will never succeed in true love.

3. Turn the situation around. If you and your partner have the basis for true love and if you both sincerely want to make it work, you should be able to overcome almost any obstacle. The process may not be easy, and you may not be able to do it on your own. As Michael and Miriam found, couples sometimes need outside help to restore focus and direction when their relationship feels like it's out of control. The critical requirement for saving a struggling marriage, however, is mutual commitment. Unless both partners are willing to invest the energy, no amount of counseling can restore the necessary core of love.

How do you know when it's time to seek outside help? Be on guard for the following warning signs:

- Certain issues keep coming up and never get resolved. Some problems evaporate naturally, even without being resolved, and these generally are not cause for concern. But others become a plague on the relationship, and even if they seem trivial at first they can become perpetual irritants. Regardless of whether you believe these issues could ever threaten your marriage, don't let them fester.

- You begin resenting your partner. Resentment usually leads quickly to anger, and anger usually leads to distrust. Without trust, true love cannot survive.

- One of you is avoiding the other. The avoidance may be purely emotional, or it may be both physical and emotional. The symptoms include an increasing amount of time spent apart, lack of intimacy when you're together, and a decrease in sexual frequency and desire.

- You or your partner fantasize about life as a single person. The signals may be as overt as a threat of divorce or as subtle as a renewed interest in single friends.

- Communication has broken down. When there is a consistent pattern of miscommunication, you will feel as if you are constantly talking across each other. One or both of you may stop listening or you may keep misinterpreting each other's messages. This often is merely a sign of laziness or preoccupation, but if not corrected it can become chronic.

- You find yourself continually complaining about your partner to family and friends. While it's important to have people in whom you can confide, when there are serious or chronic problems in your marriage it's generally unwise to lean on family members or friends for suggestions. Instead of the unbiased, constructive support you need in such situations, you're likely to receive judgmental and ill-informed advice. Your family's responses may be colored by their own interests in either supporting or breaking up your marriage, and your friends' advice usually will be slanted in your favor, either because they haven't heard your partner's side of the story or because they don't want to risk your friendship by telling you their true opinions. If you cannot deal with your partner openly and honestly, you probably are better off turning to an impartial therapist than to the people who have a personal investment in you or your marriage.

- One of you feels the relationship is out of control or is falling apart, and you can't pinpoint and resolve the cause. Sometimes this occurs after a prolonged series of arguments or in the face of a family crisis. At other times it's more internal. If either partner states a need or desire to see a marriage counselor, there's probably a legitimate reason behind it.

The most important rule is *not* to wait until the problems are overwhelming. Even in Michael and Miriam's case, there was a good chance they would succumb to the hostility they'd allowed to infest their marriage. Had they come months earlier, when Miriam first realized that Michael was not taking her discontent seriously, the wounds would have been less deep and the healing process less arduous. By the time a relationship hits the resentment stage, so much divisive momentum has built up that it often requires almost herculean strength to halt and reverse it.

Ideally, marriage counseling is not a last resort but a resource for couples with basically healthy relationships. It provides an opportunity to peel away the layers of superficial problems, focus on the strengths and weaknesses beneath the surface, and marshal those strengths to resolve ongoing problems and conflicts. Even for a unified couple, this process can be emotionally draining — opening up a relationship, after all, is like opening a Pandora's box of concealed truths — but the net result usually fortifies the marriage in a way that protects it from future crisis.

When Christine and Mark turned to counseling, neither had any thought that their marriage was in trouble. They'd been together for four years and planned to start a family in the near future. As they sat in my office, they held hands. Each listened attentively as the other spoke. I was particularly impressed by Mark's calmness. Most of the husbands I see in marital therapy are visibly anxious and usually angry at first. This tall, robust young man seemed perfectly at ease with himself and with his wife.

Christine, a willowy blonde with a penetrating, earnest gaze, explained that she had suggested they come. "The problem, in a nutshell, is that I think Mark is drinking too much. Not that he's an alcoholic, but still it scares me. He doesn't think there's a problem."

It seemed that Mark, who had recently taken a job as manager of a large furniture store, frequently went to a nearby bar with his coworkers and had as many as four or five beers before coming home. They had never actively fought about his drinking, but Christine had voiced her concern several times and he had refused to take her seriously. Finally, when she told him she was worried about him, he agreed that they needed to get an outside opinion to break the stalemate.

"For me, having a few beers at the end of the day is just a way of unwinding and getting to know the guys I work with," he explained. "I don't drink to get drunk or escape from anything. It doesn't affect my work or the way I treat Christine."

"But it sounds as if Christine feels differently," I said, suspecting that the drinking was a symptom of something else happening in the relationship.

"No," answered Christine, to my surprise. "I don't really disagree with what Mark says. He doesn't come home drunk, and his behavior hasn't changed. . . ."

"But you're worried," I reminded her. "When did you start to feel he was drinking too much?"

"It first hit me when I realized he was drinking *every* night," she said. Then she paused, looked at Mark, and continued. "But I guess I started to *worry* when we began to talk about having kids. That made me think about Mark's drinking in a different way. I mean, it's okay if he goes out with the guys now and then, but what if this turns into a habit? When we have children I want to know I can count on him to be there for us. It won't be okay for him to hang out in the bar every night if I'm about to go into labor or am home with a newborn. And it won't be a good example for our children if he continues to drink this much. I'm even a little worried about birth defects caused by his drinking."

"But I'm not an alcoholic," protested Mark. "I don't have an alcoholic's personality, and I'll never become dependent on alcohol. I could stop drinking right now if I had a good reason to, but that would mean giving up something I enjoy." He sounded frustrated, but not angry.

"You seem to be at odds with each other over something that *might* happen more than what's happening right now," I suggested. "It's quite possible that Mark's drinking will never become a problem and that he'll be a perfect father. The question is, how much of a strain is this dispute going to put on your marriage in the meantime — and for what purpose?"

Over the course of the first two or three sessions, Mark and Christine gradually came to realize that the real issue was control. Mark was afraid that Christine was trying to control him. Christine was afraid that alcohol would eventually take control of their marriage. Once these fears had been exposed, they could be measured against the trust that had always held the relationship together. When looking at the situation in context, Mark realized that Christine's concerns were legitimate, if arguable, and that his resistance had only intensified them. She acknowledged that she had no specific reason to believe that his drinking ever would become the problem she imagined, but she also pointed out that her trust in Mark had never been in doubt. It was alcohol she mistrusted. Founded or unfounded, Christine could not ignore her fears as long as Mark's drinking bordered on excess. When Mark finally realized that her concern was for his own benefit and that of the marriage — and not motivated by some irrational desire to control him — he was much more willing to moderate his consumption.

During their final counseling sessions, they negotiated a limit of two drinks, applicable to both of them, and jointly decided that Mark should cut back on his after-work visits to the bar. Three months later, when Christine became pregnant and gave up drinking entirely, Mark voluntarily quit as well.

As mild as Christine and Mark's dispute might sound, it had the potential of growing into something far uglier had they not

confronted it early on. By immediately and rationally address-
ing that single issue, they prevented it from poisoning the
wealth of trust and commitment that formed the nucleus of
their relationship. They also stopped it from proliferating into
a host of tangential conflicts, which would have made therapy
far more complicated and much less likely to succeed.

If you and your partner ever decide to turn to outside help,
you'll find a wide selection of trained professionals to choose
from. With the array of psychologists, psychiatrists, social
workers, marriage and family counselors, and members of the
clergy, the choice can be quite baffling. To avoid being overwhelmed, your first step is to determine your own needs. Many
therapists specialize either in individual or in marital therapy.
If you and your partner are seeking help to strengthen your
marriage, you need to find a professional who is trained and
experienced in marital counseling. If one of you is *not* committed to the relationship, you probably will need to start with individual therapy and then, when both of you are sure you want
to stay together, move into joint counseling.

In most cases, it's the wife who decides that counseling is
necessary and the husband who reluctantly comes along. Many
men view therapy as an unnecessary and potentially destructive
process. They may see it as an invasion of their privacy and an
embarrassment. Even if the marriage is clearly in trouble, some
men resist getting professional help because they don't want
their inadequacies as a husband to be "found out." They may
also be unwilling to confront many of the concealed problems
in the relationship. When the husband is resisting counseling,
it's often best to seek a male therapist, who may seem less
threatening. By the same token, if it's the wife who is resisting,
a female therapist may be the better choice.

If you cannot get referrals from trusted friends, your religious organization, or personal physician, go through the professional associations for a list of licensed therapists. You may
need to interview several before you find one who makes you
feel comfortable and confident, but don't let this dissuade you.

And don't be afraid to ask questions about the therapist. Unless you trust this individual's capabilities, you're not likely to entrust yourself or your marriage to his or her scrutiny. Many of the qualities that inspire this faith will depend on your own personalities and the nature of your marriage, but you may also want to look for the following general characteristics.

- A positive attitude toward commitment. Some therapists are not strong proponents of commitment. They may advocate sexually "open" marriages or occasional infidelity as a "necessary" release mechanism. In my experience, this approach usually is more destructive than constructive to the marriage. If you enter therapy as a unifying process, you need a therapist who will help you increase your commitment, not discourage it.
- A successful personal relationship of his or her own. Many well-qualified marriage counselors have themselves been divorced, but you probably will have more faith in your therapist if you know his wisdom has worked for him personally. If he hasn't been able to succeed in marriage or other intimate relationships, it's only natural to doubt his ability to help you get back on track.
- Sensitivity to both partners. The job of a marriage counselor is to bring out both partners' points of view, not to take sides. A neutral adviser is better able to do this than one who has previous experience with one partner. This is one reason why it's sometimes inadvisable to use your or your partner's personal therapist as your marriage counselor as well.
- Insight. The therapist should start to provide useful feedback right from the first or second session. This does not mean that you necessarily should like what he or she tells you, but if you feel as though you're talking into thin air or if the feedback seems utterly inappropriate, you probably should try someone else.
- Patience. Anyone who promises instantaneous results is not going to provide lasting solutions. It takes time to work

through the layers of a relationship to get to the heart of difficult issues. Some problems can be resolved in a few weeks, but often it takes months, sometimes even years. The therapist needs to be willing and able to gauge the pace of the couple so that neither partner feels too pressured, while maintaining a sense of progress from the start.

Not every couple has the kinds of problems or doubts that require outside mediation, but virtually every couple does at times experience difficulties. The important thing to remember is that these difficulties — and even the occasional doubts — are a *necessary* part of true love. As you and your partner learn to face them and work through them in a healthy, unified way, your relationship will deepen and become even more committed. Often, adversity can make you stronger, both as individuals and as a loving couple. This is just one of the ways true love grows.

Preventing Wanderlust

Fortunately, it's much easier to prevent wanderlust than it is to restore balance to a relationship after a partner has wandered. Commitment is the primary key. If you and your partner both openly accept monogamy and work aggressively to maintain the vitality of your love over time, neither doubt nor temptation will easily penetrate your marriage. Observing the rules of love described in the previous chapter will help you achieve these defenses. Another important safeguard against wanderlust is romance.

While it's inevitable that passion will ebb and flow during the course of your relationship, you need not ever surrender romance. To the contrary, it's important to make a conscious effort to sustain romance even during periods when you don't feel particularly passionate. This does not necessarily mean that you have to start buying from Frederick's of Hollywood or investing in erotic equipment. For most couples, the power of romance lies more in the subtleties than in the trappings. The following suggestions can help you cultivate these subtleties:

- Demonstrate affection in many different ways. Having sex is not the only way to experience intimacy. Talking, hugging, holding hands, even dancing can sometimes be *more* emotionally fulfilling than having intercourse. Unfortunately, some couples restrict all physical contact to the bedroom. A kiss is automatically assumed to be an invitation to foreplay. This attitude undermines the current of intimacy that, ideally, runs through everything you do as a couple. If you remain openly expressive and free with your affection, taking a walk or cooking dinner together can be as intimate an experience as going to bed together.
- Be open about your needs and expectations. Having discussed your sexual preferences when you first began dating, you may assume that you understand each other implicitly forevermore. This is a mistake. Just as people's ambitions and interests shift over time, so do their sexual desires. Both of you need to recognize this and be responsive when such shifts occur. The more open you are with each other sexually, the more likely you are to enjoy each other sexually — and the less tempted you'll be to wander.
- Have sex as frequently as necessary to satisfy your physical and emotional needs. No one can prescribe how often you need to make love. Sometimes you may be satisfied having sex once a week or less; at others, three times a week may not be enough. Problems develop when one partner's desire for sex outstrips the other's. It's important to recognize this when it happens and to work out some compromise. The resolution may involve a mutually acceptable increase in frequency, more physical intimacy when you are not having intercourse, or more masturbation for the partner with the greater sex drive. Making one partner feel obligated to have sex won't be helpful, but neither will ignoring the situation.

Even truly loving partners are likely to wander if they feel sexually unfulfilled.

• Avoid making sex routine. It's natural to schedule the activities in your life, and the more numerous your obligations become, the more you need to organize your time to fit everything in. This is especially true when you have children and their needs begin to overshadow your own. When you start to pigeonhole sex into a set weekly schedule, however, you're begging for trouble. When you routinely have sex every Saturday night after the kids are asleep, when you routinely use the same positions or listen to the same music, when you routinely expect exactly the same level of performance, the joy and excitement evaporate and lovemaking becomes a chore. Impulsiveness and surprise are just as potent after you've been married twenty years as when you were first courting. Give yourselves permission to follow your impulses, and vary the routine as often as possible.

• Preserve memories and reminders of affection. Shared experience is a major component of true love. It's important to maintain and celebrate your memories of the past. One way to do this is to document events as they happen, through photographs, journals, or other mementos. Another is to give special attention to anniversaries, birthdays, and other personally meaningful occasions. These celebrations serve as important markers that prompt reminiscences of the past while generating intimate memories for the future. Anything you can do to nurture this sense of continuity and of your history as a couple will help sustain your commitment to each other.

Perhaps the most important defense against doubt is your belief in yourself and your partner. It takes confidence and faith to overcome uncertainty in almost any endeavor, and creating a strong, lasting love is no exception. Fear of the problems and temptations that occasionally confront you will just make you more likely to deny or run from them. If instead you face them down with the belief that your love can overpower them, you may actually find that these challenges strengthen and deepen your relationship. While almost no relationship is ever completely free of doubt, your love will become less and less vulnerable as you and your partner learn to confront these internal struggles together.

PART IV

BREAKING THE FALSE LOVE SYNDROME

13

FINDING A PARTNER IN LOVE: A TEN-POINT PLAN

NOW THAT YOU UNDERSTAND the difference between true love and false love, how do you apply this information to turn your own love life around? If your romantic history is a succession of false love affairs and you're currently unattached or uncertain about your partner, your first objective is to find someone with whom you feel *confident* you can build true love.

The following ten-point plan will help you utilize what you've learned and change your dating patterns so that you begin making more appropriate choices in partners. Remember that there is no one true love waiting for you and that you cannot "find" true love. This plan will help you to identify *potential* lovers, but it's up to you and your future mate to make true love a reality.

---

1. Confront your own myths about love.

Consider your fantasies about love. If you're honest, you'll probably discover that many of your attitudes date back to fairy tale images you absorbed as a child. If you have any doubt, think about the phrases you use to talk about romance. Do you believe in "love at first sight," "falling in love," "falling out of love"? If so, you're still clinging to myths that perpetuate the false love syndrome and that hold you back from attaining true love.

Examine how you were brought up and what your family taught you about love. The success of your parents' marriage and the quality of their demonstrations of affection served as early models for romantic love. And your own success in separating from the family as you got older was important in building the self-esteem so vital in true love. Any disturbances in these early family relationships may have filtered through to your later beliefs about love.

Other clues to your underlying attitudes about love can be found in your past mistakes in romance. You might try listing each of your past relationships and examining what went wrong with each one. What types of people have attracted you? Why were you motivated to be with them? How long did it take to realize something was wrong with each relationship? Who asked to end each relationship — you or the other person? If a pattern starts to emerge, you'll know that your own choices and expectations — and not merely coincidence or "bad luck" — are responsible for your disappointments in love. In all likelihood, your personal romantic mythology has been pushing you toward false love.

Turning these myths around is not easy to do. They run deep. Some date all the way back to infancy. And because they speak to your ego, they are very seductive. But until you accept that love doesn't just "happen" and that there's more to it than being desired and feeling excited, you probably will continue cycling from one false love relationship to another.

---

2. Create a new, realistic definition of love.

Having turned your back on those dreams of romantic enchantment, you need to embrace a more mature, realistic definition of true love. To a large extent, you and your lover will build your own unique version of love, filled with intimate nuances, habits, and expectations that reflect your individual personalities. There are some generalities, however, that apply to true love in virtually every case. If you accept the following *basic* definition, you will find it much easier to stave off false love's temptations.

True love is

- an active rather than a passive experience. It doesn't happen *to* you; you *make* it happen.
- different from infatuation. Infatuation may be the beginning of false love *or* true love. It is a phase that passes relatively quickly and does not predict the success of the relationship.
- different from parenthood. Having a child requires sex, not love. Raising a child requires a type of love that is quite different from true love in a mature relationship. While having a child can complement and enrich true love greatly, it is not an automatic extension of it.
- a balance between the partners as individuals and as a unified couple. Healthy love offers both partners room to grow and satisfy their individual needs as well as to merge part of themselves in a shared identity.
- a mutual process. Before love can develop, both partners must be strongly committed both to love itself and to each other as an exclusive partner in love.

---

3. Assess your own readiness.

A ten-year-old girl may dream of love, but she is clearly not mature enough to handle the responsibility in reality. The same can be said of many men and women who are in their twenties, thirties, or even older. Before you start looking for a partner who is "mature enough for love," take a good look at yourself and make sure *you* are ready. The following suggestions may help.

Try to understand your real motivation in seeking a partner to love. Do you truly want to share your life and become deeply intimate with another person, or are other objectives more important? If you really want someone to help you have a baby, get back at your parents, take care of you, or boost your image, then you may not be ready for the reality of true love.

Are you emotionally healthy and relatively content with your life as it is? True love needs an atmosphere of normalcy and balance in order to thrive. If you are in a state of transition or crisis, you may yearn for love but probably will not be able to hold up your end of a loving relationship. Try to wait until your personal life is stable before embarking on a shared life with someone else.

Make sure that you're ready to give up being single. Living alone, supporting yourself, and establishing an independent lifestyle all help you develop as a mature individual, which in turn will make you a stronger, more confident partner in love. Exploring romance with a broad variety of partners helps you better understand what you need from a partner in love. It also contributes to feelings of self-esteem and desirability that will make you more relaxed and confident with true love. Most people need several years of independence and casual dating before they are truly ready to embark on a more serious relationship.

---

4. Reconsider what you want in a partner.

Most relationships begin with a relatively superficial attraction, but this is not enough to sustain true love. If you're going to lose your heart to someone who looks great, has money, or shows you a good time, you need to make sure that the two of you share other, deeper qualities that can unify you when the initial attraction fades. Among the most important of these are the following:

- Common desire for true love. If one or both of you still is seduced by false love, your relationship probably won't last long. Both of you need to dispel the myths and accept the reality of true love before you can turn it into *your* reality.

• Mutual goals and interests. Your love will thrive if you have compatible ambitions and religious and political beliefs and desire the same lifestyle and quality of life.

• Compatible personalities. While opposites may attract, they do not often succeed in true love. You need not be carbon copies of each other, and having *complementary* personalities can lead to a strong, secure relationship, but if you are poles apart, you may never be able to establish the sense of a common identity that is so important in true love.

• Honesty. Deceit has no place in true love. You need to be able to believe each other to develop the trust that forms the core of a loving relationship. If you know that your partner is dishonest in other relationships or in business, there is reason to assume that this deceit will also penetrate your relationship, if not immediately, then perhaps during times of stress later.

• Stability. Your partner needs to demonstrate the same emotional health and stability that you demand of yourself before attempting love.

• Maturity. True love involves commitment, effort, sacrifice, emotional strength, and determination from both partners. People who have not fully matured or established a secure individual identity are rarely able to live up to such responsibility.

If you feel uncomfortable looking so closely at prospective partners, it's probably because you're afraid of what you may discover, but the only way to know whether they possess the essential attributes for love is to penetrate the superficial images. If you then discover that the person to whom you are attracted is not capable of loving, you must decide whether to pursue a casual, probably self-limited relationship or move on. In any case, it means giving up the illusions that attracted you initially. But as distressing as this realization may be after dating someone for a few weeks, it's always easier than facing it after several years of marriage. Being forthright and demanding from the beginning gives you your best chance of finding a partner with both the desire *and* the capacity to love you.

---

5. Present an honest self-image.

While it's normal to dress up and try to impress someone you've just begun dating, trying to remake yourself is not necessarily constructive if you're hoping to initiate true love. Often, your reward will be either a fleeting attraction that evaporates when your real nature is revealed or rejection because your date resents your putting on an act. The best way to impress a potential partner is to be yourself and *not* consciously try to behave as you think that person wants you to.

If you are accustomed to being "on" with new people or if you're so nervous on first dates that it's impossible to act naturally, here are some suggestions:

- Never lie about your personal history, career, interests, or beliefs.
- Dress for the occasion and the destination, not to impress the other person. Present yourself as you would if you were going out alone.
- If given a choice of activities, request those that involve the least pressure. The more relaxed you feel, the more open you're likely to be.
- Don't disguise your mood or characteristics that you consider "weaknesses." If necessary, explain why you're feeling out of sorts or nervous, but don't play games with your behavior.

---

6. Distinguish sex from love.

Semantics and conditioning may conspire to make you think that sex and love are synonymous, but don't be fooled. "Making love," "lover," and "consummate" refer to sex, not love. And the thrill of orgasm means simply that your body has climaxed, not that you are in love. You can have an active, relatively satisfying sex life without having true love, and you can have true love without the fireworks of a sizzling sexual attraction.

It's important to recognize your own sexual needs and to satisfy them even if you are not in love with anyone. If you have a regular sexual partner whom you do not love, however, you need to be open about the situation. Unless both partners feel the same way, this can lead to disappointment, hostility, and heartbreak.

Unfortunately, women tend to have much more difficulty than men in making this distinction. Men "score" by having sex, women by attracting "love," and so the expectations that drive sexual relationships are often unequal. If you feel that sex must be accompanied by feelings of love, you'll need to be that much more critical of your partners and take that much more time to develop a relationship before consenting to sex. Don't expect love to develop *because* you've had sex, however. Physical intimacy contributes enormously to love, and vice versa, but they still are separate experiences.

---

7. Don't select a partner on the basis of others' opinions.

Turning up with an impressive boyfriend or girlfriend is often a very effective way to win approval from friends and family. Turning up with an unacceptable companion is an equally effective way to show contempt for or rebellion against family control. But as effective as these strategies may be in influencing other people's opinions, they will not bring you any closer to true love.

True love is autonomous. While it may not always be able to withstand vehement attacks, it does not *require* the active support or approval of anyone outside the couple. And, strictly speaking, it is not for anyone's benefit other than the two people in love and their future children. If your primary criterion in selecting a partner is to influence the way others feel about you, do not expect the relationship to develop into true love.

By the same token, be cautious in interpreting what others say about any partner you *are* considering for love. Friends and family members can sometimes provide useful insights, but the motivation behind their interference is not always altruistic. Try to understand not only whether their feedback is accurate but also why they feel compelled to comment at all. Never base your final decision about a partner solely on what others have advised you.

---

8. Discuss the "hard issues" early in your relationship.

Once you've found someone who possesses the general requirements for true love and with whom you feel comfortable, take a deep breath and start discussing the core issues that will confront you if you stay together. These include the following.

- Children. Do you want to have a baby together? What will the arrangement be if one of you already has youngsters from a previous marriage? If you want to have children, what is your approach to childrearing?
- Money. How much do you need to feel comfortable and secure? How do you manage your money? Who would control the budget if you were to get married?
- Career ambitions. How ambitious are you? Would you prefer a one-career or two-career marriage? Are you likely to have to move because of your work? What kind of a social life does your career demand? Can you relax your ambitions enough to put a spouse and your children ahead of work demands, as true love requires?
- Coping with crisis. Are you willing to stand by your partner even in the face of grave health or emotional problems? How much would you expect in return?
- Commitment. How will you determine when you are ready

to commit to each other? Do you want to get married? How much independence would you permit in a permanent relationship?

---

9. Apply the 90:10 rule.

By this point, you know a lot about your partner and yourself, and you're ready to decide whether to pursue a lasting relationship with him or her. Because this is such a momentous and perhaps frightening decision, you may not trust your instincts, so try using a pen and paper instead and list the pros and cons of going forward. Be sure to consider the following:

- Does your partner meet all the basic requirements for love *in general*?
  - Possesses maturity and emotional stability.
  - Has experienced other relationships.
  - Is willing to accept equality in a relationship.
  - Is willing to accept a certain amount of conflict and compromise.
  - Is able to move a relationship beyond sexual excitement and infatuation.
- Do you and your partner have all the basic requirements to love each other *in particular*?
  - Physical attraction and sexual compatibility.
  - Shared goals and interests.
  - Mutual respect, acceptance, and desire to please each other.
  - Mutual honesty and trust.
  - Realistic expectations of each other and the relationship.
  - A balance of dependence and independence.
  - A cooperative approach to problem solving.
  - A desire to share life together.
- What are the other incidental characteristics that endear your partner to you?
- What are the characteristics that you miss or dislike in your partner?

Once you've completed these lists, compare the positives and negatives. If your partner fails to meet the basic requirements for love but the list overflows with incidental traits that delight you, think twice about getting in deeper. Your relationship probably lacks the strong foundation it needs to survive. On the other hand, if the balance is ninety percent positive, but there are a few minor characteristics you don't like, you probably are being unreasonable in demanding perfection. Apply the 90:10 rule, and don't short-change your chance for love.

---

10. Give the relationship time to develop.

Getting to know each other, establishing a relaxed sexual relationship, discovering a deeper level of intimacy, and developing trust and mutuality are all essential to the grounding of true love, and all take time. Pressure and haste to make a formal commitment usually do not facilitate, but rather block the process. There is no standard schedule to use in determining when you "should" be ready to make a final commitment to each other, but most couples who succeed in love seem to require many months, or even years, together before they are secure in this decision.

Usually, one partner will be ready to love before the other. If you are in this position, try to be patient and supportive and maintain a loving attitude. If indeed the two of you meet all the necessary conditions for true love and there are not any overwhelming external obstacles (such as war, physical separation, or ill health), your relationship should survive this temporary imbalance.

Finding a partner to love is only the beginning of true love, of course. Unlike false love, true love becomes richer, deeper, and closer as it develops over time. It also becomes increasingly complex and challenging. The next chapter offers a plan for meeting the challenges and reaping the rewards of true love.

14

MAKING LOVE WORK:
A TEN-POINT PLAN

ONCE YOU'VE FOUND a partner who meets the preconditions for true love, you are faced with the awesome job of making your love work. You cannot do this singlehandedly. It takes two, both pitching in and assuming equal responsibility, to sustain a successful and growing relationship. The following guidelines, therefore, apply to both of you.

Ideally, you both will have read this book and will understand the distinction between true love and false love. This ten-point plan summarizes the information contained in the last section so that you can apply it directly to your own love life.

I. Commit yourselves.

Love is an active choice that requires a conscious and expressed commitment. For most couples, this commitment takes the form of marriage. It incorporates the decision to live together, to be faithful to each other, to share each other's goals in life, and to form a permanent joint identity.

This commitment actually has two phases:

1. Both partners must decide that they are ready to live within a permanent relationship and accept all the responsibilities and lifestyle adjustments that that entails.
2. Both must commit their love to each other and acknowledge that they are the most important people in each other's lives.

True love requires that both partners understand and accept these separate phases of commitment. As long as any doubt or reluctance remains, it will be difficult to build the necessary foundation for love.

---

2. Apply the Basic Rules of Love.

The basic guidelines of love, described in Chapter 11, govern the way you and your partner treat each other on a day-to-day basis. To recap them:

- Give and demand equality in your relationship at all times.
- Talk to each other honestly, listen openly, and offer constructive feedback.
- Recognize and confront problems directly, without letting them fester unnecessarily.
- Share the responsibility when problems occur, and work together to find a positive solution.

---

3. Maintain the balance between your individual and joint identities.

Your relationship won't survive if you are completely enmeshed in each other's lives or if you lead very distant and separate lives. You need some common ground *and* some individual activities and interests. Remember the two interlocking circles representing a healthy relationship? Keep them in mind as you structure this balance in your own relationship.

Don't expect your partner to take care of your individual problems for you, and don't feel responsible or guilty when your mate faces difficulties outside your relationship. You naturally will want to help and provide moral support, but love can accomplish only so much. It is a source of solace and strength, not an escape or a scapegoat. If you look to your partner for salvation instead of responding responsibly and maturely, your love probably will buckle under the strain.

On the other hand, it's just as important to work together to develop a sphere of interests and activities in which you *share* responsibility. This portion of your life might include children, social, religious, and political activities, as well as household matters. When troubles surface within these boundaries or when your individual problems spill over to your shared life, it's essential that you work together as equal partners to find solutions. Your love depends on your mutual ability to keep yourselves healthy as individuals and as a couple.

---

4. Avoid deep-seated competition.

Accept the fact that love is a partnership and that, as partners, the two of you *both* share each other's accomplishments. You both invest a great deal in the relationship, if perhaps in different ways. And by supporting and nurturing your love, you contribute enormously to each other's individual successes.

There is no reason to view your partner as an opponent; if you do so, it may tear the fabric of trust that holds you together. While a little competition in the form of intellectual debates or sports can add vitality to a relationship, don't allow your egos to get involved. You and your partner are not in competition; you're on the same team. Even if you are naturally competitive people, try to direct these impulses into your individual activities with other people away from home.

When your partner achieves a major victory at work or through other outside endeavors, allow yourself to take pride in it as well. Don't let yourself feel threatened or jealous. If you do, this adversarial undercurrent will gnaw away at your unity, and if allowed to continue it eventually may undermine your love for each other.

---

5. Accept that true love takes priority over other relationships.

Committing to love does not erase prior relationships or emotional ties, but it does push them back a level in priority. Being in love means placing your lover's needs ahead of those of your boss, your friends, your relatives, and even your parents. This will not stop these people from placing demands on you, nor should it prevent you from responding, but if other people's expectations conflict with your lover's and no acceptable compromise can be reached, then your loved one should take precedence.

If and when you have children, the balance necessarily will change somewhat, and your responsibility will be split between your spouse and your offspring. It is sometimes easy to lose this balance when you become a parent, but if your love is to survive childrearing, you must make a particular effort to spend time and energy on your relationship as lovers as well as tending to your children's needs.

---

6. Keep spontaneity and openness in your sex life.

One of the vital functions of true love is to provide sexual satisfaction. To sustain fulfilling physical as well as emotional intimacy, talk about your sexual preferences early in your relationship, and stay open to discussion as time passes. Don't assume that you know what your partner likes just because you've been using the same positions for five years. Your body changes as you get older, and so will the nature of your intimacy. Unless your sexual patterns adjust accordingly, one of you may become dissatisfied.

Avoid making your sex life routine. Boredom and predictability are lethal to satisfying sex. You need to maintain a certain level of spontaneity and surprise to keep your feelings of physical intimacy alive. Let your partner know when you *feel* like making love instead of waiting for the scheduled moment. Even if there is no immediate opportunity to act on the impulse, the mere expression of desire can have a powerfully positive impact on your feelings for each other.

---

7. Be flexible in the face of change.

Anticipate that your relationship will change as you and your partner develop individually, and structure your life together so that there's enough flexibility to adapt to these changes. While you can expect each other to live up to your commitments to love each other, these obligations do not extend to maintaining a set lifestyle, career, or income level for the rest of time. Your beliefs and even your personalities, to some extent, are bound to adjust as you get older. Demanding that your partner twenty years from now be identical to the person you married is not just unreasonable; it probably will destroy your relationship.

To maintain the necessary mutuality and to avoid growing too far apart, you may need to make certain compromises from time to time. This is why it's important to reevaluate your shared and individual goals *frequently*. When conflicts begin to appear between these goals, weigh each choice in terms of its impact on your future as a couple. As long as you are committed to loving each other, you cannot afford to pursue individual dreams that will threaten the relationship. You can, however, find ways to accommodate each other's ambitions by adjusting your life together. Each partner must be prepared to make some sacrifices so that both have a chance to grow.

8. Get help when you need it.

Almost every relationship hits occasional impasses, when it seems that the problems are insurmountable. Acknowledging conflicts and negotiating to resolve them may get you past them. But if you can't seem to deal with them on your own, and particularly if they linger on, threatening to become chronic, don't let fear or embarrassment prevent you from getting professional help.

If your partner asks to get marriage counseling, take the request seriously *even if you think there's nothing wrong.* The mere request is a signal that something *is* wrong, and your inability to recognize the problem makes it all the more urgent to get outside help to restore mutuality.

Don't hesitate to get professional advice about problems that, on the surface, appear minor. If you can't resolve them on your own and they continue to irritate the surface of the relationship, they may eventually begin to affect the deeper layers of intimacy. It requires far less emotional turmoil and time in therapy to resolve problems during their inception than after they've become serious wounds.

9. Anticipate false love's temptations, but don't be seduced.

Don't expect true love to shield you from the temptation to be single again or to be with someone else. These are the seductions of false love, and they probably will entice you as long as you live. The challenge is to accept them for what they are and enjoy the fantasies, but recognize that the love you are building with your partner is richer and much more fulfilling than the life you are likely to have if you give in to your impulses.

Remember that you cannot "fall out of love." When love disintegrates, it's because one or both partners have made a